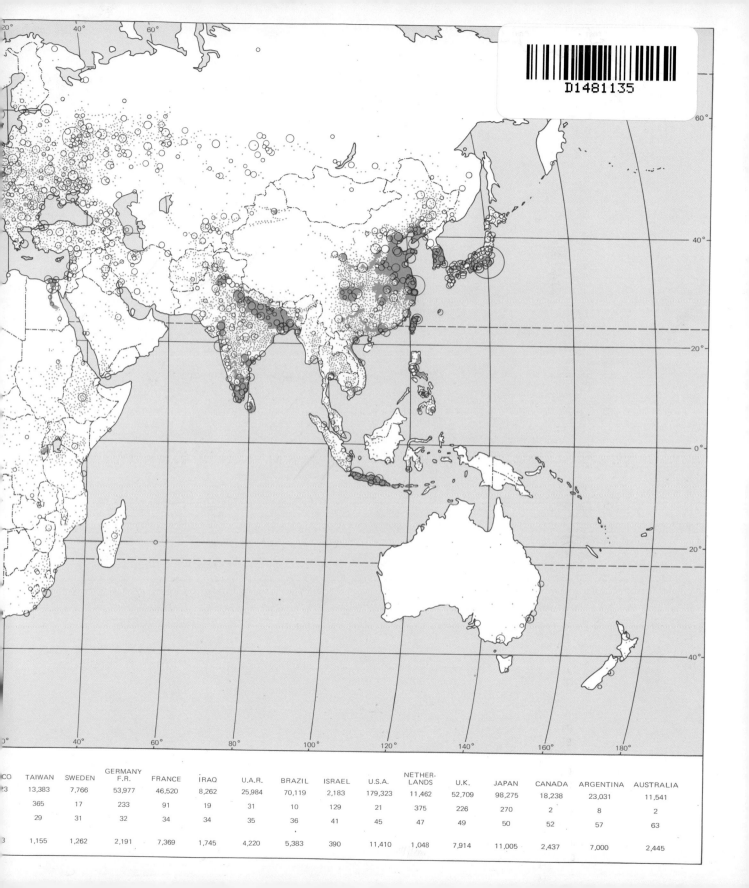

	TAIWAN	SWEDEN	GERMANY F.R.	FRANCE	IRAQ	U.A.R.	BRAZIL	ISRAEL	U.S.A.	NETHER-LANDS	U.K.	JAPAN	CANADA	ARGENTINA	AUSTRALIA
3	13,383	7,766	53,977	46,520	8,262	25,984	70,119	2,183	179,323	11,462	52,709	98,275	18,238	23,031	11,541
	365	17	233	91	19	31	10	129	21	375	226	270	2	8	2
	29	31	32	34	34	35	36	41	45	47	49	50	52	57	63
3	1,155	1,262	2,191	7,369	1,745	4,220	5,383	390	11,410	1,048	7,914	11,005	2,437	7,000	2,445

GEOGRAPHY
AS SOCIAL SCIENCE

GEOGRAPHY AS SOCIAL SCIENCE

GORDON J. FIELDING
UNIVERSITY OF CALIFORNIA, IRVINE

HARPER & ROW, PUBLISHERS
New York   Evanston   San Francisco   London

Front endpaper reproduced by permission of Oxford University Press.

Back endpaper from *Physical Elements of Geography* by G. T. Trewartha, A. H. Robinson, and E. H. Hammond. Copyright 1967 by McGraw-Hill, Inc. Used with permission of McGraw-Hill Book Company.

Sponsoring Editors: Ronald Taylor and Raleigh Wilson
Special Projects Editor: Dory Munder
Project Editor: Holly Detgen
Designer: Rita Naughton
Production Supervisor: Stefania J. Taflinska

GEOGRAPHY AS SOCIAL SCIENCE

Library of Congress Cataloging in Publication Data
Fielding, Gordon J.
  Geography as social science.
  Bibliography: p.
  1. Anthropo-geography.   2.   Social sciences—
Text-books.   I.   Title.
GF41.F53   301.29   74-1296
ISBN 0-06-042051-0

CONTENTS

PREFACE

The preface is happiness for the author. It is a tailpiece placed first in the volume in which he summarizes his aspirations and limitations. This is especially true for a textbook author, because the preface provides an opportunity to explain his approach. Thereafter, he relies primarily on the work of others to illustrate the principal themes.

Organization of the material is the author's principal contribution. This volume developed from a challenge to teach geography as social science at the University of California, Irvine. It represents an attempt to abstract the best material published by geographers and to present it in a manner that meshes with contemporary concerns in the other social sciences. This aim required the reorganization of information acquired over two decades of study and teaching so that the concepts, language, and techniques presented would be consistent with an interdisciplinary social science program emphasizing formal models of human behavior and rigorous empirical research.

Traditionally, the focus of geographical study has been spatial distributions and the content of areas. But there is renewed emphasis upon the processes which give rise to these distributions. Geography now has a theoretical emphasis, which this volume seeks to coordinate in a manner suited to introductory and intermediate courses of instruction. The methodology for the observation, classification, and precise measurement of distributions is summarized in Part One; but principal emphasis is devoted to the behavioral processes—economic, social, political, and psychological—which give rise to these distributions. Emphasis upon these processes not only facilitates interdisciplinary study but also provides a base for testing models of behavior. Through an improved knowledge of human behavior, geographers are better able to understand the spatial distributions that challenge them.

The objective of this text is to start people thinking about the human behavioral processes that give rise to distributions. It is an introductory attempt and is designed for those without previous training in geography. Should the book provoke interest in the field, then advanced courses will extend this introductory presentation and make explicit its relation with other fields. Regional courses also facilitate the testing of concepts in different cultural settings.

Physical geography is only briefly considered in this text. Apart from man's perception and interpretation of physical resources, physical processes are neglected. No denigration of physical geography is intended. It has always been more theoretical than human geography, but there is a limit to what can be effectively presented to students in any course of instruction.

PROGRAMMED LEARNING

Supplementary to the text are the programmed learning units, published separately as *Programmed Case Studies in Geography*. The programmed units enable the student to apply the concepts, techniques, and terminology presented in each chapter to geographical problems. The units reinforce themes outlined in the chapter by applying them to examples with which students should be familiar. People learn by doing: by organizing the information from text, lectures, and supplementary readings when challenged to solve problems and to respond in their own words.

Students are active participants rather than passive listeners and/or readers in this learning strategy. In each of the programmed learning units, it is not sufficient to memorize the language, techniques, and concepts of geography. Students must demonstrate their ability to use this information to solve problems before they proceed to the next unit.

The programmed units were originally prepared for computer-assisted instruction (CAI). They are not presented as computer listings for two reasons. First, CAI is still uneconomic. User costs have not fallen as was anticipated when the first units were prepared in the latter 1960s. The cost of utilizing the chapters in CAI form would be prohibitive for many colleges which urgently need new approaches to geographical instruction. Second, the wide range of languages and even wider range of equipment used for CAI make computer listings difficult to use.

Where CAI facilities are available, it is recommended that the programmed units be adapted and entered on the local system together with some of the units made available by the Commission on College Geography (1969 and 1972). There is no doubt that CAI is superior to programmed manuals if cost is not a factor. It permits individualized instruction where the student may proceed at his own pace while his progress is monitored. It also facilitates presentation of the dynamics of the behavioral processes that the geographer seeks to understand. Most students enjoy CAI. Learning is self-rewarding, as it ought to be. Tests have also demonstrated the superiority of CAI in achieving long-term learning goals.

Apart from the book's organization and its emphasis on the programmed material, little else is original. The only area in which I would claim special competence is the political process, but even here I have relied primarily on the work of others.

Footnoting ideas derived from others in most instances has been omitted. Students have complained that documentation detracts from continuity of presentation. Books and other references referred to are included in the Bibliography. Books and review summaries are listed as Suggested Readings at the end of each chapter. At the introductory level, for which this book is intended, this is sufficient. The selection of additional reading is more appropriately left for the instructor who is familiar with student interest and the availability of local illustrations.

Figure illustrations are essential to understanding the text. Each figure and caption has been edited by Richard Outwater, California State University, Long Beach, to ensure that it is consistent. Often the caption repeats the text. Such reinforcement is intentional as a learning aid.

ALTERNATIVE APPROACHES

The outline of the text represents but one of many approaches to the use of the material. Part One could be omitted from courses not intended for geography majors. Emphasis upon cultural processes with references to techniques may be preferred by those seeking a liberal education. Other courses might emphasize population geography, in which case Chapter 4 might be expanded to provide an anthropological emphasis. If such anthropological emphasis is desired, then more attention should be given to culture and cultural realms in relation to the dynamics of population growth. Within each realm economic and social development would provide themes for the consideration of the cultural processes.

The text may also be used to add intellectual challenge to introductory courses in world regional geography. Any of the several world regional geography texts could be used to provide the facts about each region with students challenged to organize information in terms of cultural processes. If this approach is used, the *Programmed Case Studies in Geography* may not be required.

Supplementary reading should be assigned. Recommended readings are listed at the conclusion of each chapter, but this is only the beginning. Reprints of journal articles are commercially available in addition to several books of selected readings. Novels should not be neglected. They provide excellent insights into human behavior and are able to illustrate themes in a more readable style than are research publications.

The eight chapters of this book were designed to be covered within a ten-week quarter. If the text is used for a sixteen-week course, then two weeks each should be allowed for Chapters 4, 5, and 6. If time is available, additional lectures on historical geography, the geography of conservation, and urban planning could explain themes that are mentioned in the text but do not receive separate attention.

Gordon J. Fielding

ACKNOWLEDGMENTS

The philosophy expressed within this volume is derived from many sources: from my teachers at Thames High School, the University of Auckland, and the University of California, Los Angeles; and from my colleagues at the University of Auckland and the Irvine campus of the University of California. The book is dedicated to Harold McCarty and Joe Spencer, for it represents an attempt to integrate the intellectual rigor associated with the Iowa school with the cultural process approach taught by Joe Spencer about the coffeepot "culture hearth" at UCLA.

Many colleagues have provided valued criticism of individual sections. Sherman Silverman, Prince George's Community College, Maryland, has been especially helpful. He has encouraged the use of case studies, suggested the quotations from regional novels, and helped reorganize the draft manuscript. However, there are still imperfections. For this reason, comments from students and professors will be welcomed so that subsequent editions might be improved.

FOR THE STUDENT

Geography is best introduced in a problem-oriented course, not a survey. For this reason the coverage here is selective. The aim is to acquaint you with some of the problems that stimulate geographical research and with the concepts, language, and techniques used by geographers in conducting that research. The course for which this text was written emphasizes human geography. It is biased toward theoretical approaches to the study of human behavior and the discussion of social problems in keeping with the emerging policy-oriented emphasis in the social sciences.

Motivating this approach are certain goals. The benefits you receive from reading this book and completing the *Programmed Case Studies in Geography* will be indicated by these goals:

1. To recognize regularities in the arrangement of phenomena as observed in the world about you or as presented on maps, photographs, and statistical tables.
2. To describe and provide examples of the major behavioral processes that contribute to the arrangement of phenomena.
3. To develop critical attitudes toward environmental problems.
4. To define the major concepts, language, and techniques used by geographers.
5. To extend your knowledge of the methodology of social science through your ability to formulate and test hypotheses.

Various learning techniques will be used to help you attain the above goals. The text introduces a topic and abstracts the results of pertinent geographical research. The general themes are covered in the Suggested Readings and in *Programmed Case Studies in Geography*. Programmed instruction is available in the form of these units or as computer-assisted instruction (CAI) or a combination of both. The form in which they are provided will depend upon the resources available on your campus.

Terms having a technical connotation are defined in the text and in the Glossary. Most unfamiliar terms are defined in a standard dictionary.

Geography is fascinating because it surrounds one always. It facilitates an awareness of the environment as it embraces both man, land, and the relationships between them, which are critical to our survival on the "thin skin of Earth." For those who enjoy travel and the reading of maps, this text will bring enjoyment by explaining the patterns of human behavior that you have observed.

G. J. F.

PART ONE

CHAPTER 1
GEOGRAPHY AND HUMAN BEHAVIOR

Husky, energetic men in sports shirts galloped up to a liquor-store window and took hold of the iron grating, heaving themselves upon it, yanking at it, twisting it. Someone was cheering in rhythm, Come on! Come on! *Glass broke behind the grating. The men got the grating loose at one end and twisted it down, their muscles bulging. Then, bending it down, they placed it neatly over the broken glass and everyone scrambled inside.* Come on, come on! They afraid!

Joyce Carol Oates (1969), p. 457.

Rioting in the summer of 1966 was an enjoyable, excitingly dangerous, and profitable diversion from the oppressive heat and dismal streets of central Detroit.

More than 250 thousand persons receiving public assistance live in central Detroit. They are mostly people who have been bypassed by technological development and for whom future prospects are bleak. They live, love, and survive in a chaotic, almost brutal manner. Alongside them are the working poor: One such family is used by Joyce Carol Oates to capsulate the moral and social conditions of central city life.

Despite the social reforms that preceded and were accelerated following the riots of 1967, there is no evidence of substantial improvement. The slums of Detroit grow at their periphery and die at their core. The area shifts but the conditions persist. At the periphery, older housing occupied by aging whites is absorbed by the immigrants from the ghetto. Left behind to surround the city center are the flophouses and unoccupied warehouses. Their only salvation is the bulldozer, but who will supply the money and who will develop the political consensus to achieve urban renewal?

Successful families have vacated the central cities to raise children in suburbia. Row upon row of near-identical, single-family homes form communities near schools, gas stations, and the supermarket. These are conformist associations. People here value equality and are pleased with their escape from older ethnic neighborhoods, but are themselves involved in a cultural transition of major proportions. Their upbringing did not prepare them for the autonomous life style of suburbia. They are involved in clubs, churches, and the Little League, yet frustrated by the dull uniformity of their life styles.

Affluent suburbanites create more diversified life styles. Grosse Pointe provides a panoramic view of Lake St. Claire. The uncluttered boulevards and elegant gardens with manicured lawns and well-trimmed trees contrast with the automobile-strewn, treeless, and power line-draped streets of central Detroit. Dearborn offers another example: a leafy suburb with the substantial brick homes of managerial and professional families. Only a few miles separate them from the central city and the suburban tract, but the social distance is immense.

Automobile men and automobile money dominate all of Detroit: in employment, commerce, and pollution of the lake and air. The choice of location was somewhat accidental as it was, quite simply, the preference of Henry Ford. However, the lakeside location of the Highland Park and River Rouge plants aided accessibility to iron ore and coal for steel making. The agricultural Midwest provided both an expanding market for automobile products and machinery and a source of employees, many of whom were unprepared for urban life.

Urbanization of people attracted to metropolitan centers like Detroit is an overriding concern in America and throughout the world. Families came to find jobs and struggled to achieve social and economic advancement. Most were successful and they or their children moved to suburbia to experiment with new life styles.

Cities like Detroit are both dynamic and, sadly enough, stagnant. The decaying core and expanding suburbs, the strip commercial districts and shopping centers, and the highways and new factories reveal patterns of human behavior that fascinate the human geographer. For this reason, urban geography and urbanization will be essential themes throughout this book.

The city is a microcosm of the world. One can assess why man chooses to agglomerate his activities into cities and within cities; how distance and accessibility affect the choice between alternative locations; what utility man achieves by using areas for different and specialized purposes; how interaction between areas is achieved in commerce, yet avoided between neighborhoods; how people perceive the city and what sources of satisfaction it provides.

These are some of the core concepts that Part One seeks to introduce and place in a geographical context. The spatial, or area-to-area, variations in Detroit introduce some of these themes. Novelists like Joyce Carol Oates and Arthur Hailey have sought to identify these variations as they explore contemporary social issues in books such as *Them* and *Wheels*. The novelist portrays aspects of behavior through individual characters, whereas the geographer abstracts elements of behavior and uses them to explain regularly recurring spatial patterns.

WHAT IS GEOGRAPHY?

Geography is a social science. It can also be a physical or environmental science, but I leave others to advance this point of view. Geography is the study of the locations and arrangements of phenomena on the surface of the earth and the processes that generate these distributions.

Traditionally, both physical and human processes were studied. This text emphasizes human processes; physical elements will only be considered in terms of man's perception and use of these elements.

Students of geography are concerned with topics such as the arrangement of urban places, the internal structure of cities, the location of industrial and agricultural activities, and the pattern of movement of people, goods, and ideas. Geographers have developed special techniques for studying and classifying these distributions and these will be introduced. However, this volume focuses neither on the distributions nor the techniques, but on the behavioral processes that generate these distributions.

The behavior of those "husky, energetic men in sports shirts who galloped up to a liquor store window" is not difficult to analyze. The riot had disorganized the power structure that had previously defined honorable behavior. *"They afraid!"* symbolizes the new circumstances. They and other normally law-abiding citizens perceived an opportunity to help themselves to items of value that were not ordinarily within their reach. Evidence of the resulting destruction remains. Many of the stores have never reopened and burnt-out structures have been leveled or remain forlornly empty.

The way in which people perceive different life styles, how they learn to achieve satisfaction from them, how they form social groups for fellowship, protection, and to obtain influence are behavioral processes. These are the ways in which men respond to, and adapt to, the physical environment that surrounds them.

A distinction is made between economic, social, political, and psychological behavior, but this classification is necessarily artificial. Human behavior is complex and motivated by several desires. Attempts to analyze spatial distributions in terms of behavioral processes necessitate the separate discussion of each process, but the totality of human behavior should never be overlooked.

The changing emphasis in geography

Geographers have traditionally emphasized spatial distributions, and detailed descriptions have been compiled for almost all parts of the world. These careful studies have concentrated on the unique features of areas in order to emphasize the differences from place to place rather than the uniformities. These unique features undoubtedly fascinate the observer and make travel enjoyable, but their study does not always advance our knowledge of human behavior.

Regional description dominated geography until 1965. The observation, measurement, and classification of geographical information during the descriptive period was essential to progress, but the emphasis on differences diverted the attention of geographers from the regular occurrences. Repetitive patterns that could provide a basis for generalizations were neglected.

Contemporary geography emphasizes the regularity in spatial organization and attempts to develop models that will explain how human behavior may account for these patterns. The substantive focus of geography—the arrangement of phenomena—remains unchanged. Changes have occurred only in the emphasis on regularities rather than differences, and in the way in which research is undertaken.

GEOGRAPHY AS AN OBSERVATIONAL SCIENCE

Although geographers carefully identify distributions and discuss the variables that cause distributions, geography is an observational, rather than an experimental science. Both observational and experimental sciences demonstrate how regular occurrences are produced by the predictable interaction of a number of variables. It is possible in experimental science, under laboratory conditions, to control and introduce the variables separately in order to observe their effect upon the situation. But in an observational science occurrences must be observed as they naturally occur. A large number of variables must be presumed to be operating simultaneously, and although attempts are made through research design to focus upon the relevant variables, it should never be presumed that these research conditions approach the controlled situation of the laboratory.

Because of the complexity of the human processes, geographers frequently utilize simplifying assumptions and surrogate variables to aid research. *Assumptions* are statements that are accepted so as to simplify the variations that are observed in most geographical situations. "All other things are equal" or "Assume a gently sloping, uniform plain" are examples of simplifying assumptions.

Surrogate variables are used when data is not available for the item under study. For example, income or education are frequently used as surrogates for social class. A uniformity of behavior is assumed for a social class and people, more often families, are included in classes based upon the income and education of the head of the household. This method is not very reliable, but for many areas it is the only information available.

Accurate data on many areas of the world is either not available or at a level of generalization that makes comparison between areas extremely difficult. Only by utilizing simplifying assumptions and surrogate variables has some progress been achieved in the identification of the core concepts in cultural geography and in developing relatively simple models of human behavior to explain some spatial distributions.

CORE CONCEPTS

Regularities in spatial distribution result from man's attempts to use land efficiently. Because of the variations in the earth's surface and the different cultural preferences of people, these regularities are seldom apparent to the untrained observer. To aid study, geographers have attempted to catalogue the patterns and identify the concepts that aid their explanation. Agglomeration, distance and accessibility, utility, interaction, and satisfaction are concepts that permeate this text. They are representative of man's attempt to maximize economic, social, and psychological return with minimum effort. Regardless of cultural preferences or system of government, these concepts appear to underlie the patterns of spatial organization.

Concepts seldom operate independently. Cities and urbanization offer the most apparent examples of the interaction of concepts: the gathering of people and the agglomeration of specialist activities within districts, the effect of distance and accessibility upon specialization and location, and the utility of some areas for residences and others for industry and commerce. Interaction between commercial areas within the city, the restriction of interaction between different social areas, and the way in which urban residents perceive their surroundings are themes that help explain urban patterns.

The concept of agglomeration

The tendency to cluster similar activities is apparent in agricultural, industrial, and population distributions. In the United States, for instance, 70 percent of the population resides on less than 2 percent of the land area. At the world scale, the polar zones and some of the deserts are virtually uninhabited, whereas most of the population is clustered along the margins and in the fertile valleys of the continents. The agglomeration of people in cities, the clustering of homes in rural townships, and the association of shops in shopping centers improves economic efficiency and provides social satisfaction. There are numerous examples of the spatial distributions that result from satisfying human needs.

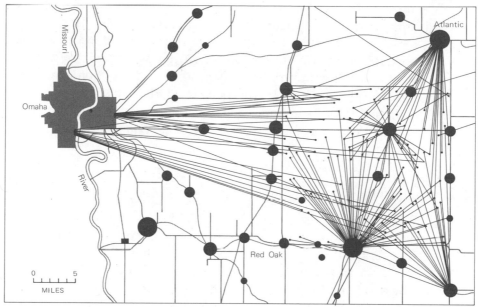

Fig. 1.1 Overlap of trade areas in southeastern Iowa. *Desire lines* connect a sample of rural customers with urban places where furniture is usually purchased. Larger urban centers, where many stores are agglomerated, are preferred over stores in smaller urban places. (After Brian J. L. Berry, H. G. Barnum, and R. J. Tennant, *Regional Science Association, Papers and Proceedings*, vol. 9, 1962, Fig. 15.)

Steel-making plants and supermarkets are two common foci for agglomeration. Sites for steel plants were chosen in Detroit because of a favorable combination of raw material sources and marketing advantages. Bulk users of steel, like machinery and automobile manufacturers, locate nearby. Agglomeration is even more apparent in the location of retail activities. A suburban supermarket is visited regularly by consumers. Drug and liquor stores, dry cleaning and hairdressing services locate nearby for the customer's convenience and to benefit from his spontaneous buying habits.

Agglomeration is best illustrated by consumer behavior. When all other things are equal, consumers prefer to visit larger centers for the purchase of specialty goods like furniture because there is a wider range of choice (Fig. 1.1). Central places like Omaha, Red Oak, and Atlantic, where numerous retail and service functions are agglomerated, attract customers from considerable distances. The larger city grows by attracting customers away from the smaller centers. As commerce declines in the smaller center, many of the residents move permanently to seek opportunities in the larger center.

Agglomeration of industry or services reduces costs of operation through joint use of transportation routes, parking, and other facilities. It also benefits buyers by offering them a greater choice. Agglomeration, therefore, results from the benefits derived by both suppliers and consumers. It satisfies an economic objective in addition to facilitating interaction. For these reasons, human endeavor tends to be clustered rather than dispersed.

The concepts of distance and accessibility

Distance and its corollary, accessibility, are fundamental to the understanding of spatial organization. Evidence of their effect is apparent in economic, social, and psychological behavior.

In a free-market economy, the location of various production activities—farm, factory, mill, and mine—are primarily determined by the costs of obtaining *inputs* (material and labor) and/or marketing *outputs* (products). In retail and service activities, the minimization of distance helps to maximize patronage. Consumers prefer accessible locations where several activities are agglomerated, and operators prefer locations that maximize accessibility to customers. Fortunately, not all enterprises are willing to pay the highest price for the most accessible land, and consumers are willing to travel different distances for different commodities. Also, accessibility requirements differ among enterprises. Competition for land is therefore tolerable, and a regular distribution of land use occurs depending on an enterprise's need for accessibility and its ability to pay for the most accessible locations.

Think about the distribution of stores in any city with which you are familiar, and you will realize how the reduction of distance creates commercial patterns. The central business district (CBD) is the most accessible location. The largest stores, governmental offices, and the most specialized business functions—such as attorneys, medical specialists, and major newspapers—are located here. Land is extremely valuable but declines in value as the distance from the center increases (Fig. 1.2 A and B).

Land values in metropolitan areas decline with distance from the CBD. Proximity to major thoroughfares or nodes of commercial activity adjacent to transit stations, each reflecting distortions in accessibility,

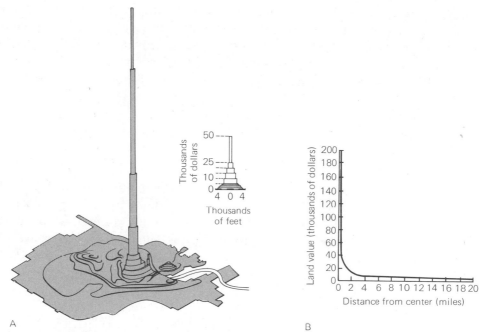

Fig. 1.2 Distribution of land values in Topeka, Kansas. (A) Three-dimensional representation indicates the extremely high values at the center and distortion from the concentric caused by accessibility along highways. (B) Land-values graph shows exponential rate of decline with decreasing accessibility. (D. S. Knos, *The Distribution of Land Values in Topeka, Kansas*, The University of Kansas, Institute for Social and Environmental Studies, 1962, Figs. 2 and 3.)

explain variations from the concentric pattern.

Even in the rural landscape the association between land values and accessibility is apparent; agricultural land adjacent to the city is used more intensively. More farmers compete for its use so it attains higher value. The first learning unit in *Programmed Case Studies in Geography*, which has been published to accompany this text, explores land-use competition and its effect on land values.

The spatial distribution of land values is one of the many patterns that geographers seek to explain. In these studies, geographers emphasize map analysis and simplified portrayals of complex patterns.

DISTANCE AND SOCIAL BEHAVIOR

<u>Distance, insofar as it promotes or limits interaction, also affects other behavioral processes.</u> Group interaction and the social behavior of groups within a society are a function of communication, which is

affected by distance between participants. Political behavior, a process of special importance to geography, is also affected by the communication, or lack thereof, among groups within a political entity. The problems of governing metropolitan areas are in no small part a reflection of the lack of communication between different social groups and even between similar social groups occupying different sectors of the metropolitan area. Political units with effective communication between members are better integrated and more effective in formulating and achieving objectives.

Communication is not limited to verbal interaction. Visual interaction is also important when explaining how human behavior affects the geography of areas. San Franciscans, for example, communicate visually with their bay. The bay is visually accessible to many. Reclamation proposals and proposals to construct the massive, two-level Embarcadero Freeway in front of the waterfront caused sufficient acrimony and unanimity to block action, even though the proposals were supported by some of the most effective political lobbies in the nation.

PERCEPTION OF DISTANCE

Psychological distance also affects man's use of earth space. The way in which man perceives distance between places can affect his travel and migration patterns. To the California student, New York and Florida are perceptually closer than Nebraska and Kansas. And the New Yorker's view of the United States is legend (Fig. 1.3): Familiar places are enlarged and places that are seldom in the news are reduced, distorted in location, and often omitted.

Man arranges cognitive space (mental space) differently from physical space. The mental map carried by individuals affects the way in which they react to proposed changes, whether these be proposed environmental changes or personal migration. Geographical distance is not the same as man's perception of distance, which is referred to as *psychological distance.*

Since many human activities involve men coming together to exchange goods and services, distance and accessibility affect behavior in numerous ways. Where distance impedes interaction, man devises communication systems to minimize its effect. Roads, rails, and telecommunication facilities are manifestations of this process. Agglomeration of people in cities is perhaps the most apparent consequence of man's desire to minimize distance in economic and social behavior.

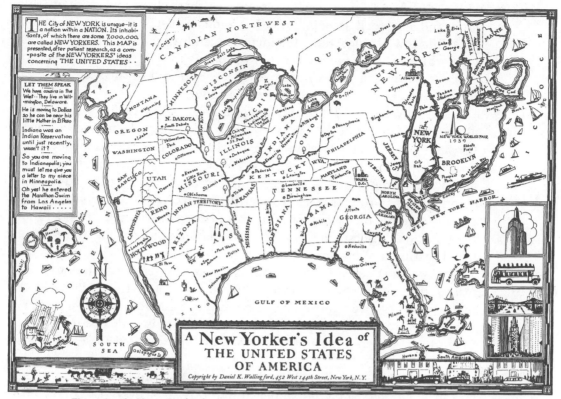

Fig. 1.3 A New Yorker's mental map of the United States. A hypothetical map that represents the perception, information, values, and attitudes of New Yorkers, by distorting location and size of states. The area extent of New York City is exaggerated as are neighboring states to the west. Information about recreation in Florida, Bermuda, Hollywood, and Hawaii distorts appraisal of those places. (F. V. Thierfeldt, Milwaukee, Wisconsin.)

Ours is already an urbanized world, and the continuing desire for interaction will intensify urbanization.

Understanding how distance and accessibility affect man's use of land is a common theme. Although it will be featured in Chapter 5, "Economic Process," it will also be considered in its effect upon social, political, and psychological processes.

The concept of utility

Utility is the value or usefulness of goods and services. It is applicable to both tangible and intangible goods like farm products, education, or affection and may be measured in monetary or nonmonetary units.

Utility is what farmers seek to maximize through choosing a particular crop and livestock association; what industrialists seek to maximize by choosing low-cost locations for factories; and what the homeowner seeks to maximize when he chooses his residence in a certain neighborhood, with or without a view-commanding location and at an acceptable distance from employment, schools, and relatives.

The physical and cultural environment offers farmers a range of alternative means to utilize resources. The dairy farmer can choose between producing whole milk for market or sending it to a factory for processing into dairy products. In choosing between opportunities, he behaves as if he were mentally evaluating them; trading the advantages of one against the other as a means of utilizing his resources of land, capital, and his own labor. If economic criteria are his sole consideration, then he will choose the opportunity that maximizes his return from the investment of his resources.

If land has several alternative uses, the farmer *maximizes expected utility* if he chooses the crop or livestock system that will yield the highest return over and above the costs of production. The additional reward for choosing the most profitable land use is called *economic rent* (Fig. 1.4), which is described further in *Programmed Case Studies in Geography*.

Utility of a good may differ between people, and identical amounts of the same good may be valued differently. Not everybody likes beer. And, even for the thirsty student who does like it, the fourth glass of beer has less utility than the second.

Although perceived utility of a good may differ, cultures and subcultures within a society have a predictable range of desirable goals. It is because groups of people seek to achieve similar objectives that the concept of utility maximization is so useful in explaining behavior.

The concept of interaction

Man is a social animal, and by and large, seeks friendship or approval. He regulates his own behavior to that tolerated by others, which he learns through interaction with parents, teachers, and friends.

Interaction creates social bonds between individuals. It is through interaction—verbal and nonverbal messages, exchange of goods, favors, and friendships—that the objectives of nations, subcultures, families, and communities are established and perpetuated. Within these groups,

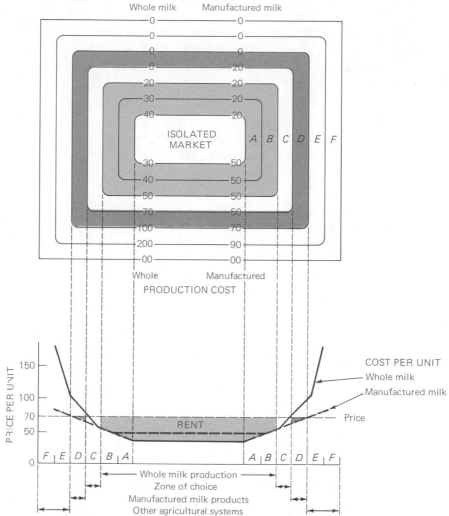

Fig. 1.4 Production cost and land rent for dairy farmers. Assume that all other things are equal except transport and milk-processing costs (production costs). Dairy farmers have a choice between producing milk for direct consumption or sending milk to factories for manufacture (butter, cheese, and ice cream). Price for either use is equivalent at 70. Let us assume that the farmers decide on the basis of which will yield the greater net profit. This is the difference between production cost and price. It costs more to process milk for cheese or butter than for fluid consumption; but, because of the reduction in bulk, the former are less costly to transport. Therefore, in our hypothetical example, the rational farmer in zones A and B would specialize in whole milk production and those in zone D in milk for manufactured produce. Farmers in C have a choice. However, for manufactured products, the hygiene requirements are less rigorous and the production schedule adjustable to seasonal, climatic changes. This would appeal to farmers when profit is near equal. Utility for the farmer embraces more than net profit. Leisure time is also valued.

shared objectives, values, and attitudes provide norms for individual behavior: They restrict the individual's choices to those that are socially acceptable and thereby influence the patterns and arrangements that result from human behavior. The concept of interaction is evident in both the behavior of small groups and the integration of larger political entities.

When the social fabric is disrupted, as in riot-torn Detroit, previously unacceptable behavior occurs. However, such dislocations are minor and are resolved by redeveloping communications between groups that have become alienated from each other. Following the riots in Detroit and elsewhere, vigorous attempts were made by universities, city agencies, and the churches to provide access to the social institutions for minority groups previously isolated in the central city. Access to institutions was intended to stimulate integration through interaction.

Using consumer travel, Murdie (1965) illustrated the effects of socially induced patterns of interaction in a comparison between the

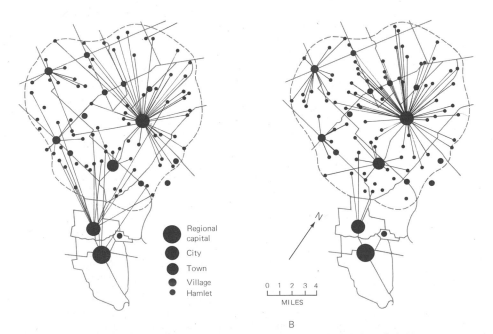

B

Fig. 1.5 Banks used by (A) "modern" Canadians and (B) Old Order Mennonites, in southwestern Ontario. Travel distance for both groups is similar, with Mennonites and moderns both traveling to larger centers. But Mennonites' travel to the regional capital is more restricted. (Murdie, 1965, Figs, 6 and 7; and after Yeates and Garner, *The North American City*, Harper & Row, Publishers, 1971, Fig. 7.19.)

travel behavior of "modern" Canadians and a Mennonite group in a section of Ontario, Canada. The Old Order Mennonites, like the modern Canadians, use modern methods to manage their farms, but in dress, domestic consumption, and mode of travel their attitudes are traditional.

Commercial farming necessitates interactions with outsiders for the financing and marketing of produce. Consequently, the two groups have similar travel patterns for banking (Fig. 1.5) and show very little difference in the location of centers or in the distance traveled to centers. However, the simplicity of the Mennonite life style, with its few household conveniences and plain, homemade clothes, reduces the need for interaction to obtain consumer goods. Here the two groups show significantly different travel patterns. The Mennonites buy only a limited range of cloth and prefer the use of the horse and buggy. Visits to regional metropolitan centers (Fig. 1.6) for clothing are not

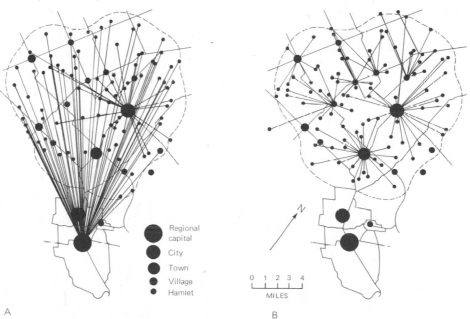

A

B

Fig. 1.6 Shopping preferences for clothing of (A) "modern" Canadians and (B) Old Order Mennonites, southwestern Ontario. Moderns prefer the regional capital over smaller centers used for banking, but Mennonites are content to use neighboring towns or villages for their limited fabric purchases. Beliefs and values (social behavior) affect the patterns of travel. (Murdie, 1965, Figs. 14 and 15; and after Yeates and Garner, *The North American City*, Harper & Row, Publishers, 1971, Fig. 7.20.)

required. By comparison, modern Canadians travel farther for clothing. The cost of traveling to the regional center is compensated by the availability of a variety of stores.

INTERACTION AND POLITICAL INTEGRATION

A cohesive political unit results from a willingness of people to work together. Generally, it implies interaction among people within a community. They are held together by mutual ties of one kind or another, which promote a feeling of identity. The object is threefold: (1) to resolve differences between individuals and to limit conflict to a tolerable level, (2) to provide collective action to promote mutual interests, and (3) to reinforce group identity. Integration as a function of interaction is a social process. However, because of its importance in spatial organization, it is identified separately as the political process.

In many new nations of the developing world, communications are poorly developed, and areas can be contrasted in terms of their level of integration. Modernization is a function of communication. The core areas of urbanization are the most developed, and the degree of modernization in outlying areas is related to their level of communication—their integration—with these centers of innovation and change (Fig. 1.7).

To reinforce the state idea, national and occasionally lesser political units attempt to restrain communication links with competing areas. The purpose is to stimulate integration through enforced interaction (Fig. 1.8).

Reduction of conflict through regulations and statutes also promotes interaction. By restricting opportunities for dispute and providing for peaceful resolution of conflict, a nation attempts to ensure that no internal group becomes alienated by unfair defeat. Where conflict cannot be resolved peacefully, as is so often the case in urban land-use control, then a myriad of political units develop in order to protect the style of living desired by each community. Land-use zoning, regulations and/or incentives for agricultural and industrial production, and the locations chosen for public investments like freeways, airports, and irrigation schemes represent political decisions in which different interests must be reconciled. *Programmed Case Studies in Geography* will allow you to study the conflict generated over alternative locations for a bisecting freeway. The case studies illustrate how community conflict develops and then is resolved through bargaining between competing interest

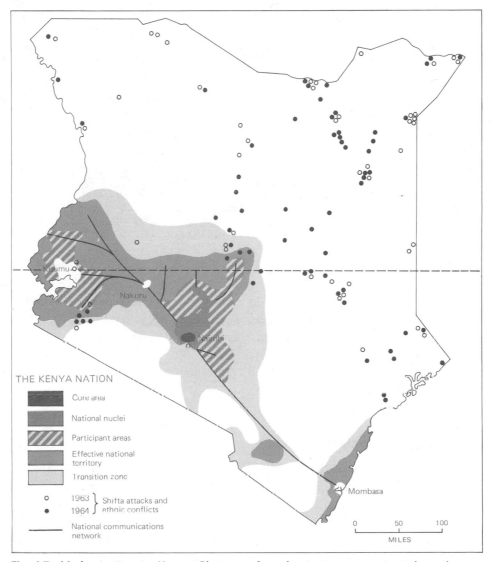

THE KENYA NATION

Core area

National nuclei

Participant areas

Effective national
territory

Transition zone

○ 1963 ⎫ Shifta attacks and
● 1964 ⎭ ethnic conflicts

National communications
network

0   50   100

MILES

Fig. 1.7 Modernization in Kenya. Plateaus of modernization are oriented to the national communications network (rail, road, and tele-communications) between coastal Mombasa and Kisumu on Lake Victoria. Nairobi is the nodal core area. Only 17 percent of Kenya's population resides in the advanced regions. Political allegiance over most of Kenya is unsettled and governmental control is fragile. The people are not integrated into the state. (After Edward W. Soja, *The Geography of Modernization in Kenya*, Syracuse University Press, 1968. Copyright © 1968 by Department of Geography, Syracuse University, Syracuse, N.Y. Reproduced by permission of the publisher.)

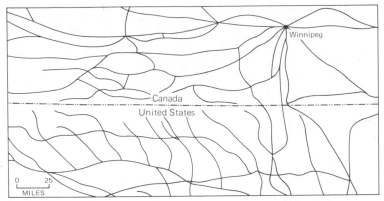

Fig. 1.8 Influence of political boundaries upon transport routes along the Canadian–U.S. border. Breaks in the network diminished interaction between the two nations. (Lösch, 1954, Fig. 85.)

groups. The resulting political decision has a profound impact upon the geography of the community.

Measures designed to foster integration of groups, communities, and nations affect the way man organizes his activities. Competition between groups is restricted and communication with other groups is restrained in order to promote integration. The dynamics and spatial impress of these social processes can be studied for families, ethnic groups, neighborhoods, or nations.

The concept of satisfaction

Are the needs of men and women inexhaustible? This is a controversial issue, but we can at least agree that there are limits on man's ability to agglomerate his goods into useful and pleasurable units. This limit is often less than the economic optimum, because the satisfied person has in some sense minimized to zero the difference between *aspirations* and *utility*. For the hungry student, the fourth hamburger has a lower utility than the second. Even before the maximum unit is achieved, he has eaten enough. He could eat more, but is generally content with a satisfactory level of achievement.

You will discover many illustrations of *satisficing* behavior, for man is usually satisfied by a reasonable level of achievement rather than by the optimum. Therefore, we must consider psychological man rather than economic man in our attempt to understand human behavior in reference to utility, interaction, and agglomeration.

Your selection of this course illustrates *satisficing* behavior. It appeared relevant and was offered at a convenient time. Most geographers teach well and grade fairly. You needed a course toward graduation. You had some, but not perfect, knowledge of other courses offered at the same time. After a brief search of alternatives, you made a satisfactory choice. It was certainly not an optimal choice, because you did not examine *all* alternatives.

Satisfaction is a psychological concept because it refers, not only to man's perception of the opportunities and resources provided by his technology, but also to the level of their utilization, which he regards as returning a satisfactory reward for his effort. In a delightful study of Swedish farming, Wolpert (1964) has shown how labor productivity of farmers falls well below maximum potential productivity (Fig. 1.9). Satisficing behavior is used to explain the divergence between actual and potential production. There are many similar examples in economic geography because the spatial patterns of farms and factories that we observe today are generally the result of capital investment during a

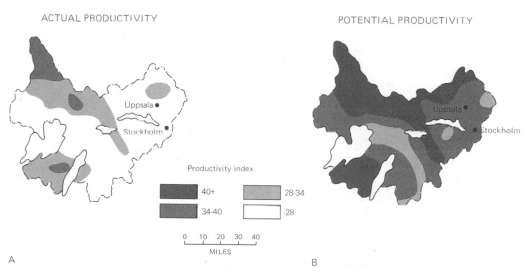

Fig. 1.9 Labor productivity on Swedish farms. In this example from middle Sweden, actual productivity, measured in 10 Swedish kroner per hour (A), falls far below potential productivity (B). Variance is explained by *satisficing* as opposed to *optimizing* behavior. (After Wolpert, reproduced with permission from *Annals of the Association of American Geographers*, vol. 54, 1964, Figs. 2 and 3.)

previous period. A reallocation of investment might increase returns, but so long as the investment continues to pay for itself operators are *satisfied* to continue rather than to abandon the investment.

Summary

Geography seeks to understand man's use of land as expressed in both pattern and process. Regularities in spatial patterns are emphasized because they offer the highest potential for developing laws about the processes of behavior. The cost of overcoming distance and the advantage of accessibility are predominant themes as they reflect man's economic, social, and psychological behavior. Distance and accessibility, utility, interaction, and agglomeration are core concepts in the explanation of these themes. But distance and accessibility alone are insufficient to explain spatial organization. The basis of human action is psychological: Satisficing, rather than maximizing, behavior most realistically explains human behavior. In addition, the geographer must recognize such limitations as the inertia of established locations, the technological capability of the society and its political objectives. Each will affect the operation of the behavioral processes and the resulting pattern of spatial distribution.

SUGGESTED READINGS

Books

A short, readable account of modern geography is provided by:

Taaffe, Edward J., ed. *Geography.* Englewood Cliffs, N.J.: Prentice-Hall, 1970.

Three texts that outline theoretical approaches to geography are:

Abler, Ronald; Adams, John S.; and Gould, Peter. *Spatial Organization: The Geographer's View of the World.* Englewood Cliffs, N.J.: Prentice-Hall, 1971, chap. 3.
Haggett, Peter. *Geography: A Modern Synthesis.* New York: Harper & Row, 1972.
Morrill, Richard L. *The Spatial Organization of Society.* Belmont, Calif.: Wadsworth, 1970.

An approach to the study of core concepts in social science is provided by:

March, James, and Lave, Charles. *The Art of Model-Building: An Interdisciplinary Introduction to the Social Sciences*. New York: Harper & Row, in press.

Periodicals

Geographical journals provide examples of the current research by geographers. There are many fine regional journals, and the *Annals of the Association of American Geographers* and the *Geographical Review* publish international articles. The *Resource Papers* published by the Commission on College Geography of the American Association of Geographers review current research in several areas.

CHAPTER 2
ANALYSIS OF SPATIAL DISTRIBUTIONS

THE FASCINATION OF geography is that it surrounds one. The houses, hotels, and hospitals; factories, shops, and offices; roads, railroads, and expressways are all elements of geography. However, the very profusion of their occurrence and their familiarity requires precise terminology and skills if the patterns are to be discerned and the causal processes understood. The objective of this chapter is to convey the skills that will enable you to observe with precision and classify distributions based upon their inherent characteristics, to measure these distributions precisely, and to present them as maps and diagrams.

The collection and ordering of data was the primary objective for geographers in the age of discovery. It is still the primary task today in remote areas. Several geographical magazines continue this descriptive tradition. They make a valuable contribution to the understanding of important social issues, and are read by a very large audience. But the geography taught in colleges is more analytical. It emphasizes the interpretation and understanding of the patterns of spatial organization.

Programmed Case Studies in Geography contains topographical maps and aerial photographs. As you are challenged to interpret information from these sources you will utilize the skills outlined in this chapter. Careful observation and description of the elements will be required and you will then be challenged to state your observations as hypotheses that can be advanced for testing. Because the units in *Programmed Case Studies in Geography* provide an opportunity to work through geographical problems, the examples cited in this chapter have been curtailed.

OBSERVING SPATIAL DISTRIBUTIONS

Geographers work with spatial distributions, so it is essential to understand the meaning of this term. *Spatial* indicates that an occurrence occupies a portion of the earth's surface. *Distributions* are assemblages of occurrences related to each other. An *occurrence* is an identified phenomenon of a specified magnitude, whereas a *distribution* is a spatial arrangement of occurrences of the same type. For example, a house is an occurrence that can be identified by location and with a magnitude indicated by its floor area, number of bedrooms, or value. Several houses of similar magnitude at different locations constitute a distribution.

Research in geography features the study of distributions rather than occurrences. Explanations based upon a single occurrence are unreliable because they do not reveal the causal process. A wide range of factors could influence a single occurrence, whereas the less important factors tend to cancel each other out when many occurrences— that is, a distribution—are studied.

The arrangement of occurrences must be precisely described, whether a study is made in the field or from secondary sources like maps, photographs, or census information. The nature of the distribution suggests which processes might be causally associated and what research strategy might be appropriate. Geographers have developed a jargon to facilitate the description of the nature, pattern, density, and dispersion of the distributions encountered.

As this jargon is used in Part Two, some of the terms are explained here. The sequence of presentation follows that recommended for geographical study: Identification of the phenomena and the nature of the distribution is followed by classification and sampling. Models of the distribution can then be constructed, and alternative explanations can be advanced as hypotheses.

The nature of distributions

Distributions are of three types: discrete, continuous, and contingent (Fig. 2.1). *Discrete* distributions consist of an assemblage of different occurrences. Houses, factories, and gas stations, when represented separately for an area, constitute discrete distributions. Each occurrence can be identified. A *continuous* distribution exists when occurrences are dependent. Air and water temperatures are continuous over an area because they are dependent upon air circulation. Required prices for agricultural commodities like cotton are also continuous since they depend on governmental policy. A *contingent* distribution occurs where the magnitude of distribution is expressed in terms of either area or time. Production in terms of bushels, tons, dollars per acre, or distance traveled per hours, and traffic density expressed as ton miles are examples of contingent measures.

Various spatial distributions can be effectively represented by different measures, but more than one type is rarely used in the same study. Comparisons between types of distributions are apt to be misleading. In general, each type requires specialized research techniques and different kinds of research models. For example, a comparison between urban land values and air pollution would be plausible but unreliable. Land values are discrete, whereas concentrations of air pollution are continuous distributions established by a few reporting stations. There are great variations in land values in areas with similar concentration of air pollutants. Relationships between them could occur by chance. There is no way of estimating the accuracy of the relationship observed between the two types of distribution.

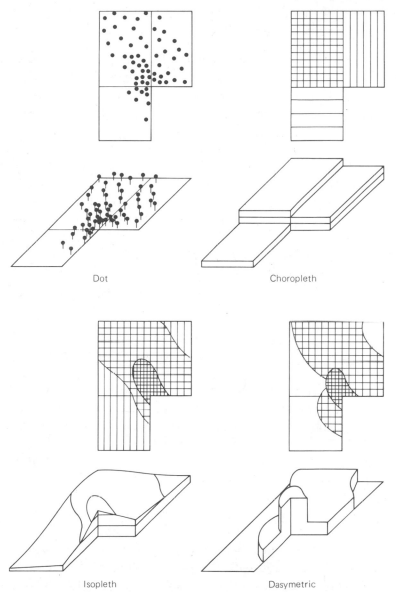

Dot   Choropleth

Isopleth   Dasymetric

Fig. 2.1 Small-scale mapping techniques illustrated by two-dimensional and simulated three-dimensional models. (Thrower, 1966, Fig. 4.)

The pattern of distribution

Once the nature and magnitude of distributions have been established, the emphasis shifts to the pattern of distribution. *Pattern* is a recurring association of occurrences that may indicate causal processes. Four types of patterns are recognized:

1. *Static patterns:* The distribution of pattern represented at a particular time; for example, the distribution of shopping centers or hospitals in a metropolitan area. Measures of location, arrangement, and magnitude can be derived for specific time points.
2. *Dynamic patterns:* The distribution displays change occurring at different time periods. For example, the spread of settlement can be shown for different times and compared (Fig. 2.2).
3. *Network patterns:* The pattern is defined by boundaries or links between nodes in a transportation system; the terms *circular, hexagonal, stellar,* and *linear* are used to describe transportation networks, and special mathematical procedures have been developed to specify structure.
4. *Normative patterns:* The pattern that "ought to be," given certain assumptions; used most frequently in location studies to indicate a pattern derived from theoretical principles that can be compared with real world patterns. The theoretical pattern of land utilization illustrated later as Fig. 2.14 is a normative pattern.

The type of pattern analyzed is dependent upon the phenomena under study and the problem that excites interest. Geographers seldom approach a study or even a field trip without an orientation or interest. And this interest often determines the type of pattern that is identified.

For example, the geographer interested in expansion and decline of shopping centers seeks to represent the date at which each center was established—a static pattern—as well as some measure of changes that have occurred through time—the dynamic pattern. If he chooses to predict the optimum location and size of shopping centers based upon population and income, then a normative pattern would be established that could be compared with the static pattern. By this analysis, a guide to the causal processes can be achieved. Pattern analysis is not an end in itself, but a step toward explaining the processes that cause the distribution.

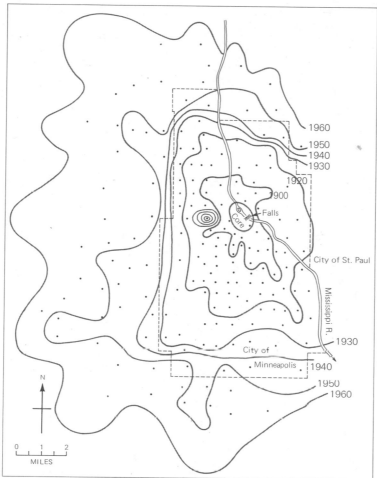

Fig. 2.2 Isoline map of settlement in Minneapolis and vicinity. Lines represent median age of housing and boundary growth rings from each construction cycle. (Adams, reproduced with permission from *Annals of the Association of American Geographers*, vol. 60, 1970, Fig. 16.)

RANDOM AND NONRANDOM PATTERNS

In the search for the processes that cause distribution, unnecessary effort is avoided by distinguishing between random and nonrandom distributions (Fig. 2.3). A *random distribution* has no discernible order and could have occurred by chance. Reliable statements about causal processes cannot be made; therefore, the problem should be either reformulated or abandoned before effort is expended on data gathering.

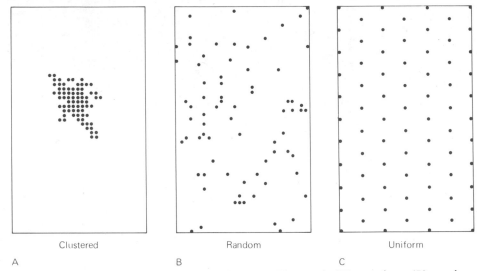

Clustered   Random   Uniform

A   B   C

Fig. 2.3 Random and nonrandom distributions. Clustered (A), random (B), and uniform (C) patterns for a discrete distribution. (King, 1962, Fig. 1.)

Nonrandom distributions exhibit arrangements that are unlikely to have occurred by chance. Either uniform or clustered distributions may occur (Fig. 2.4). Uniform patterns are more regular than random patterns: They occur in the distribution of residences in a planned subdivision or in urban centers where there is little variation in terrain and population density. In both examples the distribution results from processes creating a regular configuration of occurrences.

In clustered patterns occurrences are more concentrated than would be expected in a random distribution. The process or processes that have caused the distribution are neither uniform throughout the study area nor random. Some principle is involved and the task of the geographer is to identify the process, to hypothesize its operation, and to test this hypothesis.

Precise identification of spatial distributions is essential. Tests for randomness are the first step because effort should not be wasted on problems that cannot be solved. Nonrandom patterns are much more rewarding to investigate. Delineation of the arrangement or dispersion of the patterns, together with the identification of linear, radial, or concentric patterns, may assist further by suggesting processes that cause similar occurrences. The task appears relatively simple, but identifying, measuring, and describing spatial patterns is complex, and

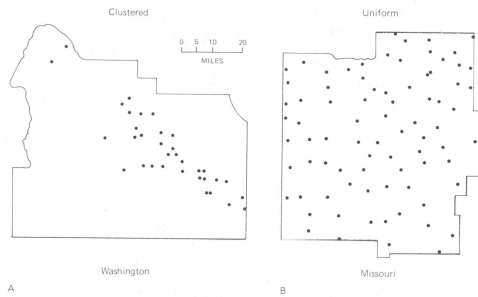

Fig. 2.4   Clustered (A) and uniform (B) distributions of urban centers. There is a clustered arrangement of towns in western Washington where centers reflect a linear arrangement along river valleys. A tendency toward uniform spacing occurs in west-central Missouri where the gently sloping terrain, property subdivision based on the quarter-section, the rectangular road pattern, and the even spread of population are characteristic. (King, 1962, Figs. 3 and 4.)

sometimes frustrating. Perhaps this is best illustrated by the example which follows.

Measuring poverty

At least one-fifth of the American population lives in poverty. But what constitutes poverty, and where do the people live? Inadequate answers to these simple questions obstruct the testing of plausible hypotheses about the real causes of poverty. Without answers, research is limited to qualitative description.

Morrill and Wohlenberg (1971) found no consensus as to what constitutes poverty. The most frequently used measure is that established in 1964 by the President's Council of Economic Advisors. They assumed that any family of four with an annual income of less than $3000, or an individual with less than $1500, lived in poverty. But income measures are misleading. Farmers, for instance, can raise part of their food and can live on less than others. Living costs also vary from area to area depending on the price of food and housing. Therefore, any threshold of poverty is open to criticism.

To correct some of the faults, the Social Security Administration (SSA) devised a more flexible set of criteria. This measure used income as a determinant, but modified the poverty threshold depending upon family size, farm or nonfarm residence, and age and sex of the head of the household (Fig. 2.5).

In addition to defining poverty there is also the problem of locating poverty families. A family unit is a discrete distribution, but most of the information on poverty must be derived from census information. Therefore, discrete information is only available as a contingent distribution, with average income of all families in a census area available as an index of magnitude. A vast amount of information is lost and the pattern of occurrence obscured by the shape of units for which census information is reported.

The distribution of poverty by counties in Illinois is shown in Fig. 2.6. The clustering of the poverty distributions in counties farthest from the metropolitan areas is apparent. However, the pattern observed is based upon the average income of the entire county, yet poverty is a discrete distribution associated with individual families. Some families in these so-called poverty areas do not live in poverty; many others live

Fig. 2.5 Average poverty thresholds for various-sized families and farm and nonfarm residences in 1959 (annual family income in current dollars)

	Nonfarm		Farm	
Persons	Actual SSA value[a]	Value used in calculation	Actual SSA value[b]	Value used in calculation
1	1,510	1,500	1,255	1,300
2	1,950	2,000	1,609	1,600
3	2,390	2,400	1,972	2,000
4	3,060	3,100	2,529	2,500
5	3,605	3,600	2,988	3,000
6	4,055	4,100	3,355	3,400
7 and over	4,985	5,000	4,117	4,100

Source: From *The Geography of Poverty in the United States* by Richard L. Morrill and E. H. Wohlenberg. Copyright 1971. Used by permission of McGraw-Hill Book Co. And from U. S. Bureau of the Census Current Population Reports, series P-23, no. 28, "Revision in Poverty Statistics, 1959, to 1968," 1969 p. 5.

[a] Using original poverty definition.

[b] Using revised poverty definition (farm thresholds are 85 percent of nonfarm thresholds, whereas these values were 70 percent of the nonfarm thresholds in the original definition).

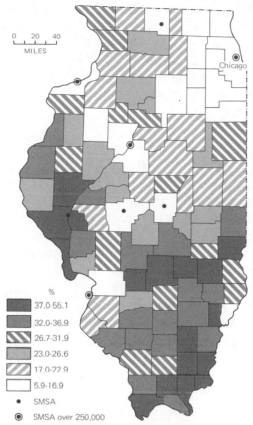

0   20   40
MILES

Chicago

%

37.0-55.1

32.0-36.9

26.7-31.9

23.0-26.6

17.0-22.9

5.9-16.9

•   SMSA

⊚   SMSA over 250,000

Fig. 2.6 Incidence of family poverty and location of larger urban centers in Illinois during 1959. (R. L. Morrill and E. H. Wohlenberg, *The Geography of Poverty In the United States*, © 1971, Fig. 3.3a. Used with permission of McGraw-Hill Book Co.)

on incomes well below the average. In central Chicago, for instance, more than one-third of the families live in poverty, yet this statistic is offset by the affluence of the suburbs, so the entire county shows a low incidence of poverty. Therefore, any attempt to explain the pattern based upon county units must recognize the inherent problems of data based upon census units.

Analysis of many important policy issues is obstructed by the inability to obtain precise information. In studies of poverty, social scientists do not have either the precise locational details or a widely accepted measure of poverty. The techniques of sampling and classification are utilized to remedy this situation. Sampling enables geographers to restrict attention to a reliable portion of all occurrences, and classification assists by grouping the products of human behavior into relatively homogeneous categories. Both techniques are utilized to reduce the complexity of spatial distributions to a manageable level.

CLASSIFICATION

Classification reduces the variety of perceptual stimuli to cognitive order. Not only do we perceive a great variety of objects, but different people perceive them differently. These objects must be categorized so that everyone knows precisely what is meant. Classification also facilitates our own thinking, for virtually all intellectual activity depends upon the categorization and the ordering of occurrences.

Retail stores appear in variety. They differ in function, size, and location. Any of these three features, or some combination of them, could provide the basis for reducing the variety to some order. Grocery stores, for instance, can be categorized as supermarkets, general merchandise, or corner grocery stores. Each attracts customers from a market area that varies in size and assortment of goods. Another way of classifying grocery stores is by value of sales. However, geographers prefer a system of classification in which there is a spatial attribute. By subdividing the group according to a classification in which there is a spatial attribute, locational factors are suggested.

The objectives of classification can be summarized as follows: to order experience, to summarize information, and to suggest hypotheses that might explain the location and arrangement of a specified category of phenomena.

Classification in geography

Occurrences of phenomena can be classified by different systems to suit analysis. Berry (1964) has suggested that classification in geography can be conceptualized as a matrix in which occurrences can be categorized in terms of activity, location, and time (Fig. 2.7).

The advantage of the threefold division is that it provides alternative differentiating characteristics that are exhibited by all occurrences. For

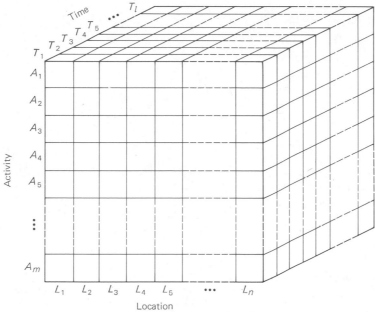

Fig. 2.7 A "matrix" for categorizing geographical information. (After Smith, 1971, Fig. 1.1; and after Berry, reproduced with permission from *Annals of the Association of American Geographers*, vol. 54, 1964, Fig. 2.)

example, poverty may be represented as an activity: There are poverty families and nonpoverty families, and a measure—usually income—that will distinguish between them may be chosen. The location of poverty families can also be identified, as can the duration or time in which families have lived in poverty. Each attribute also exhibits a range of magnitude that facilitates further subdivision.

CLASSIFICATION OF INDUSTRY

Smith (1971) illustrates this classification in his study of industrial location. Observations of industry may be placed in all three dimensions of the matrix. Each row of the matrix represents an industrial activity, while each of the columns comprises a location for which data has been compiled. In a systematic study of any one industry the observations would appear in one row of a two-dimensional matrix, representing the total information available for locations under review at a specific time. If the industry were to be compared over a number of time periods

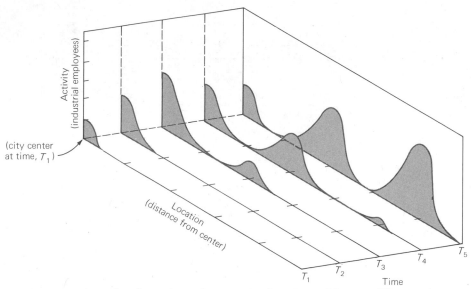

Fig. 2.8 Location of industrial employment in American cities at different time periods. During the first three time periods the intensity of industrial employment increased near the city center. In T_4 and T_5 industry has moved to suburban locations with considerable expansion employment.

so that the development processes might become apparent, then a three-dimensional matrix will be required (Fig. 2.8).

In geography the emphasis is frequently upon the study of industry in a region or area, rather than on the systematic study of a specific industry. Area-to-area comparisons involve information about different activities in the same location, which create special problems in classification. A variety of information is available, and the problem is to aggregate areas that are relatively homogeneous in terms of activities. This is what geographers call a _region_.

CLASSIFICATION OF REGIONS

One of the basic notions that pervades all subdivisions of geography is that regions of similar activities may be identified. Regions allow geographers to generalize about the complex distribution of activities that exhibit different frequencies of occurrence by location and through time. Regionalization is the identification of locations that have similar associations of activities and the linking of these relatively homogeneous locations into areas. It is essentially an attempt to bring order out of the disorder that initially appears in spatial distributions.

Figure 2.9A illustrates an idealized study area. The size of the

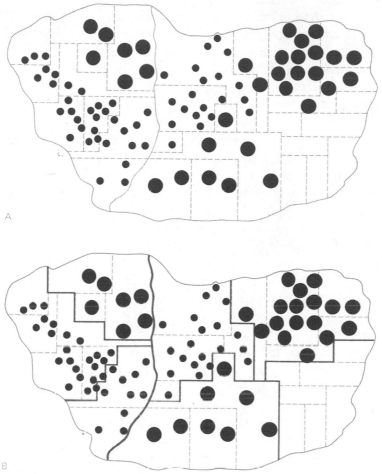

Fig. 2.9 (A) spatial distribution in an idealized study area.
(B) Generalization of distribution into regions.

large circles spatially distributed throughout this study area is proportionate to the magnitude of a specific activity (i.e., a large circle
has a far greater value than a very small circle). The broken lines and
the river delimit the study area into smaller subareas that are defined
according to some administrational criterion; for this example, these
subareas may be thought of as townships. Suppose you are asked to
describe the regional pattern that appears on the map. I do not think
this is possible because no consistent rationale has been given for the
pattern appearing on the map.

Suppose you generalize the pattern so that it depicts and summarizes the observable tendency of certain values of the large circles to cluster in specific subareas of the map. This request appears to be easier to fulfill. For example, according to the variation of the values of the large circles from place to place on the map, a reasonable regionalization of this distribution might appear as is shown in Fig. 2.9B.

A regional classification is an intellectual concept. It exists only in terms of the criteria by which it is defined. Hence, to construct a region or a set of regions, and to select a particular unit area (a township) and place it in a specific region, according to whether or not the unit area exhibits the properties of that region, is simply a matter of classification. Therefore, we may define a region as an area (1) of any size, (2) homogeneous in terms of specific criteria, (3) distinguished from bordering areas by a particular kind of association of related features, and (4) possessing some kind of internal cohesion.

It is convenient to divide regions into two classes: uniform and nodal.

Uniform regions: The uniform region is an area in which one or more distinctive characteristics are similar throughout. This similarity or homogeneity is strongest near the center or core of the region and gradually weakens toward the margins, where it is replaced by a different type of homogeneity. The boundary of the uniform region is established along the line at which this replacement occurs.

Nodal regions: The nodal region is centered upon a single node or focus. The focus is usually urban, and most often is the center of trade, communications, and circulation for the region. The unity of the region is based upon the interconnection of the places within it. All parts of the nodal region are connected to the node in some way, and their relation or connection to any other node in that particular way is less important. The boundary of the nodal region is located along the line that defines the end of the dominating influence of the node in question and the introduction of the dominating influence of some adjacent node.

A city is both a uniform region and the center of a nodal region. As an association of intensive land utilization, it can be differentiated as a uniform region from the less intensive land utilization of the surrounding rural area. However, there are many interconnections between the urban center and the surrounding rural area. Newspapers, banks, and administrative offices located in the city serve the rural community so that the urban area is also the center for a nodal region. That a city can be both a uniform and nodal region serves to illustrate that regions are not unique areas; rather, they are intellectual concepts used to classify geographical information.

CLASSIFICATION OF LAND USE

Because land use is continuous it has always presented a problem in classification. Terms like *urban* and *rural* are used to describe activity systems for which there is general agreement on interpretation. But where does the urban end and the rural begin as one travels out from the city? The urban-rural fringe designates the transitional zone where the remnants of agriculture persist amid residences and noxious activities like airports, power plants, and electrical substations.

Differentiation between *land use* and *land utilization* is also important. Land use is the use actually made of any parcel of land. House, apartment, duplex, and condominium are land-use categories, whereas the term *residential* refers to a system of land utilization implying roads, and neighborhood retail and service activities as well as social and recreational facilities. In a rural area, tree crop or row crop would identify *land use*, whereas orcharding or truck farming indicates a system of *land utilization*. generalized land use for an area (several land uses in a zone)

Classification has helped order the profusion of occurrences so that similarities between areas have become apparent. Rigorous sample designs have also helped: They provide the method for selecting a representative portion of the similar occurrences in different areas so that causal processes might be further analyzed.

SAMPLING

Science does not require the study of every occurrence of a particular activity. Rather, it is normal to test an idea against a designated portion of the total population. The unbiased selection of the test population is called *sampling*. A systematic examination of a *sample* population establishes laws applicable to the *target* population.

Selected sampling is not unbiased. It is merely a way of studying typical portions of an area. It accepts rather than tests a hypothesis and is used as a method for illustrating an idea. Case studies in economic geography are examples of selected sampling. A factory or farm is a selected sample used to illustrate the locational advantage of an area for certain types of economic activity. A traverse across a city may be selected to illustrate the arrangement of land uses. These are useful teaching aids, but selected sampling should not be confused with sampling for experimental design.

Sample design

Four types of sample design are common in geographical research: random, stratified, systematic, and a combination of all three—stratified systematic unaligned samples (Fig. 2.10). The choice of design depends on the kind of distribution under investigation. In random samples, each unit has equal opportunity to be chosen. This is the preferred method because it is possible to estimate the accuracy with which the sample values are representative of the target population. However, random samples are not suited to all studies. Stratified and systematic samples are used to restrict random selection to designated areas. They are useful in geography where tests are designed to assess variability of occurrences within an area, or when representation of different areas occupied by the occurrences is desired.

The stratified systematic unaligned sample produces the least variation between sample and *target populations*. It is a combined method that preserves the theoretical advantages of randomization and stratification, together with aspects of systematic samples. The study area is divided into regular subareas, but a different location is chosen in each subarea as the sample.

In the design of new public transit routes, management is very interested in consumer response to route locations, schedules, design of vehicles, and the service provided by employees. An opinion survey of people selected by the stratified systematic unaligned method will provide this information. Census blocks, representative of the area in which new routes are to be introduced, can be chosen at random within stratified areas. Within each block a predetermined number of dwelling units are selected again by random methods and a member of the household is interviewed. In this manner opinions of people representative of the target population (i.e., people within an area in which new routes are to be introduced) can be obtained. This information is used by manage-

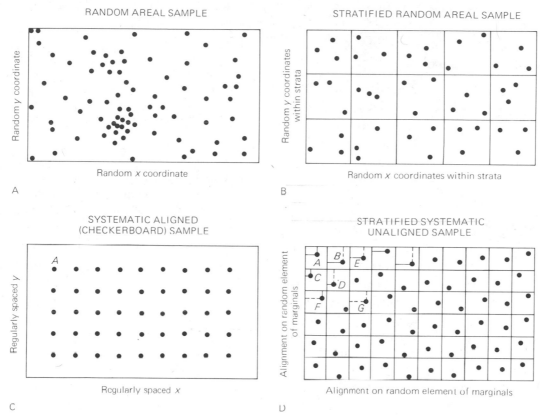

Fig. 2.10 Sampling spatial distributions. Four methods of sampling are useful in geography: random (A), stratified random (B), systematic (C), and stratified systematic unaligned (D). (Brian J. L. Berry and Duane F. Marble, eds., *Spatial Analysis: A Reader in Statistical Geography*, © 1968, pp. 92–93. Reprinted by permission of Prentice-Hall, Inc., Englewood Cliffs, N.J.)

ment to design the route structure and level of service. By finding out what people want, transit service can be designed to fulfill the perceived needs of the patrons, rather than the opinions of management. This same information can be used to direct advertising. Surveys repeated after service has been introduced provide an index of achievement.

Market analysis studies are used in many other industries to test the acceptance of a product before it is introduced to the public. Both the sampling procedure and the survey instrument must be designed with care, otherwise the results are not reliable. Information is often gathered on the occupation and personality of the person interviewed, because products may prove more attractive to some groups of people than to others.

Units for sampling

The unit for which sample information is gathered must be determined early in the research strategy. This decision is influenced both by the availability of information and by the nature of the distribution under investigation.

Either point locations or areal units may be chosen. _Point samples_ are used for continuous distributions like temperature, air pollution, or farm prices, because the occurrence at any one point is assumed to equal that which occurs over a general area. _Areal units_, like census tracts or blocks, are used for contingent distributions. When contingent distributions mask important variations in discrete distributions, as they do with poverty statistics, then a combination of areal and point sampling units must be chosen.

For research on poverty, census tracts or blocks (areal units) can be selected by a sampling method. Information can be aggregated for the entire unit or, if individual household data are required, a randomized selection of households (discrete locations) can be identified for interview (Fig. 2.11). The results can be used to characterize the target population with a known level of accuracy.

Given the complexity of man's use of the land and the frequency of geographic occurrences, sampling is an essential technique. It provides a method to test statements about the causal processes generating the distribution by studying a select portion of the occurrences. The method of sampling chosen by the investigator will depend upon the nature of the distribution, the resources available, and the precision desired. Only through meticulous care in sampling can spatial distributions be tested and efficient models of spatial organization be developed.

MODELS IN GEOGRAPHY

Models are special statements about reality. They are skeletal representations of reality that enable us to understand the nature of spatial distributions.

In geography the most frequently used model is the map, in which the arrangement of phenomena is represented in abstract form and at

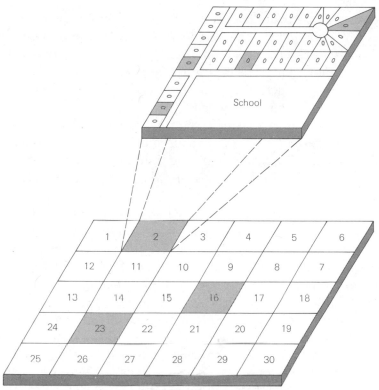

Fig. 2.11 Selecting households by random. In a relatively homogeneous suburb a random selection of census blocks (shaded areas) and households within these blocks (solid areas) will provide an estimate for the target population (all households in the suburb). If the suburb was divided socially, a means of stratifying the area would be required. The selection of sample populations is a specialized task, usually requiring a specialist in survey research.

a different scale. Maps are *analogue* models. A photograph is an *iconic* model; it captures reality but does not abstract relationships, and is usually used only for illustrative purposes or for data collection.

The most rewarding models for research are *symbolic* models in which physical properties are represented as mathematical statements. The equations that you will encounter in subsequent chapters are examples of extremely simple symbolic models. Distributions can be accounted for by changing one or more variables in these equations and comparing the results with actual distributions.

Graphic space model

Distance and accessibility were emphasized in Chapter 1 as pervasive themes in geography. The relation of one location to the centers of activity often determines land use. Although economic activities are possible at many different locations, they will be produced only at those locations from which they can be most easily marketed. Accessible locations enjoy a comparative advantage in commercial economies.

The concept of accessibility can be formulated as a graphic space model and presented as a graph or map (analogue model) or as an equation (symbolic model). If you have completed the first unit in *Programmed Case Studies in Geography* you already have been introduced to the model.

In its classic form—as propounded by the German economist Johann Heinrich Von Thünen—the model was simplified by making all things equal except cost of transportation. Transportation costs were assumed to increase with distance. Therefore, farmers farthest from the market had higher production costs due to higher transportation charges and, therefore, they could pay least locational rent.

Locational rent is the additional price an individual is willing to pay to secure the use of a favored location. In the graphic space model, land closest to the city is the most valuable because goods produced there will have the least transportation costs. Therefore, perishable or bulky goods like vegetables and milk will be produced nearest to the city.

Although the graphic space model can be used to illustrate aspects of industrial location and urban land values, it is usually associated with agriculture (Fig. 2.12). To understand the pattern of agriculture postulated by the model, five simplifying assumptions must be understood:

1. There is an isolated state, cut off from the rest of the world.
2. The state is dominated by a large city which purchases the agricultural produce and supplies manufactured goods.
3. Land surrounding the city is of equal quality: a broad featureless plain that is everywhere equal in fertility and ease of movement, so that production and transportation costs are everywhere the same.
4. Farmers attempt to maximize profits by adjusting crops in terms of the needs of the market and the costs of transporting goods to the city.

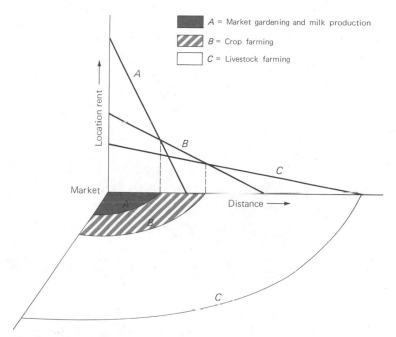

Fig. 2.12   Von Thünen's model of agricultural patterns based upon location rent. The spatial distribution is based upon distance from the isolated market.

5. The cost of transportation is the independent (causal) variable and land use the dependent (resulting) variable. Transport costs increase uniformly with distance in all directions so that the cost for 2 miles is twice the cost for 1 mile. Therefore, transport costs may be expressed as distance (Fig. 2.12).

A concentric arrangement of land utilization develops as the pattern that ought to occur (the *normative pattern*) (Fig. 2.13, left). Intensive land utilization (e.g., market gardens and milk production) is located adjacent to the city. Extensive land utilization (e.g., livestock ranching) is located farthest from the city, where distance reduces locational rent. There is little competition for the land far from the city, and goods that can be transported long distances are produced here.

Von Thünen also demonstrated the effect of improved transportation by introducing in his model a river that decreased transportation costs for lands along its course (Fig. 2.13, right). The concentric pattern is

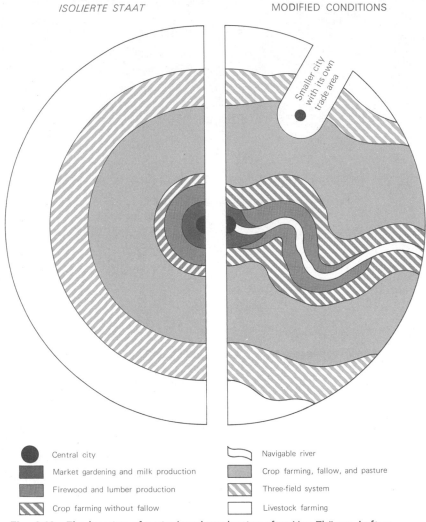

Fig. 2.13 The location of agricultural production after Von Thünen. Left, a concentric arrangement about the isolated market is assumed. Right, the influence of improved communications and alternative markets is shown under modified conditions. (Grotewold, 1959, Fig. 1.)

disrupted by the parallel bands of land use that reflect lower transportation costs alongside the river.

Symbolic model of land use

The graphic space model of land use provides a three-dimensional representation by graph and map of the relationship between distance from market and land use when all but the cost of transportation were assumed to be uniform. The agricultural landscape around any market, of course, is the result of many other factors, such as cost of fertilizer, varying crop yields, the demand for different crops, and the price differential between markets. These factors are seldom uniform. In order to assess the outcome of any changes in these variables, a statement of functional relationships in symbolic (mathematical) language is necessary.

A symbolic model conceptualizes a problem so that the effect of changes in several variables is apparent. Simple relationships can be explained in verbal terms and represented by graphs and maps, but where relationships are complex it is impossible to contemplate the problem if stated verbally. A mathematical formulation of the problem is required so that the effect of several independent variables may be assessed.

The graphic space model can be formulated so that economic rent for alternative crops can be computed using the equation:

$$R = E(p - a) - Efk$$

where

E is yield per unit area

p is the price of a unit of commodity

a is cost of production of a unit of commodity

f is transfer cost per unit distance per unit commodity

k is the distance to market

By changing the variables, alternative outcomes can be observed. Figure 2.14 shows two of a series of computer maps resulting from changes in variables. If you are using *Programmed Case Studies in Geography* you will have an opportunity to work through an example.

The computer-printed maps result from separate calculations of the above formula for 2000 locations. Economic rent is calculated for each of four activities (crops) against each location. A symbol is printed representing the activity earning the highest rent in each location. The pattern could represent farms or fields for which land-use decisions are made.

By concentrating attention on the five variables affecting economic rent and altering their magnitude, we are able to estimate the role that each variable plays in determining land-use patterns. The symbolic model not only has greater precision than the graphic space (analogue)

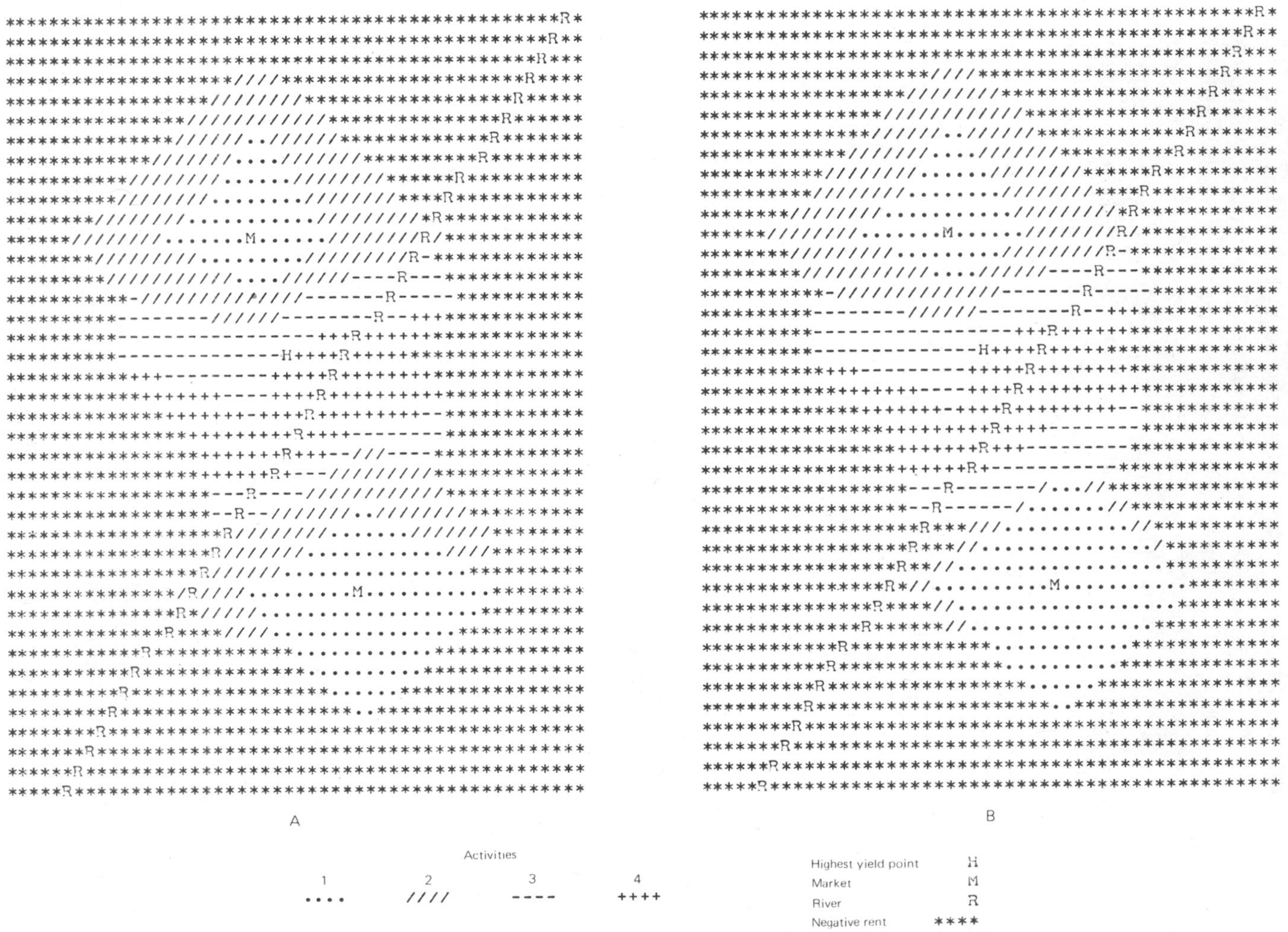

B

A

Activities

Highest yield point   H
Market   M
River   R
Negative rent   ****

1	2	3	4
....	////	- - - -	+++

Fig. 2.14 Computer simulation of rural land utilization. The activity designated is calculated separately for 2000 locations and the resultant map is produced on the student terminal. Map (B) differs from (A) because market prices for Activity 2 was decreased at the lower market center. All other variables remain equal.

model, but it also facilitates the manipulation of variables.

By designing a model for land use around cities, Von Thünen has enabled geographers to recognize similar patterns of occurrence in many parts of the world, as well as in the arrangement of land uses within cities.

Land use in cities

A concentric model of urban land use has been proposed, in which the intensity of land at the city center is explained by superior accessibility. Original housing surrounded the commercial core, but as these homes became old and therefore unsatisfactory to high-income families, they were vacated by the rich and occupied by the poor. The rich built new houses where open land was available. They surrendered the accessibility of the central city for the spaciousness of the suburbs and commuted to work. As housing aged, the sequent occupancy continues, with immigrants to the city from rural areas and foreign countries moving into the aging housing. A concentric arrangement of urban land use resulted. The commercial core became surrounded by deteriorating housing of the low-income groups with an outer ring of affluent suburbs.

Urban renewal in the 1950s and 1960s was an attempt to change the existing pattern. Old buildings at the city center were demolished and replaced by new high-rise apartments. The purpose was to attract affluent families back to the city center. However, success, as Alonso (1964) predicted, has been limited. Most affluent families prefer the spaciousness of their suburban residences over the accessibility of the central city. As a consequence, much of the cleared land in the central city remains vacant. The behavioral processes that had caused the concentric development had been misinterpreted. Only a few principally childless families were willing to exchange the spaciousness of their suburban homes for accessibility of central city apartments.

Conclusion

The geographer's search for explanations has required new classifications and sampling designs to detect the regular occurrence of similar land uses in different areas.

The progression from observation and analysis of the pattern through classification and sampling is a slow and continuing process. Heinrich Von Thünen first published his idea in 1826 and provided an analogue model. Ernest Burgess used the same model to explain urban land use in 1925. However, it was not until 1954 that Edgar Dunn formulated an adequate symbolic model. And now, modeling of the spatial pattern is no longer sufficient: Geographers and social scientists are interested in spatial distributions because the distributions and their organization are indicative of the processes of human behavior.

In the behavioral approach to social science, hypothesis formulation and testing are crucial steps to model building. These steps have been intentionally overlooked in this chapter because they deserve separate discussion. There is no general theory in social science to guide deductive questioning. Most of the research is based upon speculation about perceptual experiences. Therefore, the questions asked, and the manner in which these questions are formulated as hypotheses, is even more important than the experimental design procedures of analysis, classification, and sampling that, together with the models, have been the theme of this chapter.

SUGGESTED READINGS

The following two textbooks emphasize a similar approach to the analysis of spatial distributions. Each provides illustrations of the methods used by geographers:

Abler, Ronald; Adams, John S.; and Gould, Peter. *Spatial Organization: The Geographer's View of the World.* Englewood Cliffs, N.J.: Prentice-Hall, 1971, pp. 149–189.

Haggett, Peter. *Geography: A Modern Synthesis.* New York: Harper & Row, 1972, chaps. 1, 4, and 5.

Specific examples of the analysis of spatial distributions are provided by:

Morrill, Richard L., and Wohlenberg, Ernest H. *The Geography of Poverty in the United States.* New York: McGraw-Hill, 1971.

Smith, David M. *Industrial Location: An Economic Geographical Analysis.* New York: Wiley, 1971, pp. 1–22.

Rose, Harold M. *The Black Ghetto: A Spatial Behavioral Perspective.* New York: McGraw-Hill, 1971.

Survey research, sampling, data collection, and classification are discussed by:

Backstrom, Charles H., and Hursh, Gerald D. *Survey Research*. Evanston, Ill.: Northwestern University Press, 1963.

Berry, Brian B. J. "Approaches to Regional Analysis: A Synthesis." *Annals of the Association of American Geographers* 54(1964):2–11.

CHAPTER 3
HYPOTHESES AND RESEARCH

Developing theories and models of human behavior is of paramount concern in social science. Unfortunately, social scientists have not yet developed a well-defined body of theory which would suggest interrelationships among the variables motivating human behavior. Consequently, most research proceeds by observing patterns of occurrence and inferring the relationships between variables. The suggestion that there is a relationship between two or more variables can be stated as a hypothesis.

A hypothesis is a potential answer to a question about relationships. Hypotheses originate from the observations of events: They provide the bridge between the observed world and theory because trained observers ask questions about the relationship between events in light of existing theory. Once a hypothesis is formed, it is advanced for testing.

To assist research, social scientists transform the events of human behavior into indicators (*variables*) that can be measured. These variables may be direct indicators, like family income in poverty studies, or indirect (*surrogate*) indicators, like distance as a measure of interaction between areas. The purpose of the transformation is to obtain *measurable* variables so that the hypothesized interrelationships between events might be tested.

RESEARCH STRATEGY

Testing hypotheses may proceed by deduction or induction. *Deductive research* explains events by citing conclusions that are based upon theoretical principles or laws. *Inductive research* tests relationships between two or more events to illustrate the operation of a theoretical process. Because not enough is known of the complex interrelationships that motivate human behavior in geography, we have too few theoretical principles or laws from which we can deduce testable propositions. Most geographical research is therefore inductive.

The alternative to hypothesis testing is description. Events can be described, and the observer can become enthusiastic about the uniqueness or the commonality of occurrences. However, as society changed, the relationships described would become invalid. As an example, we might cite the former relationship between coal mining and steel production. The steel plants were originally located near the mines, but now steel is produced in many locations. If geographers had stopped after describing the original relationship, they would have failed to appreciate the complex locational factors involved, and the overwhelming desire of companies to minimize costs of production and to monopolize regional markets. Through testing the relationship between observed occurrences, a better knowledge of the locational principles has been established. Occurrences of steel plants at ports where imported iron ore and coal are available, or in metropolitan areas where there is an excess of scrap steel can be explained in terms of cost of production and market orientation. In this way, testing has identified locational factors which have contributed to the growing body of theory in geography.

Distribution of poverty

The distribution of poverty in a hypothetical area will serve to illustrate the role of hypothesis testing in geographical research. Poverty is usually associated with the elderly or families without male heads of households: families that are isolated by age or inability to work away from home. However, the most widespread occurrences of poverty are in rural areas like Appalachia and portions of the South and Midwest where the returns from agriculture are marginal and where mechanized farming has deprived many people of gainful employment. Many families in these rural areas eke out a semisubsistence livelihood at a standard well below the rest of the nation when measured by economic criteria.

To illustrate how the hypothesis helps geographers to understand the relationships between some of the variables causing poverty, let us assume there is a relatively homogeneous statistical area like a state or province that is divided into smaller census units like counties or townships. Within this territory there are three cities with more than 50,000 population, with the remaining area predominately rural (Fig. 3.1).

Information on family size is not available, so family income is used as the measurable variable indicative of poverty. Those families, regardless of size, with less than $3000 in annual income are assumed to be living in poverty, and the percentage of these families in each county provides an index of both the magnitude and distribution of poverty.

A clustering of occurrences is apparent. Counties adjacent to the urban centers have a low incidence of poverty, whereas the incidence is higher in the more isolated areas. There appears to be some relationship between interaction and poverty that deserves analysis.

Distance and interaction were identified as core concepts in geographical theory. Geographers are constantly aware of the effect on behavior when people are separated and yet expected to interact in the economic system. Familiarity with the effect of distance on spatial organization suggests the hypothesis that the incidence of poverty is

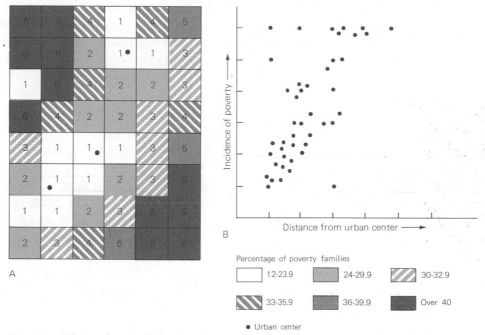

Fig. 3.1 (A) incidence of family poverty and urban centers in a hypothetical area. (B) Relationship between the incidence of family poverty and distance from urban centers.

a function of the distance from the centers of economic activity in the three cities.

This hypothesis is plausible because most economic opportunities have occurred in cities during recent decades. As people have demanded more personal services like education, entertainment, and medical care, employment has expanded in those centers that can provide these amenities. At the same time, employment opportunities have declined in rural areas as farm labor has been replaced by machines. Many families and younger people entering the labor force moved to the cities. Others felt unable or unwilling to relocate and have remained in the rural areas. Seasonal work and financial aid are their primary sources of income. The successful farmers travel to the cities often, and some even operate their agribusiness out of city offices. However, the cost of overcoming the distance cuts off the small farmer and farm laborer from regular interaction in the economic life of the city.

Both theoretical and common knowledge suggest that a relationship between poverty and distance from urban centers is plausible. The problem can be restated by the following hypothesis: That the incidence of poverty increases with distance from urban activity centers. It is hypothesized that there is a positive relationship between the two variables: As distance increases (the independent variable) there is an increase in the incidence of poverty (dependent variable). This simple relationship can be illustrated as a scatter diagram, with the dependent variable on the vertical axis and the independent on the horizontal (Fig. 3.1B).

Regression analysis is an appropriate test for the hypothesis: The distribution and magnitude of one variable may be compared with the other so that their correspondence can be assessed. Another way of explaining regression analysis is to imagine that the independent variable is a sponge and see how much of the dependent variable it can soak up through correspondence in location and magnitude. Learning Units 4 and 5 in *Programmed Case Studies in Geography* will provide additional experience in regression analysis. The procedure is broken down into steps and students are challenged to work through the steps by themselves.

Perfect correlation between distance and the incidence of poverty is unlikely. Other variables will affect the distribution so that the simple regression equation will only be able to explain part of the relationship between the two variables. Factors like the type of agriculture and the productivity of the soil, and other economic activities like mining and military installations, which are often located in remote areas, need to be included if an adequate explanation of the distribution of poverty is to be achieved. However, in the studies of poverty in Illinois, Alabama, and Iowa reported by Morrill and Wohlenberg (1971) more than half of the spatial variation in poverty was explained by distance from the nearest standard metropolitan statistical area. (SMSA).

Throughout the entire hypothesis-formulating and testing procedure, the aim is to state problems so that the relationship between variables suggested by theory might be assessed against observed occurrences. The hypothesis may be accepted or rejected, but either way it provides an important link between theory and reality.

Exploratory hypothesis

Many problems in geography are still so little understood that it is difficult to advance hypotheses that can be accepted or rejected. In

[handwritten margin note: regression analysis: explains as much as possible of the variation in the dependent variable by some measure of the independent variable.]

these problems, hypotheses are exploratory and tend to raise more questions than they answer. For example, the cause of the deterioration of neighborhoods is unknown. The sequence by which a neighborhood becomes a slum can be documented, and aspects of the demise can be selected and advanced as hypotheses for study, but the totality of the process still eludes the social scientist.

In order to clarify observations, deterioration can be hypothesized to occur in a sequence of eight steps. Each step can be studied in different cities, for it is believed that the process follows a similar course.

1. Older neighborhoods are more susceptible to decline. Senior citizens seldom have the physical or financial ability to maintain their homes in sound repair.
2. The arrival of minority families who differ in language and skin color alarms white homeowners, although the new families frequently have higher incomes and similar life styles.
3. White families disregard the caliber of the newcomers and those old families who are able to do so, move. Panic selling often results, even though studies have shown that an ethnic change does not depress property values. When more than one-fifth of the residences are occupied by minority families, white families cease to move into the neighborhood. Even middle-class families who were the early minority residents begin to desert the neighborhood.
4. When the number of families leaving exceeds the number who can afford, and are willing, to move in, residences become vacant. They become certain targets for vandalism and occupancy by "squatter" communes.
5. If there are many apartments in the neighborhood the change in tenants at this stage transforms the neighborhood very quickly. To reduce vacancies, apartment managers accept families with many children and those who are less desirable tenants. Additional demands are placed upon hallways, toilets, and utilities in the older buildings. Maintenance that was adequate for smaller families will not suffice any more. Deterioration and vandalism increases, yet landlords are unwilling to pay for repairs.
6. Public services also decline. As density increases, police are unable to cope with rising crime; fire hazards mount, and city

trash collectors cannot handle the refuse generated in crowded tenements. When the plumbing fails, halls and elevators become latrines.

7. Frequently, the building is abandoned by the owner. For some time he no longer cares. Repairs are not made, although an attempt is made to collect rents. Finally, he refuses to pay the taxes and the property reverts to the local agency.

8. Destruction may occur before abandonment. Fires set accidentally or purposely may gut the building. Vandals can be as destructive as fire. Pipes and wiring that can be sold for salvage are torn out and the building left for squatters, many of whom are junkies.

Studies of deterioration in different cities have provided geographers with an understanding of the steps of neighborhood decline, but the fundamental processes remain uncertain (Fig. 3.2). Questions arise, such as: What is the threshold of minority occupancy before decline begins; in what way are property taxes responsible; why can larger apartment complexes resist neighborhood change more effectively than smaller units; and will urban renewal change the neighborhood? Each question provides a stimulus for geographical research, which may ultimately provide an explanation for the entire process.

The United States and Canada are urban nations, yet much more is known about soil conservation and prevention of potato disease than about the conservation of residential areas and cures for urban blight. It is alarming how little urban theory has been established. We remain content with untested generalizations about the processes of urbanization while the central city becomes a wasteland occupied by people we cannot assist. Billions of federal dollars have been spent on programs intended to transform the slums: Some areas have been gilded over by new construction, but the human problems remain. The fundamental human processes that cause the sense of despair and hopelessness have not been isolated. Solutions will only be achieved by imaginative research programs that rigorously examine alternative proposals to be advanced for testing.

An exploratory hypothesis focuses study upon a problem requiring clarification. It is a way of avoiding mere description of the patterns of human behavior, because the hypothesis orients the study toward important questions. As the questions become refined rigorous testing of alternative outcomes can proceed.

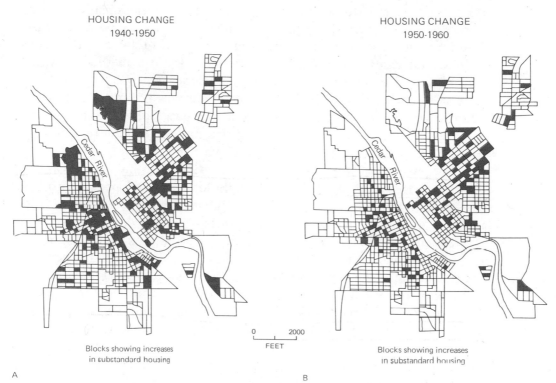

HOUSING CHANGE
1940-1950

HOUSING CHANGE
1950-1960

Blocks showing increases
in substandard housing

0   2000
FEET

Blocks showing increases
in substandard housing

A

B

Fig. 3.2 Increases in substandard housing in Cedar Rapids, Iowa, during 1940–1950
(A) and 1950–1960 (B). The outward expansion of the zone of deterioration occurs
as neighborhoods age. Urban renewal in the 1950s had begun to replace the
deteriorated zone surrounding the city center. (After Hartshorn, reproduced with
permission from *Annals of the Association of American Geographers*, vol. 61, 1971,
Figs. 11 and 12.)

Hypotheses and research endeavor

Most geographical research attempts to improve the methods by which
hypotheses may be stated and tested. Mapping, photo interpretation and
field work enhance the description of spatial distributions. They enable
the observations to be recorded accurately so that hypotheses might
be tested against real world occurrences.

The development of new techniques for hypothesis testing receives
considerable attention in geographical research. In the early 1960s
regression techniques were common. Factor analysis became popular
as geographers attempted studies utilizing numerous variables which
required reduction to representative factors. Bundles of variables were
reduced to a single index, and although the method was more complex,

the aim was still to test hypotheses about the relationship between variables. More recently, multidimensional scaling has been in vogue. The impetus was the desire to investigate problems related to the choice between alternative locations: Geographers needed a method by which attitudes toward alternative locations could be scaled.

These techniques for hypothesis testing are not unique to geography. They are common to the social sciences, and geographers have borrowed extensively. However, their use in geography to explore relationships implicit in spatial organization is distinctive.

The purpose of hypothesis testing is to improve the theoretical constructs of the discipline. Sound hypotheses are developed in order to test the relationships between theory and occurrences. Therefore, they must be developed by those with a knowledge of previous studies. Generalizations published in previous studies can be reexamined or tested for applications under different cultural circumstances. Also there are often questions left unanswered in previous studies. These offer a starting point for new questions.

Hypothesis formation is a method by which answerable questions are presented for examination. Field observation, mapping, and reviews of the literature are all important in the refinement of propositions so that research efforts are maximized. They represent the initial step in a well-established approach to research (Fig. 3.3).

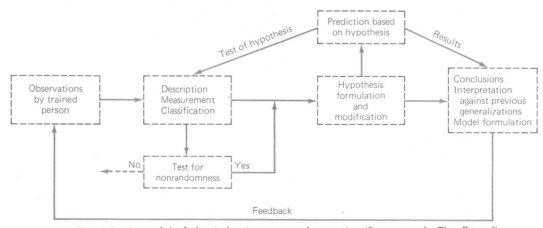

Fig. 3.3 A model of the inductive approach to scientific research. The flow diagram illustrates the process whereby a trained person observes distributions and proposes a relationship as a hypothesis for testing. The results of the test provide feedback for the discipline.

APPROACHES TO GEOGRAPHICAL RESEARCH

Research in geography is a cyclical process. New knowledge stimulates new questions, which can then be tested as hypotheses.

Initially, the questions concerned the location of elements and descriptive studies satisfied that need. However, as geographers acquired knowledge of different areas, they recognized similarities and differences *between* areas, and the questions about spatial distribution have become more complex. New methods of recording spatial distributions on maps had to be developed, and geographers began to use sophisticated data-manipulation techniques and statistical methods to test associated hypotheses. Haggett (1965) summarizes the cyclical nature of the research process and refers to sequential and parallel approaches (Fig. 3.4).

In the sequential approach, problems are defined and hypotheses are applied; their effectiveness is tested by statistical methods, and new hypotheses are evolved to explain discrepancies. The approach is conceptualized as a series of cycles.

Library or field research stimulates geographical interest in a problem, but, in order that intelligent questions might be asked, further research of related problems is necessary so that the variables, particularly the independent (Y) variable, may be defined. Information on the variables can be gathered from field study or from secondary sources like the census. Sampling methods are normally used to assure an unbiased selection of the information and certain statistical tests can be used to analyze the data for randomness and to test whether the sample is representative.

If the problem is standard and the relationships between variables well known, then regression analysis of the association can begin (Fig. 3.4, Step 7a). However, in most research the association is unknown, and mapping of the dependent variable and suspected independent (X) variables is recommended. This is the cartographic phase in which occurrence in similar locations suggest hypotheses to be tested in the second cycle of analysis.

Information on the independent (X_1) variable must be rigorously checked before analysis. Steps 5 and 6 of Fig. 3.4 replicate Steps 1 and 2 performed on the dependent variable. If the data is fairly representative of the independent variable the test of the association between Y and X_1 may proceed.

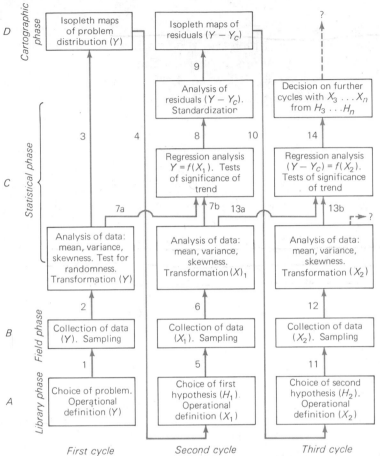

Fig. 3.4 Model of regression cycles in geographical research. (After Haggett, 1965, Table 10.1.)

This relationship may be expressed as a hypothesis in which the location and magnitude of occurrences of Y is some function of the variable X_1. This may be restated as the regression equation ($Y = f(X_1)$. The purpose is to explain as much as possible of the variation in Y by some value of, or function of, X_1. As was stated earlier, regression analysis is like a sponge: It is a technique for soaking up (i.e. explaining the association) for as much of the variation in Y by the sponge, $f(X_1)$. A perfect relationship is unlikely when dealing with human behavior. The unexplained locations can be mapped as residuals. Analysis of these residuals (Steps 8 and 9) suggest additional variables (X_2, X_3) that might provide a more complete explanation of the dependent variable.

In parallel analysis, multiple working hypotheses are presented together, rather than in sequence. Often the distribution of the dependent (Y) variable can only be explained by the interrelationship of several variables (X_1; X_2; X_3; X_n). Techniques such as multiple regression and factor analysis are used in the analysis. Before we proceed, however, an example of the sequential approach to geographical research follows.

Analysis of voting patterns

The results from an election provide excellent information on differences in the magnitude of the vote from area to area. There is a genuine interest in attempts to explain these patterns, for they provide an insight into the voter's choice. Harold McCarty, who supported a more analytical approach to geographical research during the 1960s, chose a rather whimsical illustration of the usefulness of sequential analysis. In an unpublished paper entitled "McCarty on McCarthy," he attempted to explain the voting pattern of Wisconsin residents for Senator Joseph McCarthy, a senator notorious for his attempt to purge American campuses and institutions of Communists after World War II. The problem was to explain the location and intensity of the vote cast for the senator in various voting districts of the state. The dependent (Y) variable was the percentage of all votes cast for the senator. The first hypothesis (H_1) postulated that the senator had been elected mainly by a farm vote. The independent variable (X_1) was then measured as the percentage of rural population in each voting area. Note that one percentage was being compared with another and, although rural population is not synonymous with the percentage of farmers, it provided the best available indicator.

A standard regression analysis ($Y = f(X_1)$ was then computed. About one-third of the total areal variation in the McCarthy vote could be accounted for by variations in the distribution of rural population (Fig. 3.5). The residuals from this equation were plotted and showed a high ridge in the more populous central and southern Wisconsin voting districts. The variations are represented as a choropleth map (Fig. 3.6).

In both of these areas the prediction based on H_1 had underestimated the true strength of the McCarthy vote. Familiarity with

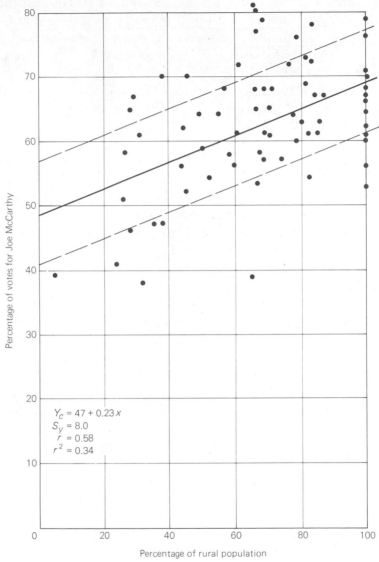

$Y_c = 47 + 0.23x$
$S_y = 8.0$
$r = 0.58$
$r^2 = 0.34$

Fig. 3.5 Percentage of votes for McCarthy related to the percentage of population classified as rural in 1950. (McCarty, 1952, unpublished paper.)

the senator's ideas was a possible reason for this discrepancy. Those areas closest to his home in Appleton would be more familiar with the man and, therefore, more likely to vote for him than rural areas farther away. Knowledge of the distance and interaction concept suggested

Positive
residuals
Negative
residuals

Appleton ●

Fig. 3.6 Residuals from regression analysis. Positive residuals
(darker areas) show where there was a tendency to underestimate
the percentage of the total vote cast for the senator. (After
Thomas, 1960, Fig. 4.)

the formulation of this second hypothesis (H_2); H_2 proposed that the
McCarthy vote was *inversely proportional* to distance from the senator's
home: the closer the district, the higher the percentage of vote for the
senator and vice versa. As distance increased, the percentage of votes
for McCarthy decreased. A linear measure of distance from Appleton
to the center of each voting district was used as the second independent
variable (X_2). When X_2 was introduced, the level of explanation rose
from one-third to almost one-half.

The ability of regression models to explain variations in human
behavior is limited both by the variety of processes affecting individual
decisions and by the inability to obtain measures for variables indica-

tive of the process geographers seek to explain. Party affiliation, current economic status, and many other variables affect the way people vote. In this instance, two measures—rural population and distance—explain almost half the observed variations. Even these independent variables are *surrogate* measures. The percentage of rural population is at best an approximate measure of the farm population eligible to vote. Also, linear distance is a weak surrogate for familiarity. Information flow between the senator's hometown and distant portions of the state are not directly proportional to distance. A "friendly" newspaper editor or radio station manager in southwestern Wisconsin could alter the obstacle of distance by providing favorable news. These are some of the difficulties encountered in social science research. Collecting appropriate data to test hypotheses is the most time-consuming activity in geographical research.

The role of explanation in geography

Geographers as social scientists are concerned with explanation more than anything else. Hypotheses are central to this task, because they provide a connection between what is known and problems yet to be solved. In any particular study the hypothesis may not be explicit, because geographers are often concerned with description, classification, and techniques for testing hypotheses. However, the desire to relate observations to models and theories is implicit in all research, and this sense of problem provides the orientation for study.

Hypotheses should be used to pose fairly specific questions about the relationships between phenomena. But as Newman (1973) has shown, geographers also use the term *hypotheses* to define more general relationships such as the steps of neighborhood deterioration. In part, this broadening of meaning is a response to the paucity of theory in geography.

Hypotheses can be investigated in either a systematic or regional context. Development in systematic studies is normal because the variables are limited and their interrelation better understood. Those who specialize exclusively in systematic studies are more familiar with studies in cognate disciplines and, therefore, are more likely to develop propositions relating spatial distributions to principles of human behavior. Regional testing of hypotheses is nonetheless important. A proposition whose truth has been demonstrated is still a generalization.

Repeated testing under different cultural situations can reveal the universality of a generalization required before it is regarded as a scientific law.

Generalizations, derived from the concept of distance and its recognized effect upon interaction, were advanced in the illustrative studies of poverty and voting patterns. Additional tests of this law contribute to the extension of the theoretical construct: The closer together people and places are located, the more likely they are to interact. In the poverty study, areas closer to the urban centers had a lower incidence of poverty because people were more likely to interact with the urban area where reliable employment is available in high-paying jobs. In the voting study, proximity to the senator's hometown increased the likelihood that voters would know him and be familiar with his policies.

The slow accumulation of knowledge about the fundamental processes of human behavior is the concern of social science. Most of this text records what is already known. It is recorded so that future social scientists may use this knowledge in formulating and testing new hypotheses in order to better understand the effect of human behavior upon spatial distributions.

SUGGESTED READINGS

Geographers have not provided readable accounts of their research strategy. Confusion over terms remains, and the following references require an understanding of geographical methodology.

Haggett, Peter. *Locational Analysis in Human Geography.* London: Arnold, 1965, pp. 277–80.

Harvey, David W. *Explanation in Geography.* London: Arnold, 1969.

McCarty, Harold H. "Use of Certain Statistical Procedures in Geographical Analysis." *Annals of the Association of American Geographers* 46(1956): 263.

McCarty, Harold H., and Lindberg, James B. *A Preface to Economic Geography.* Englewood Cliffs, N.J.: Prentice-Hall, 1966, pp. 41–86.

PART TWO

CHAPTER 4

PEOPLE, CULTURE, AND BEHAVIOR

From time immemorial the human being has been structured in such a way that his world-outlook, . . . his motivations and scale of values, his actions and intentions are determined by his own personal and group life-experience.

Aleksandr I. Solzhenitsyn

Pᴇᴏᴘʟᴇ ᴀʀᴇ ᴛʜᴇ essence of human geography: where they live, how they live, and how the behaviors that they acquire from their "personal and group life-experience" affect spatial organization. The techniques of geographical study have been the focus of Part One, but now the emphasis shifts toward the processes of human behavior.

Part Two attempts to illuminate the economic, social, political, and psychological processes of human behavior so that their operation in any particular area might be understood in terms of the "scale of values" of the occupying group. These values motivate the organization of the area so that the resources can be utilized by its occupants. As the values change so, too, will the organization of the area. Cultural geography can be compared from time to time as well as from place to place.

The Gila and Salt river valleys in Arizona are dominated today by the Phoenix metropolis. The sprawl of low-density suburbs, wide tree-lined streets, shopping centers, freeways, and smog is a response to the automobile way of life in which urban land is cheap and mobility unrestricted. But it was not always this way.

Between A.D. 500 and 1400 these same valleys were occupied by the Hohokam people who built several hundreds of miles of irrigation canals and created a sophisticated urban way of life in which the labors of a few could produce food for many. Resources were zealously conserved, and major engineering projects completed. No Indian achievement north of Mexico surpasses the Hohokam canal system for planning and coordinated effort. They were master-farmers, producing corn, beans, squash, and cotton on arid land through irrigation and water control far in advance of the farming systems known in Western Europe at that time.

Man's ability to rise above the harsh desert environment is evident in the settlement of Muertos, 6 miles south of Arizona State University in Tempe. There, hundreds of people lived in the desert 6 miles from the Salt River and were sustained by water from a canal system before Columbus discovered the New World. No other Indian people in the Southwest matched this feat. The cultural ideas imported from central Mexico were adapted to the local environment to produce a distinctive cultural landscape.

Food surpluses permitted the release of time and energy for other crafts. The Hohokam produced stone sculptures and wove fine textiles from local cotton. Recent excavations have revealed some religious architecture, but the most prominent feature of Hohokam sites is the stone-walled handball courts. Evidence suggests that these courts were placed in special arenas and that the games may have had a religious significance. But all of these achievements were to disappear a century before the Spanish explorers arrived.

The Spanish neglected the Gila and Salt river valleys. The Hohokam disappeared about 1400, and the new conquerors sought minerals to convert to riches or natives to convert to Christianity during the sixteenth, seventeenth, and eighteenth centuries. The marauding Apache tribes were inhospitable, and Santa Fe in New Mexico and Tucson were chosen as center of Spanish authority to the neglect of the former agricultural lands.

The American occupation brought families from the Middle West with a different scale of values. They sought land for agriculture rather than for minerals and Indian converts. The Swilling Irrigation Canal Company was established in 1867 to patch up and enlarge upon the historic irrigation ditches of the Hohokam and, under the Homestead Act of 1862, the pioneers took possession of the land by establishing residence. A new nucleus for settlement was established and the Apaches and Papagos were transferred to reservations. The valley land was again settled but under the culture of the American West. The ranches produced hay and wheat, rather than corn, beans, squash, and cotton. It was the surplus production from these ranches that provided the stimulus for the growth of Phoenix from a market center into a modern metropolis.

Successive groups have used the Gila and Salt river valleys differently. Each has interpreted the land resources in terms of their cultural preferences and the cultural landscape that resulted has reflected the scale of values of the occupying group.

Geographers have used *sequent occupance studies* like this brief summary of the Gila and Salt river valleys to clarify the origin of cultural landscapes. These studies begin with an analysis of populations and settlement patterns at different time periods. Hypotheses are then developed in an attempt to explain the cultural landscape and the origin of the cultural traits. People are central to these studies both in terms of demographic characteristics and their cultural influence upon settlement patterns.

POPULATION

The irregular spatial arrangement and distribution of the world population results from the adjustments that men of differing cultural traditions have made to the physical resources (see front endpaper). The adjustment has changed in the past, causing population shifts, and will change in the future as new resources are discovered or as new techniques are developed to utilize known resources.

Almost one-half of the world's 3.5 billion people are crowded onto 5 percent of the land area: on the river plains of the low latitudes and in the metropolitan centers of the midlatitudes. Most of the earth is sparsely populated and the cold deserts of the high latitudes and the arid zones of the continental interiors are virtually uninhabited.

Population distribution still reflects the original centers of cultural development in the Northern Hemisphere. East Asia with 26 percent; South Asia, 20 percent; and Western Europe, 20 percent account for two-thirds of the world's population. Within these centers and elsewhere three generalizations apply:

1. Highest densities are in areas of favorable physical environment. Irrigation is important when precipitation is seasonal or unreliable.
2. Low elevations are preferred, with 56 percent of the population dwelling below 656 feet.
3. Population clusters along the borders of continents and countries, leaving interiors empty by comparison. Two-thirds of the world population lives within 300 miles of the coast.

Where people live [handwritten annotation]

Population in developed and developing regions

Four regions—two in Asia, one in Europe, and a much smaller region in Northern America—account for three-quarters of the world's popu-

Fig. 4.1 Population by regions (1970)

	Total (millions)	Percentage	Density[a]	Annual increase (percentage 1965–1970)
Africa	344	9.5	11	2.6
Northern America[b]	228	6.3	11	1.2
Latin America	283	7.8	14	2.9
Asia	2056	56.5	75	2.3
Oceania	19	0.5	2	2.0
Europe (except USSR)	462	12.7	94	0.8
USSR	243	6.7	11	1.0
World	3632	100.0	27	2.0

Source: United Nations Demographic Yearbook, 1970, p. 105.

[a] Population per square kilometer of area. Figures are merely the quotients of population divided by area and are not to be considered as either reflecting density in the urban sense or as indicating the supporting power of a territory's land and resources.

[b] United States and Canada, excluding Mexico and Central America.

lation (Fig. 4.1). The two Asian regions differ in several demographic aspects from Europe and Northern America.

Numerically, the Asian regions are larger: eastern Asia, with China (over 760 million inhabitants), Japan (104 million), North and South Korea and Taiwan, has about 26 percent of the world's population. Southern Asia—India, Pakistan and Sri Lanka (Ceylon)—constitutes 20 percent. If southeastern Asia is included, the Asian total is 2056 million, or 56 percent of the world's population. The European region of 462 million excluding European USSR, represents 13 percent; and the smallest region, Northern America, claims 228 million, a mere 6 percent of the total.

Culturally, the European and Northern American regions are similar and are classified as Occidental cultures. The latter developed largely from traditions originating with the former. Both are technologically advanced and commercialized. Areas are specialized, living standards are high, trade and commerce are essential, and populations are urbanized. These two Atlantic regions embrace technologically advanced (developed) nations whose people, although constituting only 19 percent of the total, control 80 percent of the wealth and use 70 percent of the world's combustible energy.

Cultural attitudes toward family size, health planning, and population growth in the developing Asian regions and the developed European regions are reflected by their stage within the cycle of demographic transition. The *demographic transition* is an idealized sequence of stages that enables geographers to classify regions in terms of their population characteristics (Fig. 4.2). The four stages in the sequence

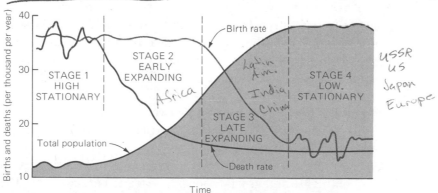

Fig. 4.2 The demographic transition. The four stages represent different growth rates corresponding to the changing relationship between birth and death rates. (Haggett, *Geography: A Modern Synthesis*, Harper & Row, Publishers, 1972, Fig. 7.10.)

are: high stationary, early expanding, late expanding, and low stationary.

High-stationary: Both birth and death rates per thousand population are high, and the population increase remains at a low but fluctuating level. The birth rate is high, but deaths from famines, wars, and diseases cancel increases.

Early expanding: The death rate declines precipitately as a result of better medical care and sanitation procedures, but the annual birth rate continues at the high level of over 35 per thousand. Life expectancy increases, and the population "explodes" at annual rates of 40 and 50 per thousand, which can mean a doubling of population within 20 years for nations like Brazil, Mexico, and the Philippines.

Late expanding: The death rate is stabilized and the birth rate begins to decline in a reflection of increased survival and an urban way of life, in which the economic cost of raising children is not compensated for by their labor as it is in farming.

Low stationary: Birth and death rates are stabilized at a low level, and zero population growth may be achieved. The birth rate fluctuates according to changing preferences.

The Asian populations are within developing nations and exhibit population growth characteristic of the first two stages in the demographic transition. Apart from Japan, population growth is rapid from natural increase. Birth rates remain high while death rates, particularly in the Philippines, Malaysia, and Korea, have been reduced by improved health care. On the Asian mainland, the regional population increase is limited by the death rate of 15–25 per thousand to 22 per thousand per annum. Even so, the 22 per thousand net increase can mean a doubling of the population in thirty-two years. With the enormous population base, this annual growth produces the tremendous population increase that alarms biologists.

By comparison, population growth in Northern America and Europe is slow. Natural increase is about 1 percent per annum (10 per thousand), with population increase being a function of migration rather than resulting from a natural increase. Both birth and death rates are low, which is typical of nations in the latter stages of the demographic transition.

Asian nations are in the second stage of the transition. In all likelihood, they will soon enter the third stage when growth rates will not be alarming. Rapid scientific and technological advances in these nations will influence human attitudes concerning work, survival, and family size, as they have in Japan. If this cultural change occurs, the contemporary population crisis may become an historical event by the year 2000.

The population geography of any area or region is not determined by environmental constraints. Rather, it is determined by the cultural abilities of the occupants. The Hohokam demonstrated the feasibility of irrigation farming in southern Arizona, but it was more than four centuries before another group of culturally oriented farmers settled these same valleys which had been neglected by the Apache and Spanish in the interval. Cultural interpretations of population patterns enable hypotheses to be developed that will explain the sequence of settlement in terms of the motivations, actions, and intentions of the occupying group.

Explaining population distributions

There is no better way of introducing the geography of an area than attempting to account for its population distribution. Population reflects the physical conditions of an area, its history of development, and the effectiveness with which the occupants have been able to utilize their cultural traditions to organize the development of these resources.

Zelinsky (1966) emphasizes the role of five genetic factors that through time, influence the distribution seldom to the exclusion of one another.

1. The impact of the physical environment
2. The economy
3. The culture of the society
4. Physical and social disasters
5. Social and political decisions

With the aid of these five broad classes of genetic factors, reasonable hypotheses can be developed to explain the arrangement and distribution of population for the entire earth's surface or any portion thereof (see front endpaper).

Canadian population

The distribution of the 24 million Canadians reflects both the physical environment and cultural attributes of various stages of economic development. Sixty percent of the population lives in the Great Lakes–St. Lawrence lowland (Fig. 4.3). Because of tidewater access through the St. Lawrence and the interaction with American commercial systems, this area has dominated Canadian economic life since Confederation in 1867. It shows no signs of decreasing, despite the settlement of the Prairie Provinces in the first decade of the twentieth century, and the popularity of British Columbia's mild coastal areas and buoyant economy.

The four major settlement areas of Canada are separated by three major barriers. From east to west the settlement areas are the Atlantic coastline, the St. Lawrence Valley, the prairies, and the Pacific coastal valleys. Separating them are the 400-mile barrier of the Appalachians, the 900 miles of the Laurentian Shield, and the 400 miles of the Western Cordillera.

SETTLEMENT HISTORY

The cultural heritage of the settlers in each area intensifies the fourfold division. British—especially Scottish—settlers pioneered development in the Maritime Provinces, whereas the French had already occupied the lower St. Lawrence. Even after Wolfe captured Quebec, the French-speaking population refused to be absorbed. Their resistance continues today, providing a delightful, occasionally troublesome variety to Canadian life. Settlement in the southern or upper St. Lawrence Valley occurred slowly. It was not until the American Revolution, when Loyalists retreated to Ontario, that the Indians were displaced. A combination of soldier settlements and private colonization schemes anglicized the area as a frontier against a feared American invasion.

Settlement of the prairies and the Pacific coastlands spread from American territories to the south. The Hudson's Bay Company had encouraged colonization, but with little success apart from trading and commercial ventures. Environmental conditions were far different from those most Western European colonists had experienced. Prairie fires, drought, wolves, coyotes, grasshoppers, and rampageous frontiersmen caused failures. Second-generation settlers from the American prairies seeking empty land, together with settlers from Eastern Europe and religious cooperatives like the Mormons, were more successful. They were psychologically better prepared for the rigors of farming semiarid lands. Experience with American dry-farming techniques and irrigation was essential to their success. But as a result, the Canadian prairies were considerably more American than the remainder of the nation.

With the completion of the trans-Canadian railroads in the latter nineteenth century, the natural barriers to interaction were reduced. Through communication, closer bonds were established between the essentially English settlements of the Maritimes, Ontario, and British Columbia. Interaction across the north-south grain of the country created the bond of identity upon which a great nation has been built. Increased communication also had an influence upon those who had not shared the English cultural heritage. They developed a pride in the vastness of their continental nation and began to participate within and to change the English-styled social institutions.

Settlement history in Canada provides a fascinating account of the advance and retreat of the frontier in response to changing social, economic, and political circumstances. For the interested student, the writings of Bowman (1931) and Clark (1959) are recommended. Writing as geographers, they provide vivid examples of how physical environments have been reinterpreted as land became available to new culture groups. The effect of physical geography and economic, social, and political processes upon the geography of Canada is apparent in the manner in which succeeding occupants have utilized their land.

THE PHYSICAL ENVIRONMENT

A combination of thin, stony soils and harsh winter climates restricts the areas of continuous settlement and integrated transport systems— what geographers call the *ecumene*—to the southern margins of Canada. Only in the Prairie Provinces does settlement penetrate far to the north. Elsewhere, northern settlement is represented by a string of isolated clusters—the mining communities that extend across the Laurentian Shield from Schefferville to Yellow Knife. With these exceptions, the north is relatively empty. Physical conditions discourage permanent settlement except along the margins in summer.

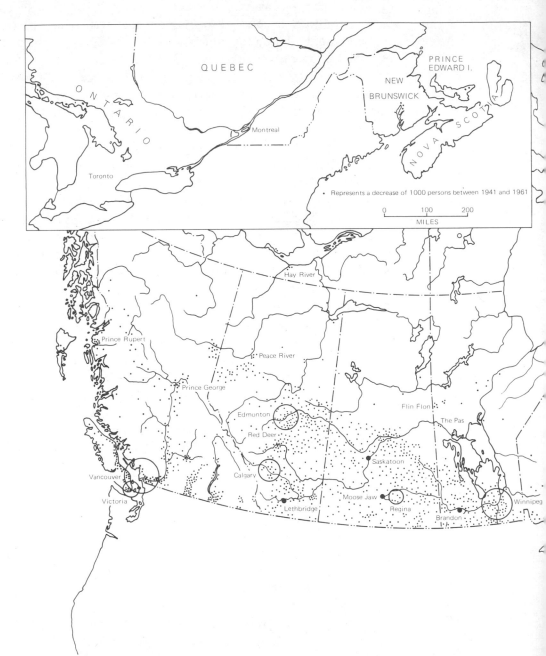

Fig. 4.3 Canadian population, 1961. (Adapted from Weir, in Warkentin, ed., *Canada: A Geographic Interpretation*, Methuen Publications, Toronto, 1968, Fig. 6.12.)

CANADIAN POPULATION 1961

○ Represents 500 Eskimos

· Represents 2000 persons

● Towns or cities of 25,000 to 100,000 persons
   in both 1941 and 1961

1,000,000 ----
500,000 ----
100,000 ---- Cities 100,000 persons and over
              in both 1941 and 1961

0   100   200   300   400
              MILES

St. John's

Corner Brook

Baie Comeau

Sydney - Glace Bay

Chicoutimi

Jonquiere

Moncton

Quebec

Halifax

Shawinigan

Saint John

Trois Rivieres

Sherbrooke

Timmins

Ottawa

Montreal

Thunder
Bay

Sault
Ste. Marie

Sudbury

Kingston

1. Cornwall
2. Valleyfield
3. Granby
4. St. Jean
5. Drummondville

Guelph

Belleville

Kitchener

Peterborough

Oshawa

London

Toronto

Sarnia

St. Catharines

Chatham

Welland

Windsor

Hamilton

Brantford

THE ECONOMY

The way in which man earns his livelihood from an area has an enormous impact upon its geography. Activities associated with the forest, mineral, and ocean resources of the Atlantic Provinces, as opposed to the mixed-crop and livestock farming of the prairies, affect the density and arrangement of settlement and the means of communications. In the Atlantic Provinces population is clustered in a few coastal towns where resources are processed. In the agricultural areas there is a fairly uniform distribution of rural population, which is served by a network of urban centers.

Urbanization of the Canadian population is a response to changing economic conditions. In a competitive economy, economic change has a profound effect on population distribution because families will move to take advantage of new opportunities and avoid impacted areas. The rural-urban migration illustrates this shift. Half of all Canadians live in medium-to-large urban centers with more than 75 percent located in urban places with populations of 500 or more. The transition from a rural to urban nation occurred as Canada began to process her own raw materials, a transition that was accelerated by wartime necessity. Small farmers and farm laborers were pushed out of rural areas by declining employment and drawn toward employment opportunities in towns. Demographic changes followed relocation because small urban families were preferred to large rural families, and birth rates declined to less than 25 per thousand.

CULTURAL INFLUENCE

Population distribution in Canada results from the dynamic interaction of man with his physical surroundings under differing cultural circumstances. Early settlers sought out the eastern coastlands that were accessible to western Europe. But as the agriculturally more favorable areas of the upper St. Lawrence and Prairie Provinces were made available, man relocated there from the Maritime Provinces and, to a lesser extent, from Quebec. The French-speaking community found it difficult to assimilate into the new, predominantly English-speaking communities, so they resettled the marginal areas of Quebec vacated by English-speaking pioneers, rather than venturing inland where Anglo culture prevailed.

POLITICAL DECISIONS

From the creation of the political units to the subdivision of land and the development of communications, government has played a prominent role in the spread of Canadian settlement. The impress of the original French and British administration remains, and upon this has been superimposed the development of national communication networks and provincial control of land resources.

The development of railways, the Trans-Canadian Highway, and the more recent airways have been politically directed to link the east—west centers of economic development and insulate Canada from the attraction of the adjoining American markets. Even the Canadian Broadcasting Corporation is subject to close federal supervision and aid.

Utilization of resources is also controlled by governmental agencies. Confederation gave jurisdiction over publicly owned land (Crown Land) to the provinces. Some provinces, for example, Nova Scotia, sold land to obtain capital, thereby losing control and quickly depleting forest resources. Other provinces learned from the Nova Scotia experience. Forest resources were conserved and a domestic pulp and paper industry developed under state control.

To conserve resources, the governments of Ontario and British Columbia placed an embargo on the export of low-value pulpwood. Pulp had to be converted into more valuable newsprint. Quebec achieved the same end by assessing lower fees upon pulpwood used locally. Through political influence Canadian provinces created substantial employment opportunities in the pulp and paper industries and were able to add value to exports.

The impress of political factors is prominent in Canadian settlement, subdivision, communications, and resource development. In turn, these elements have determined the population distribution. The prominent role of political influence upon development is not unusual. It is a feature of all former colonial areas of the New World, Africa, and the Pacific where cultures were introduced to subordinate aboriginal economies. The patterns of population observed in these areas results primarily from two influences: first, the role of the government in settling habitable areas; and second, the culture of the settlers as expressed in their needs and technological capacity to utilize resources.

The role of culture is pervasive because it affects all elements of spatial organization. The contrast between the village life styles of rural Quebec and the independent farmsteads of southern Ontario is but visible manifestation of attitudes and values that affect social life, the economy, and political organization. People fashion the resources of the areas they settle in terms of inherited experience and ideas acquired from areas with which they are familiar. New ideas are acquired slowly and only after they have been tested and modified by local innovators, so that the landscape reflects the cultural image of the people.

As the French geographer Paul Vidal de la Blache said:

> One must start from the notion that a land is a reservoir containing dormant energies of which nature has planted the seed, but whose use depends on man. It is he who by molding them to his purpose demonstrates his individuality. Man establishes the connection between disparate elements by substituting a purposeful organization of forces for the random effects of local circumstance. In this manner a region acquires identity differentiating it from others, till at length it becomes, as it were, a medal struck in the likeness of a people.[1]

CULTURE AND BEHAVIOR

Culture is the way of life acquired by learning the rules of society. Individuals and some groups may have distinctive properties, but culture overrides these by developing systems of belief, attitudes, social institutions, skills, techniques, and resources that are shared: It is learned behavior that is passed on to other members of the group through interaction. Culture does not result from genetic inheritance.

The term *society* is similar to culture. Society is an organized group of individuals possessing a distinct culture, whereas *culture* is the invisible traits of behavior that provide the organizing rules. For the convenience of presentation these "invisible traits" are represented as economic, social, political, and psychological motivations of behavior.

Man perceives the environmental resources of his habitat through the filter of his cultural preferences and in this way the human use of the land is organized. As man learns new skills and techniques his use of the land will change because culture is a dynamic process. The Chippewa Indians of northern Minnesota and Wisconsin, for example,

---

[1] Vidal, 1903; quoted in Broek and Webb (1968), pp. 28–29.

did not value the local iron ore deposits because they had not learned the technical skills that would enable them to utilize the potential resource. Yet, present-day descendants of the Chippewa have learned to work in mines, factories, and other urban pursuits that utilize the iron resources. Genetically, these people are little changed, but the attitudes and technical skills that they have learned—their culture—permits them to utilize the iron resource and its products.

Each habitat must be appraised in terms of the culture of its occupants. The same Upper Great Lakes area that the Chippewa occupy has experienced a sequence of cultural occupancy. The stony soils, coniferous forest, and lakeland have not changed, but the human use of the land has changed dramatically. The Chippewa conserved the marsh, forest, and stream as hunting grounds, whereas the French fur traders and American lumbermen and miners exploited the resources in order to obtain monetary rewards. Today recreational opportunities motivate man's use of the land: Conservation of resources has utility again because there exists demand for scenery and a sustained yield of fish, waterfowl, and wild animals.

Knowledge of the cultural traits of people is extremely important in appraising spatial organization. The individual is the unit of action, but the behavior of the individual is shaped by the social organization, attitudes, objectives, and technical skills of his culture.

The acquisition of culture

Culture results from interactions between people sharing specific areas. People become oriented to thinking and acting in similar fashion because they live, talk, and work together. Their lives are shaped by reinforcement as they relate to one another. Favorable actions are rewarded by the group while the unfavorable ones are neglected or punished. Achievements are emulated, and new ideas are tried with caution. In this manner, a repertoire of behavior is acquired that is shared by communicating with others.

LANGUAGE AND CULTURE

Language is the storehouse of culture. It is the medium through which experience is shared and stored. Each work has its cultural connotation and if this connotation is not understood, sentences are meaningless. In English we have a single word for "snow" whether it is falling, laying, packed, slushy, or driven. However, each is different for the Eskimo in whose culture snow is a more important event.

Interpretation of language is a cultural facility. The nature of a language and the way in which children learn its symbolic content structures the way in which they will think. Therefore, it is to be expected that culture will differ between different linguistic groups. Not only will they perceive information differently, but they will also think about it differently.

Nations like Canada, which contain people communicating in different languages, face a very real difficulty in establishing a common cultural heritage. The bond of a common language does not exist. The plural culture must be respected through the maintenance of local language and authority, or the political union will disintegrate.

Language is also confining. One can drop out of society, but not out of a culture. Even those who rebel against a society are forced to express, or at least think about their rebellion, within the cultural context of their own language. A similar problem confronts those concerned with social and economic development. Change is difficult to achieve when the ideas from one culture are expressed in the language of another culture. The connotations implicit in the language of the original culture are retained and the development may be perceived as alien.

Culture is the source of man's versatility and terrestrial supremacy, for it provides the motivation for both the interpretation of the natural resources and their conversion into a cultural landscape. Geographers have always been fascinated by cultural landscapes and have developed several approaches for landscape analysis.

Analyzing cultural landscapes

The surface of the earth as modified by human action is the *cultural landscape*; the analysis of which provides insight into the motivations of the cultures occupying an area at present, and in former, times.

Carl Sauer, who was for many years professor of geography at the University of California, Berkeley, is primarily responsible for the emphasis upon the cultural landscape among American geographers. In a series of studies, Sauer emphasized that the cultural landscape must be interpreted as resulting from cultural processes operating over a long period of time. The *sequent occupance* by groups with differing cultures leaves its trace upon the land, and each succeeding group takes into account the achievements of its predecessors as well as innovations borrowed from other areas. Sauer emphasized the role of fire in the development of cultural landscapes. He also noted that what historians had called the "natural prairie" had been created largely by fire, naturally, from lightning, and man-made, by hunters.

Sauer also investigated the role of agriculture in the development of the cultural landscape. As a result of these studies, he developed hypotheses about the original *cultural hearths* for agriculture and the diffusion or spread of agriculture throughout the world.

The development of agriculture was a significant cultural achievement. It enabled man to settle permanently in favored areas and produce a food surplus so that some members of society were freed from

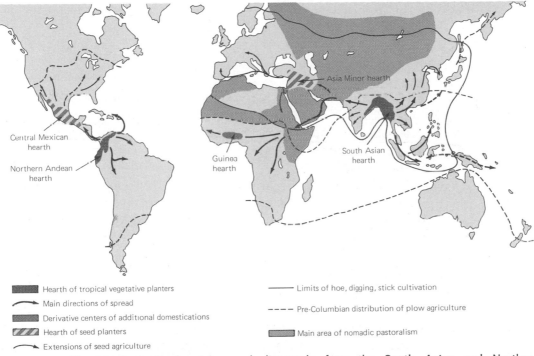

▰ Hearth of tropical vegetative planters	—— Limits of hoe, digging, stick cultivation
⌒→ Main directions of spread	
▰ Derivative centers of additional domestications	- - - - Pre-Columbian distribution of plow agriculture
▨ Hearth of seed planters	
⌒→ Extensions of seed agriculture	▰ Main area of nomadic pastoralism

Fig. 4.4 Agricultural origins and dispersals from the South Asian and Northern Andean cultural hearths. Tropical vegetables provided the original crops with seed (cereal) agriculture and pastoralism developing after the idea spread to derivative centers. (Data by C. O. Sauer, N. I. Vavilov, E. Hahn et al.; and after Erich Isaac, *Geography of Domestication*, © 1970, p. 41. Reprinted by permission of Prentice-Hall, Inc.; Englewood Cliffs, N.J.)

the daily search for food to pursue nonagricultural crafts. In his sweeping survey, *Agricultural Origins and Dispersals*, Sauer hypothesized that agriculture developed in separate *cultural hearths of domestication* in the Old and New Worlds; the idea then diffusing from these hearths throughout the world (Fig. 4.4). The South Asian hearth is supposed to have originated along tidal streams where food obtained from fishing and gathering was plentiful. The original plants may have been cultivated as a source of drugs used to stun fish causing them to rise to the surface. Such cultivation may then have been expanded to other root crops that would grow from tubers and cuttings.

The accidental observation that plants grew better on the refuse pile than they did in their wild environment may have prompted their cultivation by women, tired from roaming the forest to collect plants for the fishing expeditions of their menfolk. However, this discovery could only have been made by a superior society of fishing people, because the less successful would soon deplete a stream and be forced to move to a new site.

The origin and location of the world's agricultural hearths have been enthusiastically debated. Even Sauer has modified his original hypothesis as new evidence has been discovered. However, his work has been a seminal contribution to the literature and was the forerunner of diffusion research in geography. *Diffusion* postulates that ideas and techniques spread across areas and through time. As a result of a sequence of studies, the rate of adoption can be calculated and the affected areas identified.

Diffusion is but one of many ways in which Sauer has influenced the progress of geography. Several of his students have pursued cultural geography themes and developed more analytical approaches to the study of cultural landscapes.

THE DEVELOPMENT OF AGRICULTURAL LANDSCAPES

Although geographers constantly refer to the intensively farmed agricultural regions like the Corn Belt and Cotton Belt, there has been relatively little attention paid to the cultural traits that create these distinctive areas. Spencer and Horvath (1963) raise tentative questions about cultural causation in a study of three regions: the Corn Belt, the coconut landscape of the Philippines, and rubber plantations in Malaya. In their article "How Does an Agricultural Region Originate?" they trace the sequence of agricultural development against the physical conditions, as well as enumerating the cultural achievements of settlers in a sequence of developmental stages. Special attention is given to the farming "mentality," so as to emphasize the social and psychological elements of culture. Organizations like the Grange, the agricultural newspaper, the agricultural experiment station, as well as the attitudes of local opinion leaders, appear to have been influential in determining what crops would be selected and what farming techniques would be used. The concept of the farming mentality attempts to express the agreement among farmers on the best agricultural system. As a result, a fairly uniform pattern of land use develops throughout an area.

Spencer and Horvath say of the Corn Belt: "Taken from the point of view of psychological aspects, social processes, and cultural traditions of the settlers, the Corn Belt can be regarded as the landscape expression of a farming 'mentality.' A farming 'mentality' in this context refers to the totality of the beliefs of the farmers over a region regarding the most suitable use of land in an area."

As a summary to their three regional studies, the authors speculate about the processes of cultural causation. Six categories of cultural processes are identified. These are: psychological, political, historical, technological, agronomic, and economic.

Psychological: This refers to the way in which farmers perceive the opportunities of the land; the way they learn from their neighbors; and the subtle pressures to conform exerted on them by the rural society.

Political: This includes how governmental decisions affect original land subdivision and purchase, and how governments control imports and establish the prices for many farm commodities.

Historical: Covered in this category are how the tradition of established methods affects the possibilities that farmers perceive; the goods local merchants will supply and the products that they will purchase. A tradition of conservatism is part of the farming mentality.

Technological: Technology determines what progress is possible. For example, it was not until the advent of the steel mold-board plough that the sod of the prairie could be cultivated with ease.

Agronomic: The availability of artificial fertilizers and hybrid seed have had a similar dramatic effect upon farm production in recent decades as did the technological developments of the twentieth century.

Economic: This refers to the demand for farm produce and the cost of supplying farm inputs. The cost of supplying farm labor has been the most influential factor in determining the methods used in farming. As the cost of labor has increased, labor-intensive family farms have given place to capital-intensive farms and agribusinesses.

Spencer and Horvath were not so bold as to claim that these processes provided an analytical system for cultural geography. However, their article has had a profound impact upon geographical thought and has provided the framework for this book.

When the cultural processes are viewed as hypotheses to test the regularities observed in spatial organization, the link is apparent between the cultural geographical traditions that Spencer epitomizes and the rigorous analytical work of McCarty which was outlined in Chapters 2 and 3.

THE DEVELOPMENT OF CULTURAL REGIONS

In his articles on the "Mormon Culture Region" and, more recently, the "American Wests" (1965 and 1972), Meinig has constructed an approach to the analysis of the entire cultural landscape. Again, each area is described so that the developmental sequence of cultural occupance is evident.

The development of each cultural region is a dynamic process. A core area or nucleus is settled by people with distinctive cultural traits and the area changes as immigrants with different cultural heritages arrive, or as the economy, circulation pattern, and political organization change. The American West provides an ideal laboratory to test this hypothesis because the six original nuclei of settlement were developed separately and—in the cases of the Spanish colonization of New Mexico and of the Mormon settlements in the Wasatch Oasis—by distinctive societies (Fig. 4.5).

Meinig hypothesizes that each region passes through four stages of development that are reflected by changes in the population, circulation, political organization, and regional culture (Fig. 4.6).

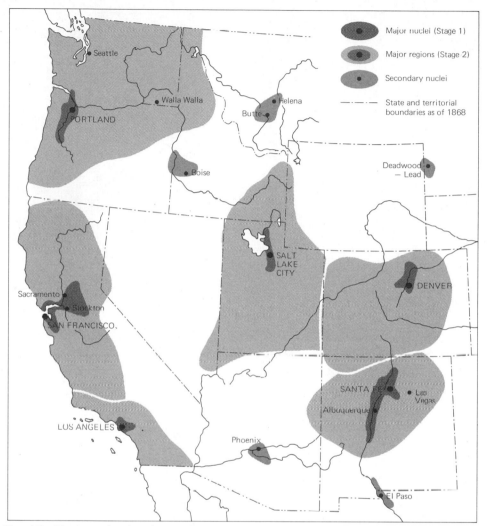

Fig. 4.5 Major nuclei for the settlement of the American West. (Meinig, reproduced with permission from *Annals of the Association of American Geographers*, vol. 62, 1972, Fig. 2.)

1. *Population,* where change is exhibited in both numbers and distribution as the region develops from the original settlement nucleus or core to a metropolitan community that dominates the entire region.

2. *Circulation,* where patterns converge on the region from outside in Stage 1 but develop into a divergent system in Stage 4, so as to provide interaction with the region and beyond.

Population

Stage	
1	Implantation of a nucleus of settlement by migrants attracted by special environmental qualities (resources, refuge, exploitable indigenes).
2	Expansion of settlement to the limit of land exploitable with available technology; the completion of the "frontier" phase of "free" land readily available.
3	Competition for development from other peoples along bordering zones; influx of new migrants, especially into new industrial and commercial districts.
4	Metropolitanization: population largely urban and suburban; commuting range brings most of the area within close contact of center; high mobility of population, much interregional contact and movement.

Circulation pattern

Stage	
1	Isolation: seasonal inflow of people; outflow only of high-valued, low-bulk, or self-propelled products; pack trains, wagons, stages; interregional communication infrequent.
2	Regional system: emergence of central places linked to regional capital; export of a few primary products; first railroads, improved roads, riverboats, first transcontinental railroad and telegraph connections.
3	Interregional network: elaboration of central place system and regional linkages; integral part of nationwide systems; variety of transport and communication systems: railroads, interurban electrics, paved highways, buses, trucks, first airlines, telephones, radio.
4	Intermetropolitan national network: elaborate metropolitan freeway system; nonstop air service to national and international centers; superhighways, unit trains, products pipelines; television.

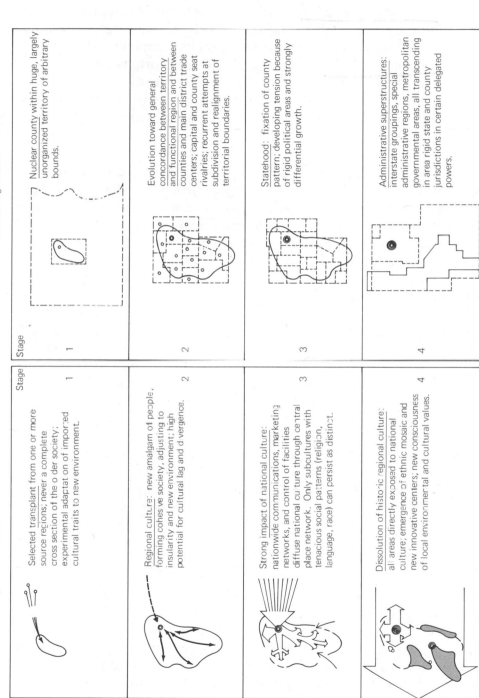

Culture

Stage

1 Selected transplant from one or more source regions; never a complete cross section of the older society; experimental adaptation of imported cultural traits to new environment.

2 Regional culture: new amalgam of people, forming cohesive society, adjusting to insularity and new environment; high potential for cultural lag and divergence.

3 Strong impact of national culture: nationwide communications, marketing networks, and control of facilities diffuse national culture through central place network. Only subcultures with tenacious social patterns (religion, language, race) can persist as distinct.

4 Dissolution of historic regional culture: all areas directly exposed to national culture; emergence of ethnic mosaic and new innovative centers; new consciousness of local environmental and cultural values.

Political organization

Stage

1 Nuclear county within huge, largely unorganized territory of arbitrary bounds.

2 Evolution toward general concordance between territory and functional region and between counties and main district trade centers; capital and county seat rivalries; recurrent attempts at subdivision and realignment of territorial boundaries.

3 Statehood: fixation of county pattern; developing tension because of rigid political areas and strongly differential growth.

4 Administrative superstructures: interstate groupings, special administrative regions, metropolitan governmental areas, all transcending in area rigid state and county jurisdictions in certain delegated powers.

Fig. 4.6 The development of a cultural region from the original nucleus of settlement to a metropolitan center and region. The four stages are indicated by changes in population circulation patterns, political organization, and culture. (Meinig, reproduced with permission from *Annals of the Association of American Geographers,* vol. 62, 1972, Fig. 1.)

3. _Political organization_, which is largely unorganized in the beginning and rather elaborate, with overlapping spheres of organization and administration in the metropolitan community.
4. _Regional culture,_ which is a distinctive transplant from one or more source regions originally, and which dissolves under the impact of nationwide communications. Only subcultures that are isolated by race, language, or religion persist as distinctive groups.

Meinig notes that the inclusion of the economic process could provide a more coherent explanation of topics included under "circulation" and "regional culture." The transformation from a subsistence primary economy, through secondary processing or manufacturing, to a modern tertiary economy, where services rather than production predominate, would help explain the development of metropolitan culture.

A similar change is evident in the political culture. Rather than emphasize administrative organization, the cultural geographer using Meinig's approach has the opportunity to explain the elitist system of governance in the original settlement where landowners dominated local affairs. As the regions became urbanized, local businessmen began to compete with landowners for political control and a moderately conservative political culture developed, in which, if an idea was good for business it gained support. Now, another transformation has occurred in the development of the metropolitan community. There are many different interest groups competing for power in the metropolis, and labor unions and employee organizations are as effective in local government as is the local business community.

Governance is made more difficult by overlapping administrative systems, which make effective government almost impossible. A metropolitan community usually moves from crisis to crisis because of the difficulty in obtaining sufficient support for programs of beneficial change.

Understanding the genesis of a cultural landscape is a difficult task. People know so little about themselves, and the cultural traits that are impressed upon the landscape are constantly changing. The historical approach that was begun by Sauer and followed by Spencer and Meinig enables geographers to develop hypotheses and test them against the cultural behavior exhibited by men occupying the same area at different periods of time. By achieving more precise knowledge of the cultural processes, geographers can explain the contrasting patterns of development.

Cultural realms

Whereas most geographical research has been concerned with small regions, there exists a demand for courses that explain the cultural geography of continental areas like North America and Africa. In response to this demand, cultural geographers have developed courses that emphasize *cultural realms*, the large areas that have some form of coherence in terms of cultural traits and that serve to differentiate areas. Cultural realms are used as a technique for classifying the impact of culture upon the spatial organization of landscapes. It is a technique that is more useful for instruction than for geographical research.

James, in *One World Divided* (1964), regards each cultural realm as "a unique segment of the earth's surface, within which there is a unique assortment of resources and habitat conditions, a unique pattern of political organizations, and an arrangement of people and production that is peculiar to the area."

Two sets of revolutionary change—the Industrial Revolution and the Democratic Revolution—have spread from the European cultural hearth, producing distinctive economic, social, and political reactions throughout the world. The people of each area have reinterpreted those ideas in terms of their own culture and in consideration of their natural resources. The result is a pattern of spatial organization that fascinates the geographer. James recognizes that the world has become sharply divided between the developed and the developing nations and between those who favor one or the other of two basic social and political philosophies: democracy and autocracy. These cultural differences are used to classify areas according to the impact of the Industrial and Democratic revolutions and to place the world into a cultural perspective.

A slightly different approach to cultural realms is used by Broek and Webb (1968). Again, the historical approach to landscape evolution is emphasized so that the cultural attainments of different people can be appreciated in terms of the origin and spread of cultural ideas. However, these authors do not select one or two criteria for distinguishing cultural realms; instead they emphasize the integration of a cultural system and the role of language and religion in sustaining cultural

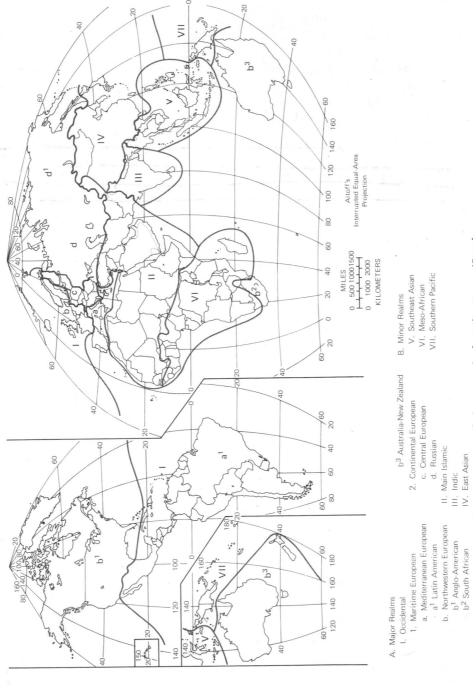

Fig. 4.7 Culture realms defined in terms of the spread of civilizations. (Broek and Webb, *A Geography of Mankind*, © 1968, Fig. 8.3. Used with permission of McGraw-Hill Book Co.)

A. Major Realms
  I. Occidental
    1. Maritime European
      a. Mediterranean European
        a¹ Latin American
      b. Northwestern European
        b¹ Anglo-American
        b² South African

    2. Continental European
      c. Central European
      d. Russian
  II. Main Islamic
  III. Indic
  IV. East Asian

B. Minor Realms
  b³ Australia-New Zealand
  V. Southeast Asian
  VI. Meso-African
  VII. Southern Pacific

MILES
0 500 1000 1500
0 1000 2000
KILOMETERS

Aitoff's
Interrupted Equal-Area
Projection

96

traits as they have been diffused from Europe and Asia (Fig. 4.7). Four major and two minor realms are identified with the important Occidental Realm which is further divided between Maritime (Mediterranean and Northwestern) and Continental Europe. In addition, the spread of these cultures through migration and settlement is recognized by designating former colonial areas—where the aboriginal culture has been displaced—with the same category as the region from which colonists emigrated. For example, northwestern Europe is placed in the same category as Anglo-America, South Africa, Australia, and New Zealand.

Both James and Broek feature the role of European culture. Europe nurtured both the Industrial and Democratic revolutions as well as the successful spread of Occidental culture to the New World. Jordan, in a more detailed study of the *European Culture Area* (1973) identifies the three basic European traits as people who (1) have a religious tradition of *Christianity*, (2) speak one of the numerous related Indo-European languages, and (3) are of Caucasian race. Also characteristic of Europe are such demographic characteristics as a well-educated and healthy people, together with a tradition of commercialized agriculture, industrial development, and democratic government.

Culture is a system of beliefs, social institutions, organizations, and modes of behavior which is made apparent through the impress of these traits upon the cultural landscape. It is convenient to think about cultural behavior in terms of economic, social, political, and psychological processes. These categories facilitate the presentation of information about cultural realms as well as providing hypotheses that stimulate research into man's role in changing the environment.

CULTURE AND ENVIRONMENTAL IMPACT

Culture is the source of man's versatility because it prepares him to learn through experimentation or by borrowing from other areas. This ability to adapt to new circumstances has been important to man in his past and will be crucial to his future survival as the resources he has learned to exploit are depleted.

The technological success of Occidental culture may also account for its demise. The industrial organization achieved in nineteenth-century Europe and perfected in twentieth-century America is based upon easily accessible mineral and fuel resources, the surplus food produced by commercial agriculture, and a superior transportation system to integrate production, consumption, and leisure. These economic traits have been supported by Christian ethics in which education, hard work, and thrift were eulogized. Through colonialism and, more recently, through economic assistance programs, these cultural traits were transplanted in the unoccupied lands of Australia and New Zealand.

But European culture—especially its mass-produced American version—is drastically out of harmony with the resources it depends upon. There is a desperate race to discover new sources of minerals and fuel, but the demand will never be satisfied. Cultural attitudes must change: A more cooperative and less competitive way of life must be developed or the resource base upon which supremacy has been established will be depleted and other cultural realms will assume control. The real test for European culture will be in its ability to adapt, rather than its ability to commercially exploit, new sources of minerals and fuel.

Population control is one way in which consumption might be checked. However, this is no longer purely a European-American problem. The very success of the urban-industrial culture has caused other cultures in Africa and Latin America to emulate the example. Nations in these realms are still in the early explosive stages of the demographic transition. The consequences of their adopting an exploitive, as opposed to a conservationalist, ethic are alarming.

World population prospects

From Malthus to Ehrlich, we have been presented from time to time with the prospect of the "population explosion." These journalistic accounts have largely overlooked man's adaptive capacity. As a result of an awareness of the population problem and the medical and legal changes that facilitate birth control, annual population growth by natural increase has declined below 10 per thousand in many technologically advanced countries.

Even in the nations of Central America, southern Asia, and Africa, where improved medical practice has resulted in annual population increases in excess of 30 per thousand, the population is not on the verge of a starvation holocaust. Famine is still common, but it is caused by political, social, and transportation inequities—all of them cultural traits—rather than by physical resources strained beyond their limits.

Take the example of African Tunisia, which borders the cultural hearth of European culture in the Mediterranean. Both the birth and death rates are high, as is typical of nations in the first stage of the demographic transition. The infant mortality rate is 74 per thousand births, whereas in most European nations it is less than 20. Tunisian diets are low in both calories and protein, famine is common, and disease strikes down many children before adolescence. However, the cause of death is social rather than physical. Only about 15 percent of the people are literate, so that European techniques of agriculture, sanitation, and health practices are known only to a small minority. And this minority has been unwilling to share its knowledge with the mass of underprivileged. Without a well-educated population, economic development and social change will not be achieved despite Tunisia's proximity to Western Europe.

The "green revolution" in developing nations has produced new varieties of rice and wheat that can triple and sometimes quintuple production. The problem lies in convincing farmers to switch from traditional methods to modern ones. Even in technologically advanced agricultural nations, production could be increased by 40 percent if only farmers would adopt already available techniques of production.

Despite the known potential for improvements, we cannot ignore current deficiencies. Twenty percent of the world's population is undernourished and 60 percent lacks one or more essential nutrients, commonly protein. Deprived families are not all found in developing nations. Also included are the poor of the technologically developed nations who are unable to participate, or intellectually incapable of participating, in highly commercialized economies.

World population and food supply is an international problem. A few affluent nations cannot survive in a world of chronic poverty, because the tensions that poverty creates upset international relations. Even in developed nations, differences between expectations and attainment create social unrest. If the political and social problems are not solved so as to provide a more equitable distribution of food, then population must be limited to an area's absorbtion capacity. The same kind of question is involved in the preservation of environmental quality. How many people can an area absorb without destroying environmental quality?

The population absorption capacity

Depending upon the economy, areas can absorb different population densities without endangering the resource balance. On the semiarid grasslands, where ranching or nomadic herding activities prevail, only one or two persons can be supported per square mile. Ranches or the territory of tribal herdsmen cover many square miles, and the animals are rotated so that no area is depleted. At the other density extreme are the central cities of metropolitan areas like Chicago, New York, London, and Paris where densities range between 40,000–60,000 per square mile. Almost all food is imported, and the population limit is imposed by the capacity of streets and railroads to transport the people and by the air to absorb the pollutants. In between the pastoral and central city extremes are the intensively farmed Corn Belt lands of the American Midwest, which will absorb between 20 to 40 persons per square mile, and the suburbs which absorb between 2000–4000 persons per square mile.

Ecological crises occur when population density or the products of human endeavor exceed the ability of the land, air, and streams to cope with the changes that man imposes. Western Kansas and Oklahoma became the Dust Bowl in the 1930s when farmers ploughed under the grassland and attempted to produce such crops as wheat and corn, which would support more intensive farming and a higher population-carrying capacity. The pollution of the air and rivers of Europe and America are other examples of how man has exceeded the capacity of the local environment to accommodate the by-products of intensive settlement. Pollution spreads far beyond the cities themselves, as is illustrated by the fish kills on the Rhine downstream from Germany's Ruhr industrial complex, and by the air pollution of the countryside. In Greece, for example, air pollution haze from Athens often conceals the monuments, and the ruins of antiquity are disintegrating rapidly due to the chemicals in the polluted air. The roadsides, littered with papers, cans, and broken bottles, are equally distressing.

Numerous other examples can be explained in terms of the changing relationship between land and the culture of the occupying group. These examples provide illustrations of how the population absorption capacity differs from place to place. They also raise the interesting question of whether the land has failed man or man has failed the land.

ENVIRONMENTAL CONTROL IN THE NAPA VALLEY, CALIFORNIA

The Napa Valley is an intensive crop- and livestock-producing area for the adjoining San Francisco market, as well as a premium viticulture area. It is also ideal for suburban expansion.

Affluent urban workers were purchasing small farms, moving their families out of the city, and commuting to work. The carefully maintained vines began to deteriorate and production was lost under part-time care. Fortunately, local governments realized the future economic consequences of eliminating viticulture and, more importantly, the pastoral landscape which attracted a lucrative tourist trade.

Local residents resented the influx of strangers, so urban and conservation interests combined to place controls upon nonagricultural land utilization. Prime agricultural lands were identified as agricultural preserves, and the farmers were offered tax benefits under the California Conservation Act to maintain their land in agriculture for ten years or longer. Sufficient land was left for controlled urban expansion around the cities of Napa and Saint Helena, but other land was protected from premature urban development.

The Napa Valley is not a unique case. Only 2 percent of the earth's surface is cultivatable and 70 percent of edible production is from this 2 percent. Because of the higher intensity of settlement on the productive land and its coastal and river valley location, these same areas have attracted urban expansion. Land for houses, roads, schools, and commerce is more valuable than the same land used for agriculture: Higher economic rent is returned so farming retreats. In the transitional stage, much land is wasted and more lies idle. The whole economy suffers from the failure to use the resources properly. At least in the Napa Valley the people, as well as their elected representatives, now have a method for limiting urban sprawl and preserving prime agricultural land. They have used the political process to reflect their cultural preference for environmental control and preservation of viticulture.

ENVIRONMENTAL CONTROL IN SOUTH LAGUNA, CALIFORNIA

Changing preferences and attitudes may have a profound effect upon population distribution in any community. The public controls land development in most communities through land-use zoning so that changes in preference for the kind of community desired should influence the decisions local officials make on zoning requests. The defeat of incumbent officials is often due to their failure to reflect these changing preferences for environmental control.

South Laguna is a small unincorporated community on the southern California coast. Although it occupies 1400 acres, most of its 4000 residents live on the gently sloping coastal shelf alongside the beach. The steeply sloping hill country that constitutes more than half the area remains in its wild state, covered with chaparral and inhabited by birds, opossums, coyote, and deer.

But the pleasant environment is threatened. New freeways and the accompanying expansion of metropolitan Los Angeles toward San Diego have placed South Laguna within commuting distance of employment centers. More people desire to live in the community and residential development of the hillsides has been proposed.

Existing residents opposed plans that would terrace the hills and replace their wild backdrop with houses and trailer parks. Under the "free-wheeling-piecemeal-any-development-is-good" urban policy of the 1950s and 1960s, local opposition to such development would have been ineffective and the intrinsic desirability of the area would have been obliterated. But, as a result of the surge of environmental consciousness in the 1970s, the political culture of Orange County has changed. A balanced ecological plan was adopted.

Five alternative plans with populations ranging from 4000 (zero growth) to 67,000 (maximum growth) were studied and their environmental impact assessed. Geographers played a positive role in the analysis of alternative plans, because the task was to evaluate man's behavior (i.e., impact) upon schools, roads, water, and sanitation as well as upon the physical environment.

The recommended plan has a population absorption capacity of 13,000 (Fig. 4.8). This will enable the environment of the hill slopes to be protected by placing these areas in natural and open-space preserves. Special property tax advantages in California make this solution attractive to landowners. Development will occur along the coast and on top of the coastal hills.

Low-rise apartments, terraced to conform to the coastal cliff, will accommodate between 30–50 dwelling units per acre. When spaced along the shoreline, they are compatible with public use of beaches and do not obstruct views of the ocean from inland. The hilltop high-rise apartments command a white-water view along 20 miles of coastline without destroying the chaparral vegetation or the hillside wildlife.

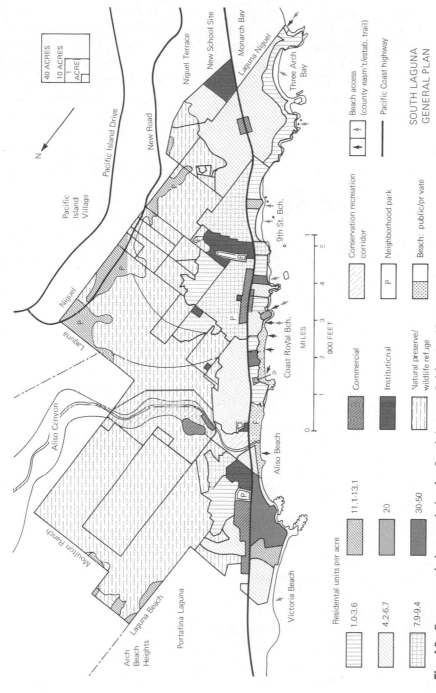

Fig. 4.8 Recommended general plan for South Laguna, California. (Committee for the South Laguna General Plan, 1973.)

Residential units per acre

	1.0–3.6
	4.2–6.7
	7.9–9.4
	11.1–13.1
	20
	30–50

	Commercial
	Institutional
	Natural preserve/ wildlife refuge
	Conservation recreation corridor
P	Neighborhood park
	Beach: public/private

Beach access
(county easm't/estab. trail)

Pacific Coast highway

SOUTH LAGUNA
GENERAL PLAN

40 ACRES

10 ACRES

1 ACRE

N

Pacific Island Drive

Pacific Island Village

New Road

Niguel Terrace

New School Site

Monarch Bay

Laguna Niguel

Three Arch Bay

Niguel

Laguna

Aliso Canyon

Moulton Ranch

Arch Beach Heights

Laguna Beach

Portafina Laguna

Victoria Beach

Aliso Beach

Coast Royal Bch.

9th St. Bch.

MILES
0 1 2 3 4 5

1000 FEET

The zero-growth alternative, although attractive to some residents, was politically untenable and uneconomic. Existing public facilities could accommodate additional users, even requiring them if investments were to be amortized without raising property taxes. Also, the continual press for development by hillside landowners would have eventually overcome local opposition. The recommended plan does allow the landowners developments that will yield satisfactory returns on their investments. By concentrating development, their costs for roads and utilities will be reduced substantially. Some have even admitted that they are financially better off under the program of controlled development.

ENVIRONMENTAL CONTROL ON THE RUHR RIVER, GERMANY

The phenomenal industrial success of West Germany during the 1960s has concentrated more people and more factories in older industrial districts like the Ruhr Valley, which contains 40 percent of German industry, including 80 percent of the country's coal, iron, steel, and heavy chemical capacity. The effluent from these new factories has further polluted the air and tributary streams like the Ruhr River. Among the several alternative courses of action available to the government were:

1. To control expansion and curtail economic growth
2. To relocate industry in less favorable areas which would increase costs of production and reduce efficiency
3. To intensify methods for pollution control

The Ruhr River, which flows through the region to the Rhine, is relatively small, encompassing about half the flow of the Potomac near Washington. The volume of industrial effluent is very large—actually exceeding the flow of the river itself during the dry season, yet people and fish still swim in the Ruhr River.

Control has been achieved through the economic process. Water quality is defined in terms of the pollution absorbtion capacity that will still enable fish to survive. Laboratory tests are conducted to determine what levels of various types of pollution are lethal to fish, and the amount of pollution is calculated from each source in terms of its fish-killing capacity. Limits are established for each source.

Once the limits of pollution have been established a price is put on the polluted effluents, and each source is free to adjust its operation any way it chooses so as to minimize costs of operation. In older areas where there are many factories, the cost of polluting is higher so that newer plants are attracted to locations where the pollution level is lower and the cost of polluting is reduced. On one tributary, the entire course has been converted to an open sewer; it has been lined with concrete and landscaped, but no attempt is made to restrict polluted effluent. A treatment plant at the confluence of the tributary with the Ruhr River processes all waste water at low cost. Therefore, the price of pollution for all factories is low, and the major polluters are encouraged by the pricing mechanism of competitive economics to locate along this tributary. The social cost caused by the pollution of one stream is also low if pollution of the main river is averted.

Revenues from the pollution charges are used to conduct research, to monitor water quality, and to operate waste-treatment facilities at dams where costs are reduced through economies of scale and the minerals recovered.

Although the system is not entirely free from political control and regulation, the emphasis upon the pricing mechanism makes this example of environmental control different from that of the Napa Valley and South Laguna. The people desired to limit pollution of the streams and they have been reasonably successful in achieving such control through the economic process, even though the Ruhr collects effluent from one of the world's most concentrated industrial areas.

POPULATION, POLLUTION, AND CULTURE

In all three areas—the Napa Valley, South Laguna, and the Ruhr River—there was an economic motivation to concentrate additional development into favored areas. The consequences of this development were inconsistent with the cultural preferences of the people, but they have used the political process to control their environment.

In the Napa Valley, urban development was clustered into existing urban areas and the viticulture land was protected by tax incentives favoring agriculture. In South Laguna, the ability of the local authority to control development through land-use zoning was used to preserve the steeply sloping hills and to encourage intensive settlement along the coast. In the Ruhr, authorities imposed a market solution. Industries were taxed by the amount and toxicity of their effluents, and these funds were used to reclaim the water and remove pollutants before the cleansed water was allowed to enter the Rhine.

Each case study illustrates how man controls his own impact upon an area through economic, social, political, and psychological processes so that the human use of the land reflects the culture of its occupants. Studies of population and land use in the present or past are an excellent way to clarify the role these cultural processes play in spatial organization.

Because economic, social, political, and psychological traits of cultural behavior can be identified, they provide a fruitful source of hypotheses to explain spatial organization, and special problems like population growth and environmental conservation. This process orientation also facilitates the exchange of ideas between geographers and social scientists. However, it must be remembered that the division of behavior into processes is artificial at best, and it has resulted in errors. Since behavior frequently involves different processes acting simultaneously, the analysis of spatial organization must employ the techniques of analysis introduced in earlier chapters so that aspects of behavior can be abstracted for study. Happily, the new methods of inquiry or analysis developed by geographers during the 1960s help us to investigate some of the contradictory hypotheses that still abound.

In the following chapters each cultural process will be considered separately. The aim is to present the achievements of the creative minds that have struggled to arrive at plausible answers, and to present additional problems that merit the geographer's attention. But do not expect too much: Because people know so little about their own behavior, knowledge about the impress of cultural behavior is also incomplete.

SUGGESTED READINGS

The geographer's approach to population studies is outlined in more detail in:

Haggett, Peter. *Geography: A Modern Synthesis*. New York: Harper & Row, 1972, chap. 7.

Trewartha, Glenn T. *A Geography of Population: World Patterns*. New York: Wiley, 1969.

Zelinsky, Wilbur. *A Prologue to Population Geography*. Englewood Cliffs, N.J.: Prentice-Hall, 1966.

The dynamics of population growth and methods for estimating future population are outlined in:

Bogue, D. H. *Principles of Demography*. New York: Wiley, 1969.

Case studies in population geography with a cultural emphasis are provided by:

Berger, Carl. "The True North Strong and Free." In *Nationalism in Canada*, edited by P. Russell. Toronto: McGraw-Hill, 1966, pp. 3–26.

Beyer, Glenn H., ed. *The Urban Explosion in Latin America*. Ithaca, N.Y.: Cornell University Press, 1967.

Warkentin, John, ed. *Canada: A Geographical Interpretation*. Toronto: Methuen, 1968, chaps. 2, 7, 8, and 9.

It is difficult to find satisfactory discussions of culture and its role in geography. The interested reader should consult:

Broek, Jan O. M., and Webb, John W. *A Geography of Mankind*. New York: McGraw-Hill, 1968, chaps. 2 and 3.

Clark, Andrew H. *Three Centuries and the Island: A Historical Geography of Settlement and Agriculture in Prince Edward Island, Canada*. Toronto: University of Toronto Press, 1959.

James, Preston E. *One World Divided: A Geographer Looks at the Modern World*. New York: Blaisdell, 1964, chap. 1.

Jordan, Terry G. *The European Culture Area: A Systematic Geography*. New York: Harper & Row, 1973, chap. 1.

Kluckhohn, Clyde. "Culture and Behavior." In *Handbook of Social Psychology*, vol. 2, edited by G. Lindsey. Cambridge, Mass.: Addison-Wesley, 1954.

Skinner, B. F. *Beyond Freedom and Dignity*. New York: Knopf, 1971.

CHAPTER 5

THE ECONOMIC PROCESS

The Yir Yoront tribe of Australia is an essentially Paleolithic society. They are aboriginals. In this "Stone Age" society a complex trade pattern was observed by the first anthropologists. These people used stingray tails for spear points and special flat stones for axe heads. The stingrays could be caught locally. The axe heads came from 400 miles to the south from another tribe. There were many tribes in between that traded spear points in one direction and axe heads in the other. In the Yir Yoront village people could exchange 12 stingray spear points for one axe head. The spear points apparently became more valuable as they moved south. A hundred and fifty miles south of the village the exchange ratio was one spear point for one axe head. And presumably (the anthropologist was not actually able to travel to the southernmost point) farther south one spear point could be exchanged for several axe heads.

Adapted from Sharp (1952), p. 75.

EXCHANGE IS THE ESSENCE of the economic process. Different places on the earth's surface are suited to different activities, and goods are exchanged between them. When a place contains a scarce resource or is more inherently productive, people are willing to compete for its use by exchanging something of value.

Accessible places are the ones most eagerly sought. Many people seek to exchange something of value for the use of land with multiple uses, for example, the central city, and such competition increases the price. Land in remote areas, however, attracts little competition and therefore demands a lower price. Likewise, products of the land will be exchanged for different amounts at different locations. The Yir Yoront, for example, are willing to exchange more spear points per axe head on the coast than at inland locations, because transportation cost adds value to the axe heads.

Locations for economic activities are chosen with a conscious attempt to maximize "something of value," which we call *utility*. The selection of a location that will maximize utility is the economic process in geography.

Because places differ in their productivity and accessibility, and because the goods produced differ in demand, areas of the earth's surface are occupied by contrasting land uses. Economic activities like agriculture, mining, industry, and commerce are neither spread evenly over the earth's surface, nor distributed in random fashion: Regularity in distribution does occur. By focusing upon these regularities, and interpreting them in terms of economic behavior, geographers are able to explain part of the complex patterns of spatial distribution.

No attempt is made here to describe all that is known about spatial distribution of economic activities. This presentation is selective, with emphasis upon those simple models that will clarify the complex distributions. Reasonable models of agricultural and industrial location and the location and spacing of commercial centers have been developed.

UTILITY AND EXCHANGE

Utility is the core concept through which economic behavior might be understood. It is the value of a commodity's usefulness, which may be measured in monetary or nonmonetary units like love or aesthetic pleasure. It is what a farmer attempts to maximize by choosing a particular location and crop or livestock association, what the industrialist seeks to maximize when he chooses a location for a factory, or what a storeowner seeks when he constructs a commercial building.

The value or usefulness of goods & services

Choosing locations for gas stations represents an attempt to achieve utility by maximizing the profit from the sale of gasoline and automobile services. There are two general types of stations: those located near residential areas, which emphasize automobile services, and those adjacent to major highways, which emphasize gasoline sales.

Stations that emphasize gasoline sales demand accessible sites and owners will bid (exchange) a premium price for the use of land at the intersection of major thoroughfares. However, many potential sites are unavailable or already occupied by other commercial functions that can pay a higher price for the use of the land. This is the case in the central business district (CBD) where commercial land returns higher locational rent to land, and gas station operators must seek less costly sites on the fringe or combine their stations with parking garages in the CBD.

Outside the CBD a range of potential sites is available. But if too many are purchased for gas stations, the value of each will fall. The amount of gas purchased is finite, and without adequate sales, a station cannot operate profitably. Therefore, stations outside the CBD should locate on accessible sites in areas where there is a demand for additional service.

Many stations fail to yield an income over and above costs. Despite the size of the gasoline market and the presumed expertise of the major oil companies in selecting locations, failure is not uncommon. Information on travel patterns and consumer demand is inadequate, and decisions on location are often made with considerable uncertainty. When supply exceeds the demand for the service, some stations will close, because they have no utility.

Utility need not be exclusively economic. Where income does not exceed costs, the operator, whose salary is included as a cost of operation, may choose to continue in business although the equivalent capital could be exchanged for a higher return in another enterprise. The individual incurs an *opportunity cost* in order to achieve a noneconomic utility like job satisfaction. This kind of behavior is more common in agriculture, where systems of land use persist although other systems would yield a higher return if the farmer were willing to change. The demand or cost of production for the agricultural product may have changed, but the producer is unwilling to alter his method of farming.

Supply and demand

It is customary to think about exchange behavior in terms of *supply and demand*: the amount of goods and services people are willing to supply for different levels of utility (usually expressed as money), and the amount of these goods that individuals are willing to purchase. Both supplier and consumer are attempting to maximize utility. Their

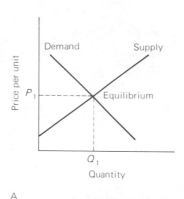 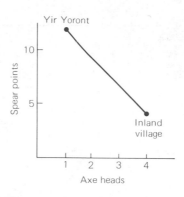

Fig. 5.1 (A) Supply and demand at one place. Both supplier and consumer are satisfied at price (P_1) for quantity (Q_1). (B) Demand at different places. Spear points purchase fewer axe heads in the coastal Yir Yoront village than in inland villages.

preference for alternative levels of the goods can be represented in a two-dimensional space so that the intersection of the supply and demand curves represents equilibrium (Fig. 5.1A). At this point both the supplier and the consumer are satisfied by the utility they receive through the exchange.

If the price is increased, fewer units will be consumed; if it is decreased, more will be consumed. However, demand is satiable. There is a limit to anyone's demand for most goods. Similarly, there is a price below which it is unprofitable to produce the good. At the equilibrium point—where the curves intersect—the supplier is maximizing utility through income while the consumer is satisfied. Both are improved by the exchange.

The supplier's costs include, not only production, but also marketing, of which transportation is a major element. Distance over which the good must be transported may cause the price to vary from place to place. The demand for axe heads illustrated this additional cost: They were more valuable on the coast than at inland areas where they were produced (Fig. 5.1B).

The role of distance

The separation of producer and consumer creates an inconvenience that must be overcome by adding transportation to production costs. In theories of economic location this cost is known as the *friction of*

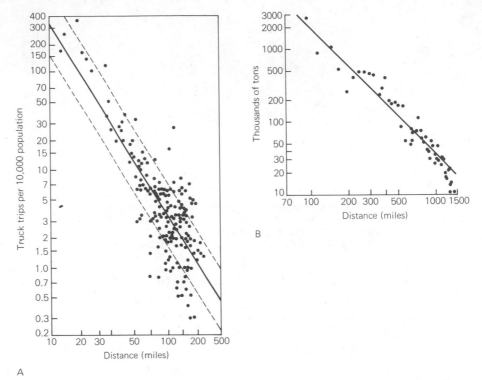

Fig. 5.2 Distance-decay regularities for the number of truck trips in the Chicago region (A), and class–1 railroad shipments in the United States (B). (Yeates and Garner, *The North American City*, Harper & Row, Publishers, 1971, Fig. 4.1; and after Helvig, 1964, Fig. 18; and after Isard, 1956, Fig. 12.)

distance, because the distribution of goods from any center decreases with distance from the center (Fig. 5.2). Locations adjacent to markets enjoy lower production costs than do locations farther removed. Both the costs of receiving raw materials and of distributing the products are lower. However, land near the major markets—usually metropolitan areas—is limited. Producers must be willing to bid a higher price for the use of this land or move to less costly areas located farther from the market.

When the product is easily transferred, as are wheat or aluminum ingots, the source of supply need not be close to markets. Although they could be produced adjacent to the market, they are replaced by products like milk, vegetables, or fabricated aluminum structures, which are costly to transport. Products that are easily transferred tend to be produced away from the market in areas where land cost is not bid up by competing uses. Processing is another means of overcoming the cost of transportation. Milk is converted into butter and cheese in remote areas. It is more efficient to ship the less perishable and more valuable product than it is to transport whole milk. The ease with which commodities can be transferred affects the patterns of commodity flow and locations of production.

There are many ways whereby farmers and factory managers may adjust production to decrease transportation cost. The comparative advantage of different areas is assessed and a production strategy chosen. Goods that are low in value generally move only short distances, whereas high-value goods are able to sustain the cost of longer movements. Shopping behavior illustrates this generalization. People travel only short distances to supermarkets, yet they will drive many miles to a specialized "automobile row" when choosing between alternative cars. Therefore, supermarkets are dispersed amid residential areas, whereas automobile sales are aggregated in accessible locations to facilitate comparison shopping.

Agglomeration

The aggregation of like and interrelated activities reduces the cost of transportation and facilitates exchange. Although locational decisions are made on an individual basis, additional economies are achieved by clustering similar activities. These economies, plus a certain element of imitative behavior, contribute to the development of commercial, industrial, and agricultural patterns.

Agglomeration of commercial activities into regional shopping centers provides a familiar example of clustering for mutual benefit. Specific sites are chosen because of their superior access to transportation routes and the availability of sufficent land. One or two major department stores provide the main attraction. Other convenience stores are located between the major stores to encourage shoppers to add purchases impulsively. This increases the sales and growth of the center. Toy, candy, and book stores fall into the convenience category, as do restaurants and accessory stores. Agglomeration increases both sales and the ability of the center to attract customers from greater distances because they can satisfy several needs at one stop.

In industry the location of a raw material or a transportation advantage may be the original reason for a clustering of activities. Often the original reason for location becomes less important, but the agglomeration remains intact for social and psychological reasons. Industrial locations alongside ports illustrate these reasons: Originally proximity to the transshipment of goods at the port provided the incentive for industrial developments like flour mills and machinery manufacturers. However, as sources of the raw materials changed, and as distribution costs for manufactured products increased, suburban locations have become more economical. Yet, industrial location near the port persists as a result of the inertia of established locations and individual resistance to change. People are content with the location because utility is achieved through noneconomic satisfactions.

Optimal or satisfactory locations

Although we can assume that producers will seek the most profitable locations, it is misleading to assume that producers seek to optimize their returns. Both individual and organizational decision making is concerned with the selection between satisfactory alternatives; only in rare occurrences is an optimal location chosen. There are two major reasons for this:

1. Information on all possible sites and costs of operation at those sites is seldom available. The decision-maker has only a selected sample of the possible information.
2. Social and psychological processes affect the decision. The farmer or industrialist might be unwilling to leave the area where he has established friendships in order to secure a more profitable location. Liaison between subsidiary units of a corporate structure also affects the choice.

Established regions also have an advantage over developing areas. Individuals and corporations avoid risks. They tend to reduce risk by locating in established areas rather than at new sites that might be more profitable at first, but that could be affected more severely by changing economic conditions. In Chapter 1, Wolpert's study (1964) was used to illustrate the spatial impact of the Swedish farmers' contentment with satisfactory, rather than optimal, returns. Actual labor productivity fell far below potential productivity. Apparently, many farmers were content with returns from existing investment and were unwilling to risk the additional investments needed to intensify productivity, although this would increase profitability.

Similarly, an entrepreneur faced with the prospect of locating a new electronics plant will tend to limit his search to areas with which he is familiar. For instance, if he limits his choice to three cities, he can then select one on the basis of his own experience or on the basis of a detailed examination of each city. He might even hire an economic research firm to conduct such studies for him. The more information he has, the more he reduces the uncertainty about the choice. Even if he employs a professional consultant, he cannot be assured that he has chosen the optimal location in terms of profitability because the choice was restricted to three cities, and information about these cities would be selective and incomplete.

The comparative advantage in economic behavior

Choice of location for economic activities is decided by many factors affecting the cost of the operation. It is difficult to construct a *numerical* or *quantitative* scale against which alternative locations can be compared. If we wish to do so, we must reduce the problem to a few essential factors, such as transportation costs and land rents, which we will do later in this chapter. In most instances, however, we are required to assess a location's *comparative advantage* over competing locations in *qualitative* terms.

Comparative advantage is a comparison of environmental, social, political, psychological, and economic attributes of one location with those of competing locations. Different activities have different requirements, and locations that might be unsuitable for one will be ideal for another. For example, hill country may be unsuitable for wheat farms or industrial sites, yet it is preferred by sheep ranchers and homeowners.

Locations will also vary in their resource endowment. The oil and gas fields of Alberta provide an industrial resource with which few areas can compete, yet manufacturing in Canada still clusters along the Great Lakes and the St. Lawrence Valley (Fig. 5.3). These areas enjoy market and labor advantages as well as the geographic inertia of long-established operation.

Economic activities are virtually excluded from extensive areas of

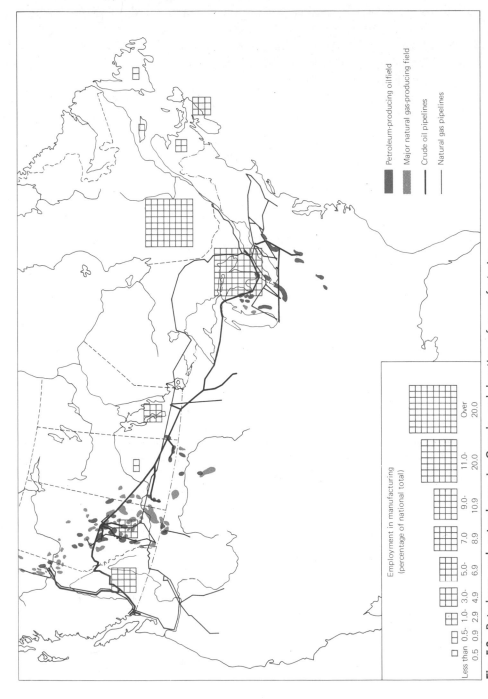

Fig. 5.3 Petroleum and natural gas in Canada and location of manufacturing employment. Whereas the major sources of fossil energy are in western Canada, manufacturing remains in the east adjacent to the major markets. (After *Oxford Regional Economic Atlas: The United States and Canada*, 1967, pp. 92–95, 116 and 117. Reproduced by permission of Oxford University Press.)

Petroleum-producing oilfield

Major natural gas-producing field

Crude oil pipelines

Natural gas pipelines

Employment in manufacturing
(percentage of national total)

Less than 0.5- 1.0- 3.0- 5.0- 7.0- 9.0- 11.0- Over
0.5   0.9   2.9   4.9   6.9   8.9   10.9   20.0   20.0

the earth's surface. Usually these are remote areas, like most of the Laurentian Shield in Canada and the nonirrigated arid lands of the American Southwest. Activities such as forestry and ranching are feasible, but the cost of producing and transporting goods to markets renders these areas uneconomic. The comparative advantage of these areas is less than that of alternative producing areas. Only high-value commodities whose bulk can be reduced through processing (e.g., mineral extractions) are economic.

The cost of overcoming distance—the *friction of distance*—is a key variable in location theory. There are numerous possible locations for most enterprises, but it is the cost of marketing goods that most frequently determines whether production will be economically feasible. For example, the least cost-producing areas for winter flowers in America are Southern California and Hawaii. Yet growers using hothouses that are located on expensive land within eastern metropolitan areas compete successfully with the more distant growers. Because of its pervasive effect on economic location, distance is commonly used as the independent variable for location models of all categories of economic activity, whether they be primary, secondary, or tertiary.

CATEGORIES OF ECONOMIC ACTIVITY

The division of economic activity into primary, secondary, and tertiary activities provides a convenient method of classifying the arrangement of phenomena based upon the method of production.

Primary activities: These include mining, forestry, and the farming of land and sea resources. These activities occupy most of the earth's surface.

Secondary activities: These encompass the processing and/or manufacturing of primary products so as to increase their value and usefulness. These activities are clustered in a few locations; usually near markets but not exclusively so.

Tertiary activities: These include the financing, transporting, marketing, and selling of primary and secondary products. These intangible services, essential to the system of exchange between producer and consumer, are located in market centers.

The disadvantage of such a division is that it is based upon the supply (production) aspects of economic behavior rather than on the demand (consumer) aspects. Production occurs in specialized areas, whereas patterns of consumption by households are similar across a wider area. Models developed to explain particular categories of production like agriculture are specific to that activity. More general models of economic behavior can only be developed by focusing upon demand.

The production orientation results from the availability of data. Census information lists the results of economic behavior in terms of agricultural and industrial production. By comparison, there is a paucity of reliable information on the location of consumption, and this more general aspect of economic behavior has been neglected.

The volume of information about production has also encouraged descriptive, as opposed to theoretical, approaches to economic geography. So much effort has been devoted to describing the patterns that the analysis of causes has been neglected.

Recent emphasis upon consumer behavior in tertiary activities is the exception. Availability of information on the volume of consumer sales at different locations enabled the testing of hypotheses about consumer behavior. These studies have led to the development of a model concerned with the size and spacing of such central places as towns and shopping centers, known as the *central place theory*. The generality of the theory has done more in a decade to advance understanding of economic behavior in a spatial context than have previous generations of descriptive studies on economic production.

The models of economic behavior to be introduced are of two types: *choice* and *exchange*. Explanation for the location and magnitude of tertiary activities is based upon choice behavior, where the consumer must select between alternative opportunities. The problem is to estimate the probability of a consumer traveling to center A as opposed to B, C, or D, when the cost of travel to each competing center and the attraction of that center can be estimated.

Exchange models will be utilized in subsequent sections to explain the patterns of land use in urban and rural areas and the location of industry. In an attempt to simplify the factors of economic production, assumptions are used to reduce the exchange problem to one or two key variables, so that an optimal location may be selected for an activity in terms of the key variables.

LOCATION OF TERTIARY ACTIVITIES

The location of tertiary activities is generally in agreement with population: the more people there are in an area, the greater the number of tertiary activities offered. Differentials in wealth do create variations, but people within each cultural realm, regardless of wealth, demand a similar range of goods and services. Therefore, the location and arrangement of commerce and public and personal services reflects the demand created by people.

Tertiary activities can be divided into four categories:

1. *Distributive* activities that include people employed in the wholesaling and retailing of primary and secondary products. Warehouses, supermarkets, bars, and hamburger stands are familiar examples of such activities.
2. *Financial* activities that facilitate the production and marketing of produce through banking, insurance, and real estate activities.
3. *Governmental* activities that protect both producers and consumers, and facilitate the marketing of commodities. Included are all persons employed by local, state, or provincial and central government service. Teachers and university employees, whether they are in state or private institutions, are placed in this category because they work to enhance the capability of individuals as producers and consumers.
4. *Personal services* that include such activities as hospital and medical care, hotels, and entertainment.

Each category includes similar types of activity that are designated as functions. Supermarkets, for example, may differ from one another in franchise name, but each is an example of a similar function. Each function requires a level or threshold of demand before it is viable, and the number of functions present in any central place is indicative of the magnitude of demand at that place.

Models of tertiary location

Tertiary functions are specialized to serve particular consumer markets. If consumer preference changes, then a tertiary function normally fails. Seldom can its function be modified as is possible in agriculture or industry. Sometimes a hairdresser can adapt to changing demand by diversifying, but the usual response is to close. Demand for the commodity or service is crucial to the survival of a tertiary function at specific locations.

Economic models conceptualize exchange as a function of supply and demand (Fig 5.4A). *Demand* is the different quantity of goods and services (e.g., the hamburgers noted in Fig. 5.4A) that an individual will buy at different market prices. *Supply* is the various quantity sellers are willing to provide at these market prices. The point of equilibrium is where the supply curve intersects the demand curve. At this price (P_1) a sufficient quantity of hamburgers (Q_1) will be produced to satisfy the consumer demand at a price attractive to both seller and consumer.

Schedules for exchange will vary with a person's utility for hamburgers and money. Figure 5.4A represents utility for an American college student. His parents would probably value the hamurgers less and be willing to pay less. In comparison, the British college student would pay more. Meat pies and fish-and-chips are the British substitute, and hamburgers are perceived as having greater utility, and, therefore, command a higher price per unit.

Distance and economic behavior

Whereas the exchange schedule tells something about the occurrence of commercial activities, it will not explain distribution. Commercial activities that supply popular, low-priced goods like hamburgers will occur frequently. However, the cost to the consumer includes, not only the market price, but also the cost of travel to obtain the good.

The cost of travel will increase sharply at first and then more gradually (Fig. 5.4B). This additional cost can be incorporated into the price schedule. As price to the consumer increases with distance from the marketplace, the quantity demanded will decline (Fig. 5.4C). Let us assume that the price at the marketplace is P_1. At this price the amount Q_2 will be demanded. At distance d the price increases to P_2 and the quantity falls to Q_1. At distance r, the additional cost of acquiring ham-

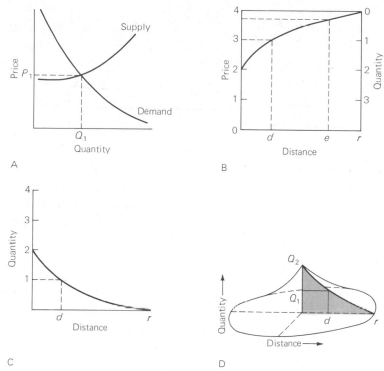

Fig. 5.4 Relationship between demand distance and price of a good. (A) Various quantity of hamburgers demanded at different prices. This reflects a student's preference (utility) for hamburgers. Suppliers are willing to offer more hamburgers as the price increases. Below a minimum price, none are available. (B) Price varies with distance. Demand is also affected by the cost of travel, which can be indicated as an addition to the cost of the goods. At r, the price is 4, and quantity falls to 0. (C) As distance increases, the quantity purchased decreased as a result of travel cost. (D) Demand at different distances from stand can be represented as a spatial demand cone. Assuming travel is equally easy in all directions, then the range will be a perfect circle. This circle is the outer limit of the demand cone under which the quantity consumed decreases with distance. The price increases because of transport cost. (Fig. 5.4D after Brian J. L. Berry, *Geography of Market Centers and Retail Distribution*, © 1967, p. 61. Reprinted by permission of Prentice-Hall, Inc., Englewood Cliffs, N.J.)

burgers makes them unattractive. How many times have you desired a hamburger at 2:00 A.M.? All the local stands have closed except the all-night diner five miles away. Will you drive there, go hungry, or eat a candy bar from a vending machine in your dormitory?

THE RANGE OF A GOOD

A declining demand for a good with its distance from a market can be conceptualized by rotating Fig. 5.4D so that quantity demanded at the marketplace becomes the vertical axis, and price, which varies with distance, becomes the horizontal axis. The *range of the good* is the distance that people are willing to travel to purchase goods and services at certain prices. In our example of the hamburger, the maximum range is r. The concentric area beneath the demand cone is called the *market area*, the *hinterland*, or *complementary region*.

Should the price of hamburgers decrease, or the cost of travel become more economical, then the range of the good would increase. If the price increased, there would be a corresponding decrease in range.

Commercial functions seldom maintain an ideal market area. Competition from other stores in adjoining locations creates zones of competition at the margins where consumers may choose the center they will patronize (Fig. 5.5). Competition for customers in this zone of consumer indifference is intense, because it is essential that stores maintain a level of demand in order to amortize costs of operation. Only then can they supply goods and services at reasonable cost.

THRESHOLD OF DEMAND

A certain minimum number of sales is required before any good can be offered to the consumer. These sales are required to bring a firm into business and keep it operating. Market analysts applying geographical techniques can calculate the potential demand beneath each demand cone. Sales are estimated by: (1) counting the number of people within the potential market area of a store; (2) calculating the prob-

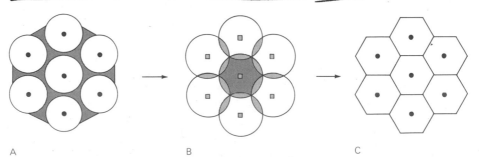

A   B   C

Fig. 5.5 Emergence of hexagonal trade areas. To serve interstitial areas, trade areas overlap. When the points of intersection are joined, hexagonal trade areas are constructed which cover the area without overlap. (Yeates and Garner, *The North American City*, Harper & Row, Publishers, 1971, Fig. 7.26.)

able use by people at varying distances from the store; and (3) estimating the price they would be willing to pay for each unit.

Threshold can be defined as a minimum level of demand required to support one establishment of a function type. Normally, it is expressed as the minimum number of people required to support one establishment of a functional type.

The threshold required by different functions is based upon the nature of the goods offered and how frequently they are demanded. Goods and services used daily such as food, automobiles, telephones, and schools have low thresholds. Goods like specialty clothing, and services like heart surgery, museums, and universities require larger threshold populations. They are used occasionally by a minority of the population and can only survive at accessible locations within major metropolitan areas. It is customary to designate as *lower-order* goods and services, those that are required frequently. Those that are required less frequently are *higher-order* goods and services that are offered only at places accessible to a major metropolitan market. Figure 5.6 lists a range of services and provides estimates of threshold populations required in Phoenix, Arizona. Automobile travel is convenient in Phoenix, and commercial areas are dispersed in a multinuclei urban area. Therefore, the apparent cost of travel is less and there are fewer commercial functions serving larger threshold populations than you would expect to find in older cities.

A CENTRAL PLACE

In addition to satisfying the demand for goods and services from a market area, commercial functions also create employment opportunities and stimulate consumer demand. Because employees also wish to minimize travel costs, they reside nearby. Agglomerations of homes and buildings or a settlement develop near the commercial core which serves, not only the settlement, but also a hinterland or market area where there is insufficient demand to warrant duplication of functions. The foci of commerce are *central places*: centers that serve areas— urban or rural—larger than themselves, and for which they serve as the center of a complementary region.

In rural areas, central places may be villages, towns, cities, or regional centers. In metropolitan areas they are represented by convenience shops, neighborhood and convenience centers, and the CBDs, which serve as regional centers. Each central place offers its threshold

Fig. 5.6   Threshold populations for selected functions in Phoenix, Arizona (1964)

Central functions	Number	Threshold population	
Service station	887	859	Low-order
Auto repair	619	1,231	functions
Motel	473	1,612	
Physicians	426	1,789	
Bar	426	1,789	
Beauty shop	353	2,159	
Insurance agency	321	2,375	
Barber shop	307	2,483	
Clothing store	283	2,694	
Dry cleaner	283	2,694	
Liquor store	175	4,432	
Used car	158	4,852	
Convenience grocery	141	5,406	
Restaurant (fully licensed)	141	5,406	
Bank	103	7,410	
Jewelry	86	8,864	
Hardware	63	12,100	
Lawyer	58	13,143	
New car	58	13,143	
Appliance sales-service	57	13,374	
Florist	51	14,947	
Sporting goods	48	15,881	
Hotel-motel	45	16,940	
Savings and loan associations	43	17,728	
Animal hospital	40	19,057	
Camera shop	30	25,410	
Movie theater	30	25,410	
Car wash	26	29,319	High-order
Mortuary	24	31,762	functions

Source: After Dunbier, 1964, unpublished.

population offers a range of functions for the complementary region of which it is the center. The nature and variety of these functions will depend upon the market range of the goods, the services it offers, and the market area it controls. A hierarchy of central places is exhibited in both urban and rural areas. And if adjustments are made for size of trade area and settlement density, each serves a comparable threshold population (Fig. 5.7).

Hierarchy of central places

Consumers choose between competing central places on the basis of proximity and the range of functions available. Other things being equal, a consumer will choose the nearest place. However, where sev-

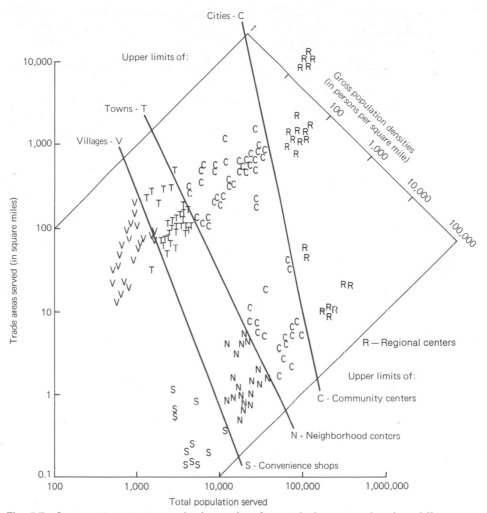

Fig. 5.7 Systematic variation in the hierarchy of central places is related to differences in the density of settlement. (Brian J .L. Berry, *Geography of Market Centers and Retail Distribution*, © 1967, p. 33. Reprinted by permission of Prentice-Hall, Inc., Englewood Cliffs, N.J.)

eral competing stores offer similar goods a consumer may decide that the additional cost of travel will be repaid through the advantage of comparison shopping. CBDs and community shopping plazas are able to attract customers for this reason.

Because the larger commercial districts serve a greater threshold population, they also offer *higher-order* goods and services. For this reason, they are often referred to as *higher-order central places*, whereas the neighborhood centers and towns and villages are *lower-order central places.* In addition to the higher-order goods and services, higher-order central places also offer lower-order goods for the adjoining market area.

Classifications of central places are based both on the number of different business activities (i.e., the number of functions) and the type of business performed by the central place. Lowest-order central places like hamlets or minimum-convenience centers have fewer than ten functions, whereas higher-order cities and community shopping centers have in excess of sixty (Fig. 5.8).

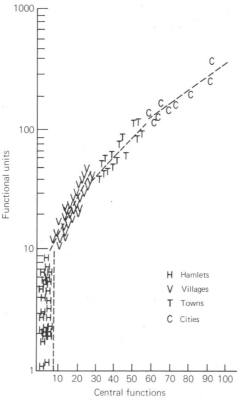

Fig. 5.8 Classification of central places based upon number of central functions. Hamlets have fewer than five and cities more than sixty types. More than one unit of each type is present in higher central places. (Brian J. L. Berry, H. G. Barnum, and R. J. Tennant, *Regional Science Association, Papers and Proceedings*, vol. 9, 1962, Fig. 7.)

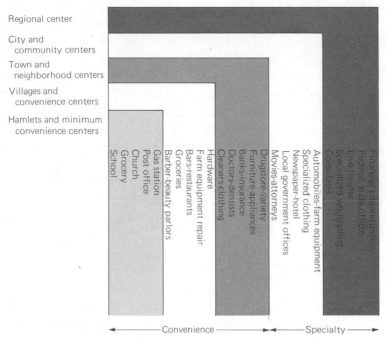

Regional center

City and
  community centers

Town and
  neighborhood centers

Villages and
  convenience centers

Hamlets and minimum
  convenience centers

School
Grocery
Church
Post office
Gas station
Barber-beauty parlors
Groceries
Bars-restaurants
Farm equipment repair
Hardware
Cleaners-clothing
Doctors-dentists
Banks-insurance
Furniture-appliances
Drugstore-variety
Movies-attorneys
Local government offices
Newspaper-hotel
Specialized clothing
Automobiles-farm equipment
Consulates
Specialized wholesaling
Live theater
Federal, state offices
Financial administration

◄———— Convenience ————►◄——— Specialty ———►

Fig. 5.9 Types of central places with functions characteristic of
both urban and rural settlements. Higher-order central places
have the functions of lower-order central places as well as the
functions that are characteristic of their own level.

The type of function will also differ. A city will have city-level
functions such as specialty clothing stores together with hotels, hospitals, and administrative activities in addition to bars, service stations,
churches, and schools, which are characteristic of village-level functions (Fig. 5.9).

The school system provides an example of the hierarchy of tertiary
functions. A village will contain one elementary school for children
from rural families, whereas a town will have one or more, and possibly
a high school (two functions) as well. In a city, there will be several
elementary schools and at least one high school, in addition to junior
highs, and possibly a college. Both the number of functions and the
number of educational establishments increase in higher-order central
places.

A hierarchy of central places exists in any area. Centers at different
levels offer different functions. However, central places of similar
level—but separate from one another and controlling their own market

area—will duplicate functions. A nested hierarchy exists because the market areas of higher-order central places embrace lower-order central places. For example, a city might provide newspapers and professional and administrative services for several towns and villages, each of which will provide lower-order goods and services.

Retail outlets are duplicated because it is cheaper to move goods in bulk. Therefore, central places develop wherever there is sufficient threshold population for the goods. The goods are then distributed from warehouses in the metropolitan areas to the central place, since this minimizes the travel cost for consumers. If tertiary functions are not easily available, consumers will go without a given product or find substitutes. For instance, if there is no bakery, people will bake their own bread with materials that can be more easily transported than fresh bread.

Usually consumers have a choice of centers as well as a choice between stores offering the same goods. Other things being equal, they will make this choice based upon the distance they must travel and the range of functions they will have available at competing centers. The operation of this choice behavior creates a nested system of central places ordered in terms of size and spacing.

Central place theory

The principles of commercial location are derived from the *central place theory*: a theory about the size and spacing of tertiary activities developed by Walter Christaller in 1932. It is a simple theoretical model, based upon deductive reasoning, about consumer demand and the willingness of entrepreneurs to provide goods and services to satisfy this demand.

Like most location theories, central place involves assumptions, most of which are similar to those postulated by Von Thünen in his model of agricultural location. We assume that there exists:

1. A relatively homogeneous plain without physical obstacles
2. Uniform population characteristics, even distribution, and uniform purchasing power
3. Uniform transportation costs where it is equally easy for a person to move in any direction

These assumptions create an *isotropic* or uniform surface upon which the effects of economic processes can be observed. In addition, Christaller assumed that the evolution of the economic landscape was solely related to the development of tertiary activities, and that consumers would act rationally.

From these assumptions, <u>Christaller hypothesized the existence of concentric market areas that would cluster in *hexagonal patterns* so that each trade area would be tangential to six others.</u> Highest-order central places would offer the greatest range of goods and services. However, within the market area of the highest-order central place, there would exist locations at which entrepreneurs could compete by offering lower-order functions that consumers would require more frequently, and for which they would be unwilling to travel. Each succeeding lower level would occupy one-third of the higher market area (Fig. 5.10).

Another way for you to conceptualize the hierarchy is to consider that the market area of each city would embrace three towns, and

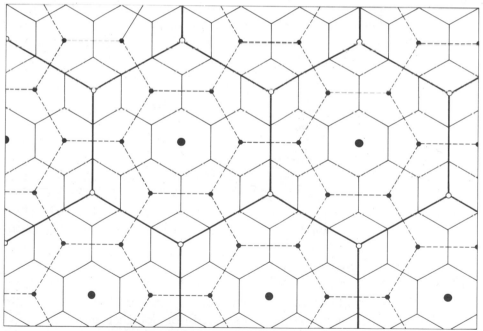

Fig. 5.10 Part of the Christaller K - 3 settlement pattern. Only the three largest levels of centers are shown on the diagram. Each succeeding lower level occupies one-third of a higher market area. (Yeates and Garner, *The North American City*, Harper & Row, Publishers, 1971, Fig. 7.27.)

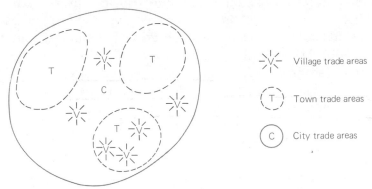

Fig. 5.11 Schematic representation of the nesting of trade areas. (Yeates and Garner, *The North American City*, Harper & Row, Publishers, 1971, Fig. 7.23.)

that the market areas of these three towns would each contain three villages (Fig. 5.11).

Christaller's hypothesis regarding the location and spacing of towns as centers for tertiary activity has had a profound impact upon social science research. Christaller himself tested the theory in southern Germany and there have been numerous other applications. Generally, these studies have substantiated that:

1. As population of central places increases the number of functions also increase, but at a decreasing rate.
2. Higher-order functions are found only in higher-order central places that are the largest population centers.
3. In any area there exists a hierarchy of central places. There are few high-order central places and many lower-order ones.
4. Central places of corresponding order contain similar central place functions.
5. Thresholds for different functions vary with the culture of consumers.

SOUTHWESTERN IOWA AND CONSUMER TRAVEL

A comprehensive demonstration of settlement patterns within a central place system has been provided for southwestern Iowa (Berry et al., 1962). The area was well chosen because the gently sloping land and relatively uniform distribution of rural population approaches an isotropic surface. A hierarchy of central places has developed with Omaha

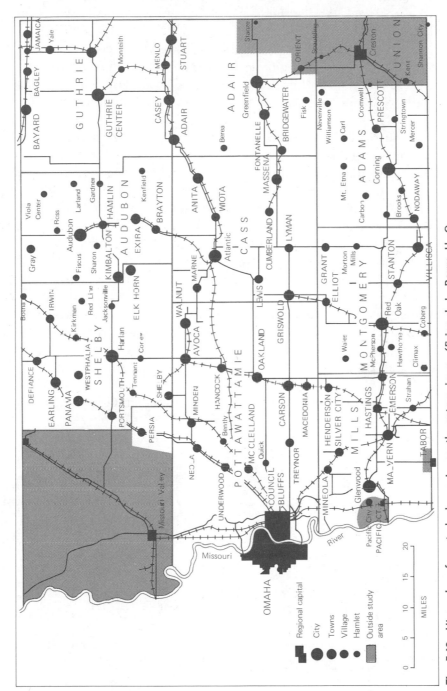

Fig. 5.12 Hierarchy of central places in southwestern Iowa. (Brian J. L. Berry, H. G. Barnum, and R. J. Tennant, *Regional Science Association, Papers and Proceedings,* vol. 9, 1962, Fig. 1.)

—Council Bluffs as the highest-order location (Fig. 5.12). In addition to the regional capital there are eight cities, twenty towns, thirty-six villages, and thirty-five hamlets.

With the exception of hamlets, lower-order centers occur more frequently than do higher-order ones. The reduction of services in hamlets is explained by the declining rural population in America and the ability of the remaining population to travel by automobile to larger centers.

Because of the transportation network, the pattern of distribution does not resemble the hexagonal pattern hypothesized by Christaller. The rectangular subdivision of the American Midwest has produced a corresponding road and rail network. Settlements originating at intersections in this network produce linear patterns, with cities separated by at least one town and several villages. Hamlets are more common in areas of lower-population density like Adams County where they are protected by distance from competing towns.

An analysis of travel desire lines within southwestern Iowa indicated that consumers seemed to select the closest central place for the purchase of goods of different orders. Higher-order places attracted consumers from greater distances and controlled larger market areas than did lower-order centers. A distinction was made between urban and rural travel because for urban consumers the market was often within the same settlement.

Clothing purchases are a city-level function (Fig. 5.13). Atlantic, Red Oak, and Council Bluffs are preferred shopping areas because comparison shopping is available where many businesses offer the same

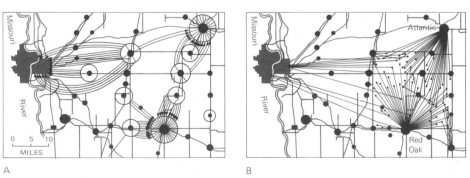

Fig. 5.13 Shopping preferences for clothing in southwestern Iowa: (A) urban dwellers; (B) rural dwellers. (Brian J. L. Berry, H. G. Barnum, and R. J. Tennant, *Regional Science Association, Papers and Proceedings*, vol. 9, 1962, Fig. 17.)

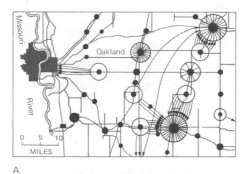
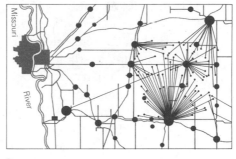

A   B

Fig. 5.14 Shopping preferences for dry cleaning services in southwestern Iowa: (A) urban dwellers; (B) rural dwellers. Brian J. L. Berry, H. G. Barnum, and R. J. Tennant, *Regional Science Association, Papers and Proceedings*, vol. 9, 1962, Fig. 14.)

product or service. The additional consumer attraction of the regional capital upon the neighboring towns diverts consumers away from closer, but smaller, competitors like those in Oakland.

Dry cleaning is a town-level function (Fig. 5.14). It is frequently demanded and there is little variation in price and quality. Atlantic and Red Oak are unchanged, but towns like Oakland and Carson are independent of the dominance by the regional city.

Groceries are a convenience good, and consumers are willing to travel only short distances for their purchase (Fig. 5.15). The cities and towns each have several enterprises, and within the market area of each village there is a sufficient threshold of rural population to support this function.

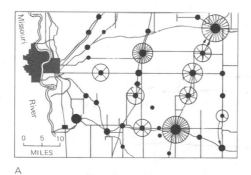

A   B

Fig. 5.15 Shopping preferences for groceries in southwestern Iowa: (A) urban dwellers; (B) rural dwellers. (Brian J. L. Berry, H. G. Barnum, and R. J. Tennant, *Regional Science Association Papers and Proceedings*, vol. 9, 1962, Fig. 11.)

CENTRAL PLACES WITHIN METROPOLITAN AREAS

Within metropolitan areas a hierarchy of commercial areas is present that is comparable in function to the settlements in southwestern Iowa Consumers still attempt to minimize travel cost, but because the population density is much higher, threshold populations are achieved within smaller market areas. By comparison with rural areas, commercial functions (stores) are larger and more specialized and require larger threshold populations (see Fig. 5.7).

The actual pattern of trade areas in a city like Chicago is quite complex. Major regional centers occur in the newer suburbs and the older, but more affluent, suburbs to the north (Fig. 5.16). Specialized clothing, home furnishings, and camera stores are functions that occur only at this highest level. Community shopping centers offer city-level functions. They are the downtown commercial districts of older suburbs where clothing and hardware stores, radio and television repair, movie theaters, and banks are characteristic. Neighborhood centers are the equivalent of the rural town. They are oriented to supply convenience requirements such as groceries, drugs, variety goods, personal services, and liquor.

Analyzing commercial structures within metropolitan areas is made additionally complex by the ease of movement enjoyed by urban residents. The strip commercial districts, with limited parking, cater to those who shop by car. Elsewhere, specialized commercial districts have developed for the furniture and automobile trades. These offer convenience buying for high-order, infrequently needed goods like furniture, automobiles, and medical services (Fig. 5.17).

The CBD is the single largest concentration of commercial activity. It serves as the center for the metropolis and an extensive hinterland. The CBD is:

1. An area of intensive land use
2. An area of vertical development, rarely more than a mile square, where a considerable premium is paid for the personal interaction in business and commerce
3. An area of daily population fluctuation with few permanent residents
4. A focus for inter- and intracity transportation
5. A center for specialized professional, financial, and governmental activities

6. An area that is specialized internally into subareas with specific functions (Fig. 5.18)

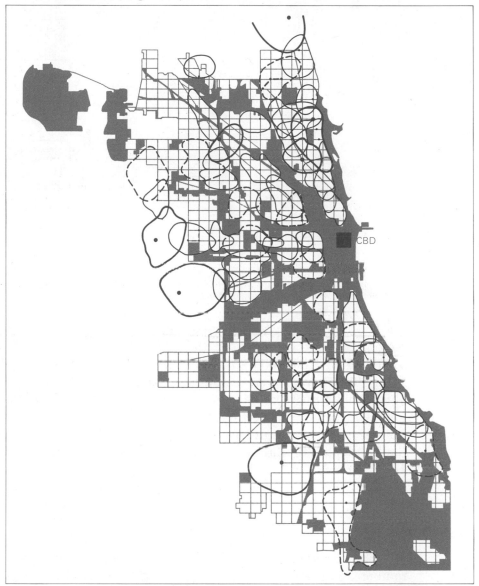

Fig. 5.16 Trade areas for convenience goods in Chicago. Note overlapping customer trade areas around major Chicago shopping centers. Width of lines indicates size of shopping centers (dots). Dark gray areas are industrial and commercial sites. (Simmons, *Changing Pattern of Retail Locations*, University of Chicago, Department of Geography, Research Papers, 1964, Fig. 8.12.)

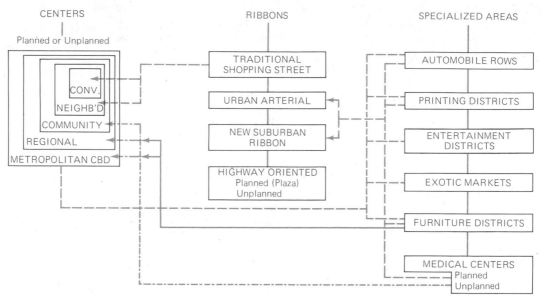

Fig. 5.17 Major components of the urban business pattern (Brian J. L. Berry, *Commercial Structure and Commercial Blight*, University of Chicago, Department of Geography, Research Papers 85, 1963, Table 2.)

The CBD is the highest-order central place for the metropolis and region. In urban nations like the United States and Canada, activities in the major metropolitan centers dominate economic, social, and political life. There is even an international hierarchy because the financial and administrative centers of New York, London, Tokyo, Moscow, and Peking dominate the world. A hierarchy of lower-order centers are nested into each of the most powerful central places. An understanding of the principles of the central place theory—market areas, thresholds, and hierarchical arrangements—helps explain the pattern and the reasons why spatial distributions are structured the way they are.

Growth of cities

Modern society is dominated by a few megalopolitan centers. Even remote areas are affected by commercial, financial, and political decisions emanating from these centers. However, the centers themselves are sustained by the resources drawn from their hinterland: they expand only by marketing the surplus from primary and secondary activities.

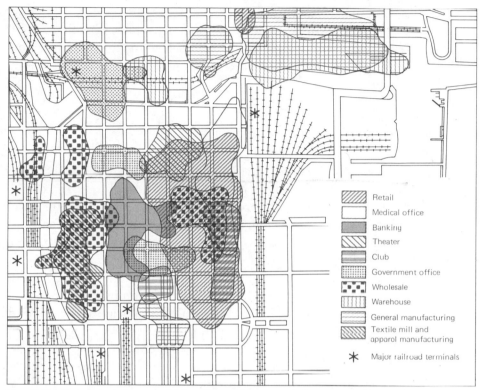

Fig. 5.18 Functional areas within Chicago's central business district. (Brian J. L. Berry, *Geography of Market Centers and Distribution*, © 1967, p. 52. Reprinted by permission of Prentice-Hall, Inc., Englewood Cliffs, N.J.)

The growth of large cities has been made possible by three general factors:

1. An efficient agricultural system that produced a surplus to sustain the urban population
2. Scientific discoveries that made possible the mechanization of industry in large factories for which urban location was preferred
3. Development of an efficient transportation system to transport raw materials and distribute the finished products

Tertiary activities are the essence of urban life, yet tertiary activities are dependent upon the exchange of surpluses from primary and secondary activities. Therefore, the location and arrangement of primary activities like agriculture and secondary activities like industry is best understood within the context of exchange between producing areas and centers of consumption. An exchange model, with distance from markets or raw materials as the independent variable, provides the basis for explaining the location of both agricultural and industrial production.

LOCATION OF AGRICULTURE

Agriculture is central to all economic activities. Not only is it man's principal occupation, it is also the source of raw material for manufacturing and the fulcrum for retail activities. Most of the earth's inhabited surface is occupied by agriculture. Those areas in which agriculture is too difficult or unrewarding are virtually unoccupied (see back endpaper).

It is usual to distinguish between commercial (production for profit) and subsistence (production for domestic use) agriculture. This is useful when classifying agriculture, because the final disposal of the crop affects the way in which the land is used.

Areas differ in terrain, soil, and climate as well as their human capacities. These differences have given rise to fascinating geographical distributions (which are summarized on the map of world agricultural regions, back endpaper). The effect of agglomeration is readily apparent in the tendency for regions to specialize. The major controls over land use that provide areas with the comparative advantage for specialist activities are:

1. Patterns of human behavior
2. Inherent attributes like terrain, climate, soil, and original vegetation (inherent attributes of place)
3. Location in references to markets (accessibility)

Patterns of human behavior

Human behavior is a complex, but essential, factor in assessing the potential usefulness of an area in terms of the culture of the occupants. It includes among other things the following patterns.

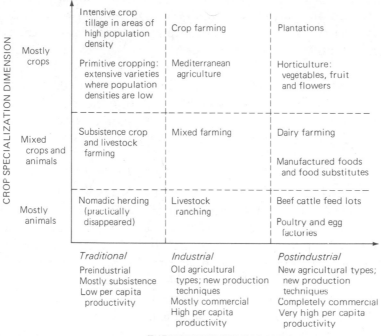

Fig. 5.19 A two-way classification of agricultural systems. Crop and livestock specializations associated with economic systems. (Ronald Abler, John S. Adams, and Peter Gould, *Spatial Organization: The Geographer's View of the World*, © 1971, Fig. 10.3. Reprinted by permission of Prentice-Hall, Inc., Englewood Cliff, N.J.)

Degree of modernization. Traditional societies (preindustrial) seldom can arrange systems of commercial agriculture. Subsistence agriculture prevails, with exchange through barter and ceremonial gift giving. Productivity per capita is low (Fig. 5.19). Industrial economies modernize, intensify, and commercialize traditional systems. Subsistence farming is transformed into commercial counterparts. In postindustrial societies production and marketing are specialized, yielding very high per capita productivity.

Food preferences. <u>Dietary habits exert influence upon production by establishing demand</u>. The preference for rice in Asia and potatoes in Western Europe affects the cropping program. Similarly, the religious disdain for pork by followers of the Moslem and Jewish faiths affects livestock patterns in areas where these religions predominate. Cattle keeping for religious purposes is another example of how cultural preference affects agriculture. India, for example, has more cattle than any other nation, but not for beef consumption.

Willingness to innovate. Many farmers are unwilling to experiment with new crops and methods of production, even though these methods can be shown to be profitable in the short run. Satisfaction with returns from familiar crops affects production patterns even in postindustrial societies.

Political influence. One means of resisting change is for farmers to lobby for governmental subsidization of traditional agricultural systems. Rather than allowing the market process to force change as demand shifts to reflect new consumer preferences and/or to favor new and more economical producing areas, governments subsidize established agricultural enterprises. Cotton and sugar, for example, could be imported to the United States more economically than they can be produced here, but farmers resist the economic process that would require them to produce these crops more economically or to cultivate more specialized crops. For very good reasons, farmers and farm organizations resist the change from agricultural conditions with which they are familiar. They attempt to offset competition from areas with superior attributes by requesting political controls.

Inherent attributes of place

Crops and animals to some extent thrive under different environmental conditions. There are optimal conditions for each crop. A specific crop may be produced elsewhere, but only at greater cost or with lower yield than in the optimal zone. Eventually, the cost of overcoming environmental disadvantages makes production unprofitable (Fig. 5.20).

Climate is the most pervasive environmental influence. In the case of horticulture, and especially for citrus fruits, climatic requirements establish sharp limits for production. Soil requirements are more easily overcome with fertilizers, soil additives, and drainage. However, areas with soils high in inherent fertility, like the American Midwest, enjoy a comparative advantage for cropping systems. Slope

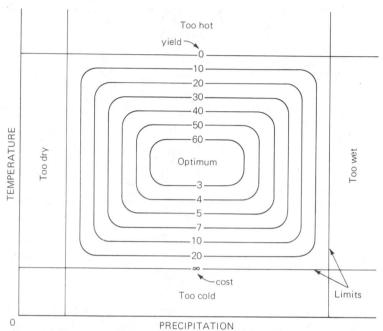

Fig. 5.20 Optima and limits schema. For any crop there is an optimal combination of temperature and moisture. Nonoptimal conditions increase costs of production until yield drops to zero and costs are prohibitive. (Harold H. McCarty and James B. Lindberg, *A Preface to Economics Geography*, © 1966, p. 61. Reprinted by permission of Prentice-Hall, Inc., Englewood Cliffs, N.J.)

increases costs of operation because the land is more difficult to cultivate; therefore, more intensively farmed land is on the more gently sloping plains.

Various attempts have been made to construct models of agriculture based upon environmental influences, but they have not been successful. Agriculture is a human system, and human behavior is not determined by environmental influences. Man takes account of the physical attributes of sites, and then adapts systems of agriculture, and the site itself, to his needs. Seldom are the physical attributes a determining factor. A wide range of crop and livestock combinations can yield a profitable return on most land. Man can even modify the physical attributes of the land itself through irrigation, temperature modifiers, fertilizers, and drainage. Environmental influences may explain local variations, but the regional patterns of agriculture are determined by human processes in which the accessibility between the producing area and market is prominent.

Accessibility to markets

Distance between the producing area and market affects agricultural production because the cost of transporting goods over this distance is a production cost that farmers must absorb. Areas close to the market enjoy a comparative advantage over similar areas farther removed. Farmers in these latter areas, although possessing ideal environmental conditions, must produce other crops or accept lower returns.

The location of plantation agriculture in accessible areas—along the coast or navigable waterways, in tropical Africa, South America, and Southeast Asia—reflects the role of distance (see back endpaper). Many other areas are suited for commercial production of tropical crops, but production from remote areas is precluded by the cost of transporting crops to coastal ports.

Distance, or the cost of overcoming distance, exerts a pervasive influence upon agricultural land use. It directly affects farmers and is therefore an appropriate variable for attempts to provide a model of agricultural land use. In addition, it is a continuous variable for which data, either as linear distance or cost, is readily available.

When the problem of agricultural location is simplified to the cost of transporting products to market, a relatively simple exchange model can be outlined. Since a wide range of crops can be grown in most locations, the critical factor becomes the cost of transporting the product to market. Distance, or the cost of overcoming distance, becomes the independent variable while the return to the farmer for alternative crops becomes the dependent variable. The farther any area is from the market, the higher the costs of production and the lower the returns per acre.

Competition for access to markets creates a spatial ordering of land use. Farmers cultivating crops like vegetables—which are highly productive per acre but cannot be transported easily—are willing to pay a higher rent for the use of land adjacent to the market in order to reduce their transportation costs. Crops like wheat, which are not as highly productive and whose product can be shipped with ease, allow the farmer to exchange location advantage for land of lower rent. This advantage is expressed as *locational rent* which, you will remember, is the additional profit over and above production costs that accrues to land because of its superior location.

In the introductory section of this chapter, the principles of exchange were emphasized in relation to the achievement of utility. In the following section, an attempt will be made to show how farmers choose crops on the basis of an exchange between costs of production and returns for their effort. We assume that farmers are attempting to maximize something of value or utility. This is the additional return over cost for the use of land in a specific way. To simplify the problem, all costs are assumed equal except transportation cost.

The Von Thünen model

The German economist-landowner Von Thünen recognized this spatial organization of land use and, in 1826, outlined the model that we still use (see Fig. 2.12B). In order to simplify the problem he assumed that:

1. The agricultural region was uniform in environmental attributes.
2. There is only one marketplace.
3. Transportation is uniform and transportation costs increases uniformly with distance from the central marketplace.
4. All farmers are rational economic men, who use land so as to maximize profit, and who have complete knowledge of production costs and market prices.

SINGLE CROPS

First, let us assume there is only one crop, say vegetables, produced in the region. Price for 1 acre of output at the marketplace is $800. It costs farmers $200 to produce the crop on farms. Now if the farmer produces right at the market and has zero transport (marketing) costs, his net profit will be $600 (Fig. 5.21).

Unfortunately, this is unrealistic: Farmers do not locate at the center of the city. Location at A is more reasonable: Here the cost of marketing the crop is $170, allowing $430 as net profit. Since vegetables are bulky and perishable their cost of transportation increases quite rapidly with distance, so that the net profit falls to $200 at location B and $25 at C. Locational rent is the difference in net profit for 1 acre of

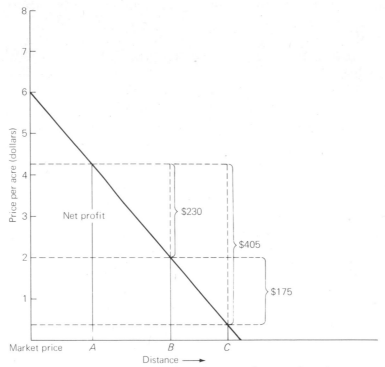

Fig. 5.21 Locational rent at varying distances from market. The comparative transportation advantage (superior location) of A with respect to B is $230, and to C it is $405. With a market price of $800 per acre of output and on farm production costs of $200 everywhere, the gross return before transport costs equals $600 per acre.

vegetables between farms at C and B ($175), C and A ($405), and B and A ($230).

MULTIPLE CROPS

As a second case, let us allow three crops to be produced—vegetables, corn, and wheat—with farmers choosing only one. (Fig. 5.22A). The net profit for vegetables remains the same. Corn and wheat are not as valuable as vegetables and return lower gross profits per acre. However, they are less costly to transport; and transport of wheat is even less costly than that of corn, so the decrease in net profit is more gradual for wheat as its transportation cost increases.

Thus, a concentric spatial organization of crop results (Fig. 5.22B). All farmers, whether they grow vegetables, corn, or wheat, could max-

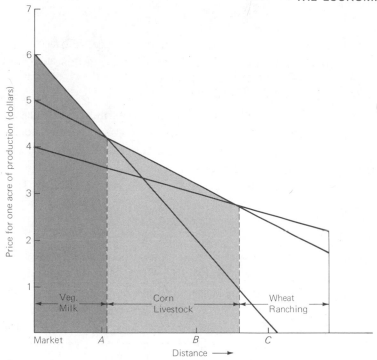

A

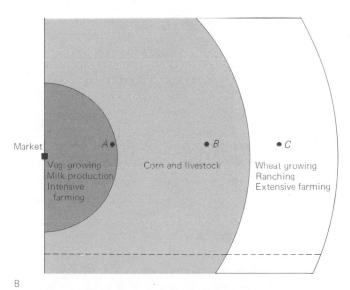

B

Fig. 5.22 Locational rent for competing land uses. Small vegetable farms with intense applications of labor and capital predominate adjacent to the market. Large wheat ranches with low per acre applications of labor and capital utilize remote areas. Systems of agriculture are exchanged to maximize economic rent.

imize profits between *A* and the marketplace. However, the returns per acre from vegetables are greater. This enables vegetable growers to bid a higher price for the use of the land.

You must remember, of course, that we have assumed an exclusive economic motivation on the part of these farmers: that they will choose locations and crops to maximize the net profit. They accomplish this by exchanging accessibility to market for more land of lower price and planting crops that are less costly to transport than vegetables. Therefore, the spatial organization that we observe results from an economic process.

RELAXING THE ASSUMPTIONS

Elements of the Von Thünen model may be recognized in the *zonation* of agriculture around metropolitan markets. Dairying and horticulture are usually adjacent to markets, whereas corn and wheat areas are farther removed. However, the patterns in the real world are obscured by the influences that were eliminated by the assumptions for the model. Let us now relax some of these assumptions and observe the results (Fig. 5.23).

Uniform environment. Areas differ sharply from each other in environmental conditions. The dry interior plains of New South Wales are unsuited for dairy farming and are used for fine wool growing. The steeply sloping land that surrounds many metropolitan areas is unsuitable for cropping so that the concentric zones of agricultural use are set back or distorted to parallel terrain (Fig. 5.23C). These environmental variables can be included in the conceptual model by allowing crop yield to vary within the area as it does in reality. Areas of higher yield can distort the concentric pattern by enabling distant producers to offset the cost of transportation by their higher per acre yields and lower, on-farm, production costs. Irrigated areas with superior climatic advantages and well-drained soils of high inherent fertility utilize this advantage in horticulture so as to compete with producing areas closer to markets. Specialized agriculture in California and the other southwestern states are classic examples of this influence.

Single market. Farmers are seldom dependent on just one market unless the government controls the marketing of their produce. Competition between alternative markets for farm produce is usual. Therefore, the zones of land-use intensity may coalesce or even surround minor

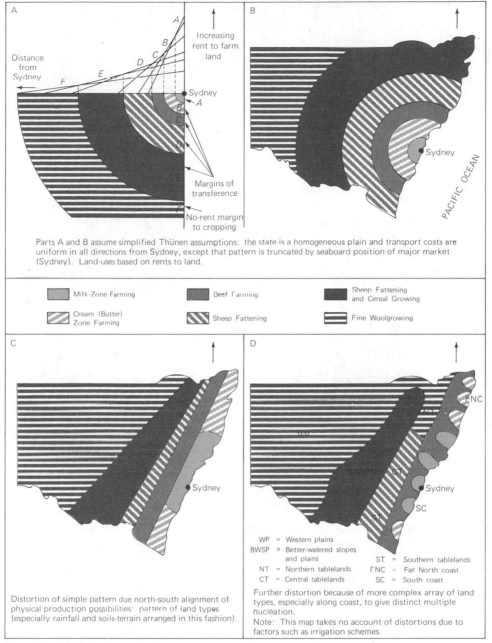

Parts A and B assume simplified Thünen assumptions: the state is a homogeneous plain and transport costs are uniform in all directions from Sydney, except that pattern is truncated by seaboard position of major market (Sydney). Land-uses based on rents to land.

Legend:
- Milk-Zone Farming
- Cream (Butter) Zone Farming
- Beef Farming
- Sheep Fattening
- Sheep Fattening and Cereal Growing
- Fine Woolgrowing

A — Distance from Sydney; Increasing rent to farm land; Margins of transference; No-rent margin to cropping

C — Distortion of simple pattern due north-south alignment of physical production possibilities: pattern of land types (especially rainfall and soils-terrain arranged in this fashion).

D —
WP = Western plains
BWSP = Better-watered slopes and plains
NT = Northern tablelands
CT = Central tablelands
ST = Southern tablelands
FNC = Far North coast
SC = South coast

Further distortion because of more complex array of land types, especially along coast, to give distinct multiple nucleation.
Note: This map takes no account of distortions due to factors such as irrigation schemes.

Fig. 5.23 Model of types-of-farming regions in New South Wales. Diagrams suggest how present-day land-use patterns might be explained by a Thünen locational model which takes into account the combined influences of distance from main market (transfer costs) and price-cost relations as affected by land types. The stages of the model involve progressive relaxations of simplifying assumptions; but the end result still assumes that farmers are basically economic men, and it ignores the complicating effects of factors such as radial transport routes and irrigation schemes. (J. Rutherford, M. I. Logan, and G. J. Missen, *New Viewpoints in Economic Geography*, 1966, Fig. 2.5. A. H. & A. W. Reed, Sydney, Australia.)

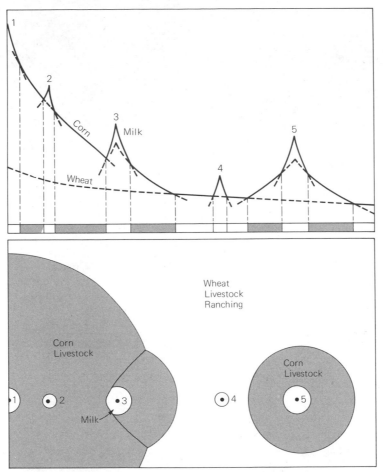

Fig. 5.24 Rural land use in response to multiple markets. Production of milk and vegetables for local requirement are nested within regional agricultural patterns. (After E. Hoover, *The Location of Economic Activity*, © 1948, Fig. 6.2. Used with permission of McGraw-Hill Book Co.)

markets (Fig. 5.24). The nesting of milk-producing areas within areas producing other animal products and crops is perhaps the most frequently occurring illustration of the influence of competing markets (see Fig. 5.23D). In New South Wales, milk-producing areas are focused about the coastal markets, whereas beef farming is the predominant agricultural activity along the coast with the animals being sold to packinghouses located in the largest market centers.

Uniform transportation costs. Accessibility from all points of a region is never equal, and transportation costs seldom vary uniformly with distance. As when you ride in a taxi, the first quarter mile costs more than succeeding units of distance, so too with the transport of agricultural produce: The first mile is more costly than the twentieth. In reality, the gradients of declining net profit would be more gradual than the diagrams have indicated. The assumption that transportation costs are uniform is unrealistic; they vary with distance and within sectors of any region. A more realistic presentation would require a variety of transportation costs within the area. Improvements in transportation also distort the concentric pattern of land use. Roads, railroads, and rivers improve accessibility, and land use changes to reflect this economic advantage.

Intensive and extensive systems. Capital- and labor-intensive systems of land use are clustered about the most populated areas where capital and labor are concentrated. Remote lands are occupied by extensive systems of agriculture like pastoralism and commercial grain growing. The products of these latter areas must be shipped to the major market centers in eastern and southern Asia, western Europe, and northeastern North America.

Rational farmers. Few farmers, even those associated with agribusiness corporations, make decisions exclusively on the basis of economic return. As has been shown previously, they seldom have complete information on alternatives and are content with "satisfactory," rather than "optimal," returns. Traditional practices, investment in equipment, established marketing patterns, and many other influences tend to make farmers conservative about innovations. In addition, cultural food preferences and religious proscriptions influence decisions.

Toward a more realistic model of land use

The Von Thünen model provides a simple but extremely useful *analogue model* of exchange behavior. It helps us understand the rudiments of decision making by farmers. However, as the above discussion of the assumptions has indicated, it can be improved and represented as a *symbolic model* (Rushton, 1969; Dunn, 1954). Equations have been developed that allow economic rent to be estimated for different crops by including variables indicating:

1. Market price in different markets
2. Yield as it varies for each crop within the region
3. Transportation cost as the rate varies with distance
4. Production cost as a way of incorporating the advantage of location adjacent to transportation corridors

Learning Unit 6 in *Programmed Case Studies in Geography* allows you to investigate a model of this type. It will expand upon your knowledge of the Von Thünen model as illustrated in this chapter. If you have computer terminals available, you may vary the assumptions and run the program to observe the results. If such terminals are unavailable, then you will be challenged to interpret computer maps similar to Figs. 5.25 and 2.14.

DISTANCE AND LAND USE AT THE MICRO LEVEL

In addition to its macro effect upon agricultural regionalization, <u>distance also affects individual decisions as farmers seek to economize on effort.</u> The most intensively used fields are those closest to the farmstead. They are usually closely subdivided and, when animal husbandry is involved, higher in productivity because the addition of manure and urine increases fertility of the land. On a New Zealand dairy farm, distant pastures are of poorer quality and often are reserved for hay and silage.

Where farmhouses are clustered in villages the decrease in land-use intensity is zonal. Farmers operate parcels of land in each zone and use them at different intensities. About the Sicilian village of Canicatti, vines and olives receive the highest application of labor and are located within 2 miles of the village. Beyond a distance of 2 miles, arable land for wheat and barley predominates because these crops require less attention (Fig. 5.26). On distant fields, farm work is concentrated into seasonal activities performed cooperatively or by contract.

Man is an economizer. Farmers, like the rest of us, conform to the principle of least effort so that land-use patterns at both the farm and regional level reflect a zonal gradation of intensity. Von Thünen conceptualized this principle as a model of human behavior in which intensity of use diminishes with distance from the market. A similar principle is invoked as an explanation for industrial location.

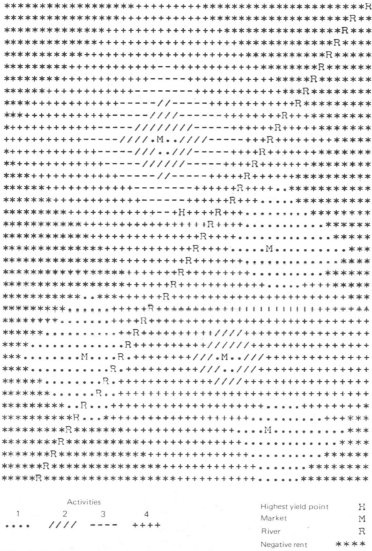

Fig. 5.25 Computer map of land use. There are four different activities (crops) for which different prices are paid in each of five markets (M). Yields for all crops vary with distance away from the optimum location (H).

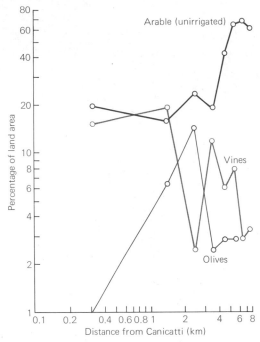

Fig. 5.26 Land-use intensity about Canicatti. As distance (in kilometers) increases from the village, the percentage of land devoted to labor-intensive crops—vines and olives—declines and unirrigated cropland for wheat and barley increases. (After: Chisholm, 1967, Table 6, p. 63.)

THE LOCATION OF INDUSTRY

Compared with agricultural and commercial activities, attempts to represent the elements of industrial location as a simple model of economic behavior is a frustrating experience. Choosing locations for industries is a complex decision, with considerations given to:

1. Location of resources and markets
2. Changing demand for products
3. Transportation costs for assembly and distribution
4. Variations in manufacturing costs; principally in labor cost, but also in land cost, costs of heating and cooling the plant, disposal of waste, and corporate and inventory taxes

5. Scale of operations
6. Techniques of production—labor-intensive or capital-intensive
7. Governmental policy that serves to encourage industry to locate in special areas by guaranteeing markets, providing land and/ or trained employees and tax deductions
8. Agglomeration economies achieved through availability of specialized services and interindustry linkages between suppliers and customers within specialized manufacturing regions
9. Availability of capital
10. Amenity factors, such as superior schools, or location adjacent to a college or university, which offers a pool of prospective employees. Mild climate, cultural amenities, and suburban locations are especially attractive to management.

Admitting the complexity of elements underlying the spatial organization of industry does not keep us from seeking generalizations that will lead to models explaining some of the behavior implicit in the decisions. First, industry is more clustered than population (Fig. 5.27). There is a definite market orientation as entrepreneurs prefer to locate plants within major markets, usually metropolitan areas, and cover the added cost of shipping products to smaller markets by the economies of scale achieved in large plants. And within the metropolitan area itself, manufacturing is concentrated near the CBD, along transportation corridors, and in suburban industrial parks. Industry normally occupies less than 10 percent of all urban land.

A second generalization recognizes the role of transportation. Both the assembly of material and the distribution of the finished product involves transportation (Fig. 5.28). When other elements are assumed to be equal, then transportation cost provides a basis for evaluating alternative production sites. Varying amounts of assembly cost can be exchanged with distribution cost so that alternative locations can be compared. However, to assume that transportation costs are independent is misleading. As Fig. 5.28 indicates, decisions on alternative locations are interrelated with prior considerations about techniques of production (whether cheap labor is to be substituted for expensive equipment), scale of enterprise, and use of materials (raw or semi-processed). These prior considerations influence the search for a location at which time the role of transport cost in determining least-cost locations becomes critical.

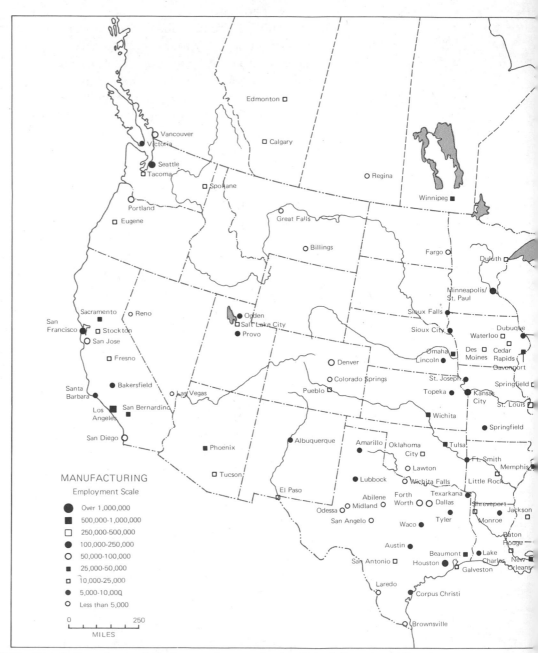

Fig. 5.27 Distribution of manufacturing employment in the United States and Canada. (*Oxford Regional Economic Atlas: The United States and Canada*, 1967, pp. 116–117. Reproduced by permission of Oxford University Press.)

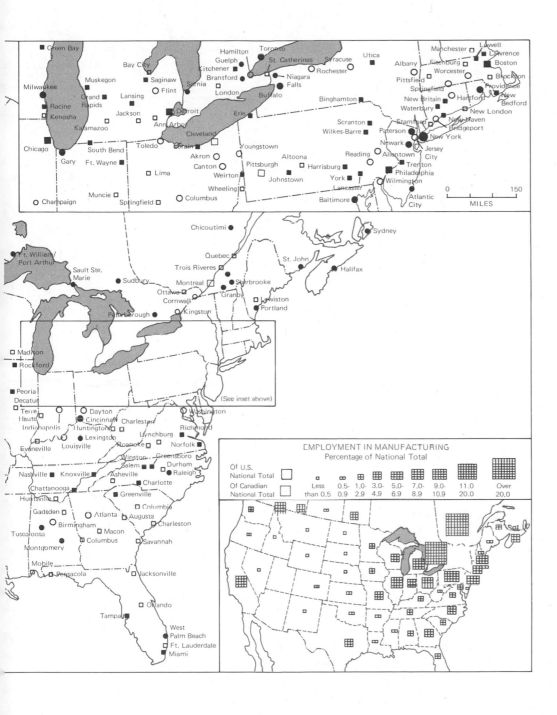

EMPLOYMENT IN MANUFACTURING
Percentage of National Total

	Less than 0.5	0.5-0.9	1.0-2.9	3.0-4.9	5.0-6.9	7.0-8.9	9.0-10.9	11.0-20.0	Over 20.0
Of U.S. National Total									
Of Canadian National Total									

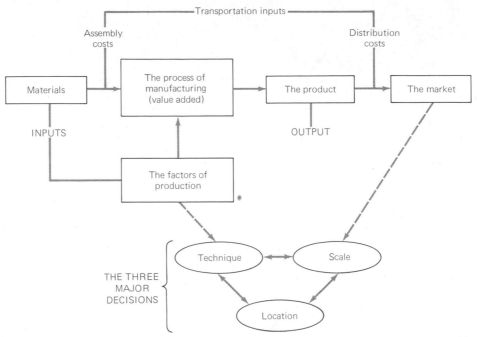

Fig. 5.28 Variables in industrial location. Transportation costs affect both the assembly and the distribution. However, the effect of transportation costs will depend upon prior decisions concerning techniques of production, scale of enterprise, and location of the plant in reference to raw materials and markets. (David M. Smith, *Industrial Location*, 1971, Fig. 2.1. Reproduced by permission of John Wiley & Sons.)

Alternative locations

By utilizing Fig. 5.28 and assuming that decisions on the capital, labor, and material inputs, the techniques of production, and the scale of the enterprise have been made, <u>industrial location</u> then can be considered a <u>function of the exchange</u> between assembly costs and distribution costs. In the simple case, assuming that all other elements are uniform and that transportation costs are proportionate to distance, location can be at the raw material site, at the market, or anyplace in between (Fig. 5.29A).

Case 1: Let us designate as Case 1 any location that can be exchanged for another without increasing transportation costs. The manufacture of pencils would be one such example since transportation cost is negligible and the commodity can be stored easily.

Case 2: When assembly costs increase at a faster rate than distribution costs, location at the production place is an advantage (Fig. 5.29B). Fruit canning fits this description because canned fruit can be distributed more economically than ripe fruit can be assembled.

Case 3: Where manufacture adds weight and where materials are universally available, for example, water for carbonated drinks and beer, then location at the market has the advantage (Fig. 5.29C). For beer, the raw materials—the flavoring, hops, barley, malt, and sugar—other than water are easily assembled. Distribution costs determine location unless, of course, consumers are willing to pay a premium for beer "brewed from pure Rocky Mountain spring water."

Case 4: In Cases 1 through 3, we have assumed transportation costs to be linear, that is, to increase at a constant rate as distance increases. Therefore, it would seem that places at the raw material site and at the market enjoy a locational advantage over intervening places; however, this has not been true historically. Linear cost increases are unrealistic: Transportation costs actually increase more rapidly over the first few miles than over the last few (Fig. 5.29D). There are also loading and unloading costs to consider. Cities at the break point in transshipment, at river, ports, and railroads, gained their initial manufacturing advantage because of the costs involved in transferring (i.e., loading and unloading) goods and the opportunities this has presented for manufacturing. Industrial complexes developed at these transshipment places have provided the economic base for metropolitan growth. The Great Lakes ports in both the United States and Canada are excellent examples of this effect of transshipment costs upon industrial location.

Flour milling provides a good example. Wheat is grown in Saskatchewan, North Dakota, Kansas, Washington and, to a lesser extent, in other states and provinces. Flour milling is an important industry in these areas, but the major centers for milling in Minneapolis, Toledo, Buffalo, and Montreal are many miles from the wheat lands. These places have achieved importance in flour milling because breaks in the mode of shipment, between rail and water or between lake- and ocean-going boats, have created an opportunity for manufacturing. Frequently, this opportunity originated when transportation technology was less sophisticated than it is today, but the industry persists despite techno-

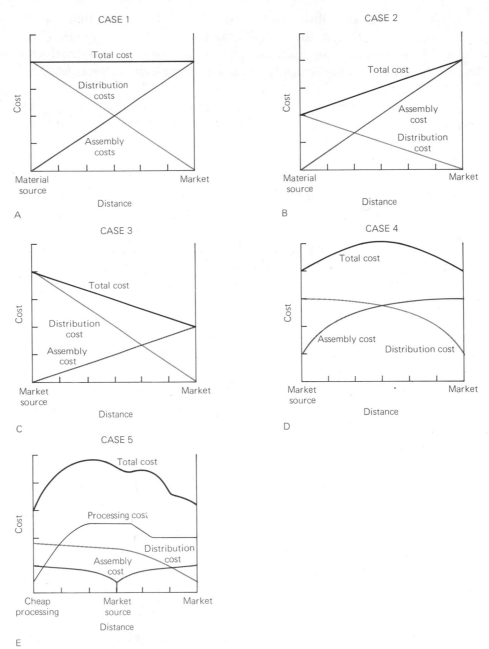

Fig. 5.29 Industrial location under different assumptions. Only assembly and distribution costs are considered in Cases 1–4. Distribution cost includes transporting raw material as well as distribution. Case 5 introduces the effect of processing costs that are lowest in a place with cheaper labor and/or fuel.

logical improvements such as the St. Lawrence Seaway, which allows oceangoing boats to penetrate to Chicago and Duluth.

Case 5: Let us further complicate the problem by introducing a third place that enjoys an advantage of cheaper labor or power source (Fig. 5.29E). For convenience, the raw material source has been centralized. Assembly costs increase as material is transported to the market or the third, low-cost processing place. The lowest-cost place is at the market, but it is not substantially superior to the places with low processing costs. Location of electronics plants in foreign countries would be an example of this.

These five cases illustrate the simplicity of the industrial location theory when transportation costs are the sole consideration. However, they also illustrate the precariousness of the exchange involved. Costs of transporting different commodities vary. Also, processing costs and the many other elements of industrial production may influence the choice for the location of an industrial plant. It is the range of variables that may enter into the decision that frustrates attempts to provide a simple but satisfying model of industrial location.

Classification of industry

Industry may be classified in many ways; however, the one that serves to illustrate the economic process of exchange and the role of transportation cost is based upon the association between assembly and distribution costs (Fig. 5.30).

RESOURCE ORIENTATION

Industries that utilize bulky or perishable raw materials normally seek locations close to the source of raw material. Mining illustrates this type of location. Production is oriented to the spatially restricted sources of raw material. Here, at the source, the ore is refined to eliminate waste material and concentrate the mineral. Small special-purpose towns develop around these extraction centers. Once the resource is depleted, their population decreases and they become ghost towns if no substitute economy is available.

Aluminum smelting is a special case in which the source of cheap electric power is a critical factor in the transformation of bauxite—

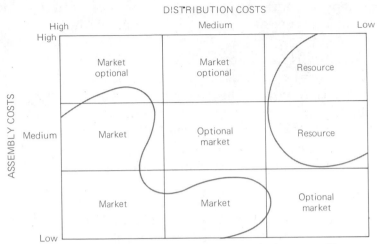

Fig. 5.30 Classification of industry by locational orientation. Plants processing raw materials with high assembly and low distribution costs are resource oriented. Plants with high distribution costs compared with assembly costs are market oriented. Where locational choice is optional, market orientation generally prevails.

aluminum oxide—into alumina ingots that are shipped to markets for processing into lightweight but bulky finished products such as window and door frames. Bauxite occurs widely, but sources of cheap hydro-electric power are limited to previously glaciated mountain areas like those found in British Columbia, Quebec, Norway, and southern New Zealand.

MARKET ORIENTATION

The location of market-oriented industries having high distribution costs is positively correlated with the location of population. The bottling of soft drinks, beer, and milk are good examples of such industries. So, too, is the baking of bread and the production of building supplies. Other industries like printing and the production of office equipment and supplies locate within their market because of the need for speedy service and the personal relationship which develops between supplier and purchaser.

Location in major metropolitan market areas conveys two additional advantages for industries whose distribution costs exceed assembly costs:

1. A large volume of sales produces economies of scale that offset the distribution cost to distant markets.

2. The separation of major metropolitan centers makes it possible for regional producers to dominate a particular market. The cost of product may be slightly higher, but because they are near customers, they are able to manufacture to satisfy local demand. This is true for steel-fabricating plants, petroleum refineries, furniture makers, and the manufacturers of electrical components.

OPTIONAL ORIENTATION AND THE IRON AND STEEL INDUSTRY

Many industries can be either market or resource oriented because of their ability to rearrange (exchange) the techniques of production so as to maximize the profitability of alternative locations. Usually several raw materials are used in the production process and many markets are supplied. A metropolitan or market location prevails in most instances. Metropolitan areas offer an inherent demand for goods, and provide access to a pool of trained labor. It is for this reason that a market orientation is indicated alongside optional choice locations on Fig. 5.30. Normally, the nontransportation elements of industrial location are influential in determining location for these industries, as there are many inputs of production that can be rearranged to suit different sites. Alternative locations for the iron and steel industry in the United States illustrate how this rearrangement occurs.

The iron and steel industry has always been highly transport oriented. Sites near raw material sources commanded an early advantage, but the increased use of scrap steel and imported ore, and improved technology have resulted in an increase in production near markets (Fig. 5.31).

In the eighteenth century, because up to 10 tons of coal were required to smelt 1 ton of pig iron, blast furnaces concentrated near the supplies of coal in Ohio and Pennsylvania. As technology improved, less coal was required. This enabled distant ore resources, particularly those in the Mesabi Range in Minnesota, to be used. Steel making shifted to more accessible industrial sites—fairly close to, but not on, the coal fields—such as Cleveland, Erie, Chicago, Detroit, and Youngstown, where coal and iron ore supplies could be brought together and steel making integrated with industrial plants.

The availability of high-grade imported ore from Latin America and northwestern Africa, together with the reuse of scrap steel, aided development of a market orientation. Philadephia and Baltimore have become major producers in the East, as have Houston in the Southwest

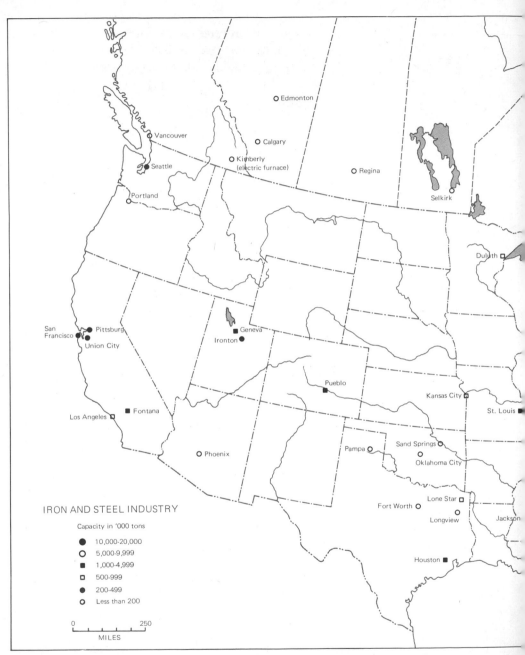

IRON AND STEEL INDUSTRY

Capacity in '000 tons

● 10,000–20,000
○ 5,000–9,999
■ 1,000–4,999
□ 500–999
● 200–499
○ Less than 200

0   250
MILES

Fig. 5.31 Location of iron and steel industry. Plants are both raw material and market oriented. Lakeside and coastal locations have a transportation advantage because of the lower cost of shipping raw materials and finished products. (After *Oxford*

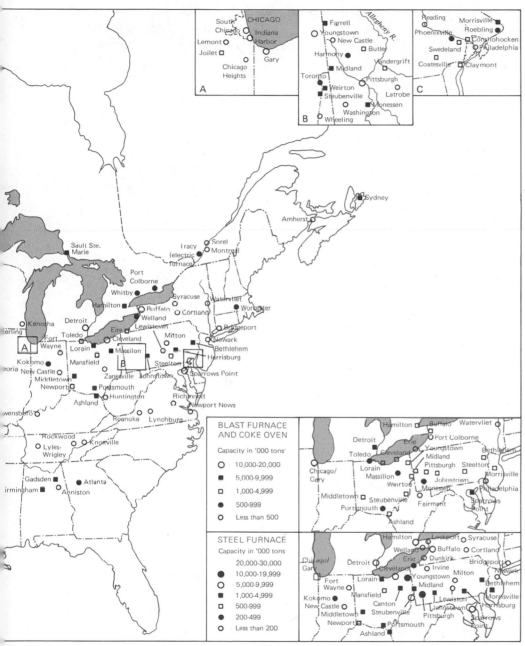

Regional Economic Atlas: The United States and Canada, 1967, pp. 100–101. Reproduced by permission of Oxford University Press.)

and Los Angeles in the West. San Francisco and Seattle also produce a small quantity of steel from scrap. The shift from raw material to industrial, and more recently, to a market orientation reflects a changing technology that has increased the ability of market centers to compete with resource-oriented centers.

The pattern of iron and steel production reflects both the inertia of the original locations and the comparative advantage of market-oriented production where scrap is combined with imported ore and pig iron. Maximum-profit plants have been developed in varied locations by substituting different techniques of production. Wages, although they represent 25 percent of production costs, are not a crucial consideration because they are almost uniform as a result of unionized labor. And any production cost advantage that one area may achieve is soon canceled by the high cost of distribution.

The cost of overcoming distance protects local steel markets, although there is substantial variation in the production techniques used in each region. Exchange between regions is limited, because substitution of raw materials and fuel has enabled production to occur in places with different capabilities. Distance remains a factor in determining modern industrial location, and models based upon the friction of distance still enable us to outline the essence of industrial location. However, the computation of the cost of assembling and distributing material is never as simple as has been inferred by the models presented earlier in this section. Choosing locations for industry is a specialized task, with a variety of consulting firms offering this service to major corporations.

Even within a metropolitan area there is a range of alternative locations for industry. Inner city sites offer established transportation services and access to low-paid workers. However, most new industry is moving to suburbs where highly automated plants are established on spacious sites with access by freeway. Industry like commerce is present in different forms and functions within the metropolitan area. Specialized urban land-use zones, not unlike the specialized zones identified by the Von Thünen model of rural land use, can be identified.

THE LOCATION OF URBAN ACTIVITIES

There have been several attempts to generalize the Von Thünen model into an urban land-use model. Although these models help us to conceptualize urban land-use patterns, they leave much to be desired on several accounts.

1. Urban economic processes are complex. There is no single market, so housing, and industrial and commercial markets have different foci. Each requires separate models.
2. Locational choice precludes other alternatives so that when one location is chosen for one activity it eliminates others. In agriculture, fields may be used for different crops each year, but it is difficult to change factories into homes.
3. Many more people are involved in urban land use who make decisions on comparatively small units of land.
4. Economic processes in urban areas, especially for residential use, are obstructed by social and political processes.

Notwithstanding these criticisms, it is useful to provide a conceptual overview by presenting the concentric, sector, and multinuclei models of urban land use (Fig. 5.32). All three are based upon the principle that there is a limited area of high-value, intensively used commercial land in the CBD, and that both land value and land-use intensity decline with distance from, or accessibility to, the center.

A concentric model

The concentric model is a direct replication of the Von Thünen model using urban land use that decreases in intensity from the CBD (Fig. 5.32). The zonation of urban structure consists of:

1. A business, administrative, and retail core—the CBD—comprising those activities that require access to the entire urban area and that are able to pay for this accessibility
2. A transitional zone, formerly containing manufacturing plants and homes of the most prestigious families, but now afflicted by urban blight. It is characterized by the following mixture of land uses: warehouses, some central manufacturing, and parking lots; tenement housing, skid row, and transportation facilities; and high-rise apartments where urban renewal has occurred on view-commanding locations
3. Multifamily apartments and older single-family residential areas occupied by low-income families

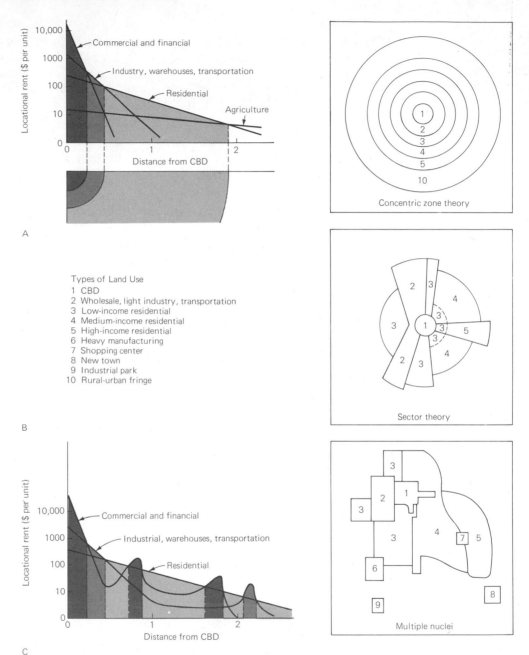

Fig. 5.32 Generalized models of urban land use. (A) The idealized gradient of land rent is conceptualized as a function of distance from the central business district. Urban structure is concentric. (B) Concentric zones are distorted into sectors by the effect of improved accessibility along transportation corridors. (C) Nuclei of commercial land occur at the CBD and near the intersection of major transportation routes. They are separated by residential land so as to produce a multinuclei urban structure.

4. Single-family homes with increasing lot sizes occupied by medium- and high-income families.
5. Peripheral manufaucturing and wholesale activities in single-story, parklike settings
6. The rural-urban fringe with some commuting

The ideal concentric structure with decreasing intensity of land use seldom occurs. The nearest approximation to the ideal comes in port cities that are economically dominated by export activities. Planned cities like Adelaide in Australia, where the CBD is surrounded by magnificent parks, also preserve the concentric pattern.

The sector theory

Although the concentric nature of land use in the central city is often preserved, the outer zones are affected by variations in accessiblity along transportation corridors (Fig. 5.32B). A railroad or freeway will distort the concentric pattern. Sectors of industrial and warehouse use parallel the corridor. High-value housing moves away from this corridor and low-value housing is on the other side of the tracks. Cities that have developed around railroads or along highways like Fresno, California, and Calgary, Alberta, exhibit sectoral patterns.

Multinuclei theory

Both the concentric and sector models have shortcomings when applied to the modern metropolis in which automobiles have increased accessibility to many nodes of activity. Even with a relatively uniform physical environment as is seen in cities of the American Midwest, land rent does not decline uniformly with distance from the CBD. There is a noticeable peaking at the intersections of transportation arteries. This reflects the additional rent that commercial activities are willing to pay for accessible locations. As a result, several commercial nuclei exist throughout the metropolis (Fig. 5.32C).

Adjoining the CBD are wholesale and light manufacturing zones and remnant neighborhoods occupied by older, poorer, and frequently poverty-level families. Extensions of the CBD extend along major arteries toward high-income residential areas as the result of the attempt by managers of CBD corporations, who dwell in the leafy suburbs, to minimize their journey to work. Like the Sicilian farmer, top management also adheres to the principle of least effort.

Elements of all three models of urban structure can be observed in most metropolitan areas. Competition for land of superior location or accessibility provides a partial explanation that enables students to grasp the broad outlines of urban structure. The CBD represents the site of maximum accessibility and land value (Fig. 5.33). Land value decreases toward the periphery but is modified by two elements: (1) major transportation corridors that have ridges of higher value; and (2) intersections of major corridors that create secondary peaks—nuclei of commercial uses such as shopping centers—at fairly regular distances from both the center of the city and each other.

Urban land values may be represented as a conical hill with ridges, peaks, and valleys (Fig. 5.34). Accessibility and amenity factors under-

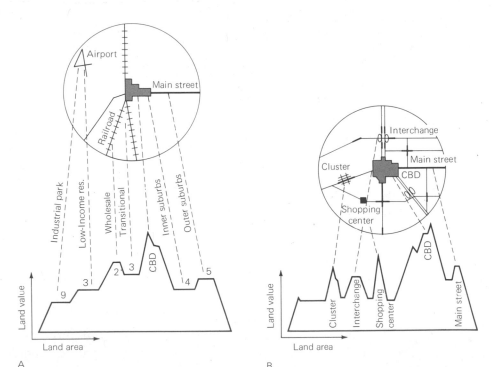

Fig. 5.33 Urban land values. In both sector (A) and multinuclei (B), land values peak at the center and decrease toward the periphery. (Rothwell et al., reproduced by permission from *The Professional Geographer*, vol. 23, 1971, Fig. 3.)

Fig. 5.34 Diagrammatic representation of urban land values. Peaks of value are associated with commercial and industrial use of nodes of superior accessibility. The valleys are occupied by residential land or are vacant. (Brian J. L. Berry, *Commercial Structure and Commercial Blight*, University of Chicago, Department of Geography, Research Paper No. 85, 1963, Fig. 3.)

lie the structure, with commercial and industrial activities the most susceptible to change with improvements in transportation.

Both in urban and rural areas people are willing to exchange resources—effort, time, and money—to obtain something of value or utility. Commercial locations that will maximize sales, industrial locations that will minimize costs, and agricultural locations that will maximize economic rent are eagerly sought. As a result of this economic behavior, reasonable models of commercial, industrial, and agricultural use can be developed.

Distance has been integral to all models for the location and arrangement of economic activities. The cost of overcoming distance adds to production costs so that an efficient enterprise in any area soon loses advantage when it must transship goods to distant markets. Distance enables other enterprises to compete. It also compels enterprises to develop technological changes to offset the comparative advantage of places with superior location. In this manner, the economy of regions becomes diversified and creates additional challenges for geographical analysis.

Despite its pervasive nature, the economic process seldom provides an adequate explanation for spatial organization. The models presented in this chapter are abstractions. They have been plausible, only because all other things have been assumed equal. Such economic landscapes never exist. Therefore, for adequate explanations of spatial organization, we must combine our knowledge of economic behavior with information about the social, political, and psychological bases of behavior.

SUGGESTED READINGS

General

March, James G., and Lave, Charles. *The Art of Model-Building: An Interdisciplinary Introduction to the Social Sciences*. New York: Harper & Row, in press.

McCarthy, Harold H., and Lindberg, James B. *A Preface to Economic Geography*. Englewood Cliffs, N.J.: Prentice-Hall, 1966, chaps. 1–5.

McDaniel, Robert, and Eliot-Hurst, Michael E. *A Systems Analytic Approach to Economic Geography*, Publication No. 8. Washington, D.C.: Association of American Geographers, Commission on College Geography, 1968.

Rutherford, John; Logan, J. I.; and Missen, G. J. *New View Points in Economic Geography*. Sydney, Australia: AH and AW Reed, 1966.

Agricultural activities

Chisholm, Michael. *Rural Settlement and Land Use: An Essay in Location*. London: Hutchinson University Press, 1962.

Dunn, Edgar S., Jr. *The Location of Agricultural Production*. Gainesville: University of Florida Press, 1954.

Gould, Peter. "Wheat on Kilimanjaro: The Perception of Choice Within Game and Learning Model Framework." *General Systems* 10(1965): 157–166.

Gregor, Howard F. *Geography of Agriculture: Themes in Research*. Englewood Cliffs, N.J.: Prentice-Hall, 1970.

Harvey, David W. "Theoretical Concepts and the Analysis of Agricultural Land Use Patterns in Geography." *Annals of the Association of American Geographers* 56(1966):361–374.

Wolpert, Julian. "The Decision Process in Spatial Context." *Annals of the Association of American Geographers* 54(1964):537–558.

Industrial activities

Greenhut, M. L. *Plant Location in Theory and Practice.* Chapel Hill: University of North Carolina Press, 1956.

Smith, David M. *Industrial Location.* New York: Wiley, 1971.

Tertiary activities and urban structure

Berry, Brian J. L. *Geography of Market Centers and Retail Distribution.* Englewood Cliffs, N.J.: Prentice-Hall, 1967.

Berry, Brian J. L., and Horton, Frank E. *Geographical Perspectives on Urban Systems.* Englewood Cliffs, N.J.: Prentice-Hall, 1970, chaps. 7 and 12.

Marshall, John U. *The Location of Service Towns.* Toronto: University of Toronto Press, 1969.

Yeates, Maurice H., and Garner, Barry J. *The North American City.* New York: Harper & Row, 1971.

CHAPTER 6
THE SOCIAL PROCESS

Howler monkeys in Panama sometimes occupy the same tree with cebus monkeys. The two species, feeding side by side, do not interact. The conversations of one group are neither directed to, nor attended to, by the other. They share physical space and food, but not social space.

Surrounding my home are three aged palm trees, each sheathed in a skirt of old fronds. One tree is exclusively occupied by English starlings, but the other two are the guarded nesting trees for orioles. They drive out starlings, but allow sparrows to nest amid the lower fronds.

Along Telegraph Avenue, Berkeley students pass amid "street people" and local residents. Each group can be distinguished by their dress, grooming, and chatter. They are in different streams of social life: all primate; not quite separate species, but obviously separate subcultures who share territory but seldom interact socially.

GROUPS WITH DIFFERENT value systems produce significantly different spatial distributions. In considering the economic process, we simplified the real world by assuming that all other things were equal, that people's actions are independent and economically motivated, and that men organize their activities to maximize productivity from a given set of resources. However, behavior reflects, not only rational choice based upon economic criteria, but also awareness of alternatives, aversion to risk taking, and the individual's social values and mores. The effects produced by these social influences differ among groups. Individuals are socialized to these values through interaction, so that decisions are patterned after modes of behavior acceptable to the group. Even though they may reside within the same community, individuals appraise alternative courses of action differently.

The purpose of this chapter is to provide an awareness of these social influences and the concepts that are used to explain the differences in spatial organization arising from social behavior.

PATTERNS RESULTING FROM SOCIAL BEHAVIOR

Spatial patterns resulting from social behavior are of two kinds:

1. *Status patterns* that result from the social characteristics of individuals; including distribution of socioeconomic class, religion, family status, race, and political affiliation
2. *Patterns of movement* that reflect the interaction between groups of people at separate locations. The flow of people, goods, and ideas from area to area can be mapped, and explanations tested against the resulting patterns.

It is important to remember that the significance of these patterns should not overshadow the underlying social processes that created them. Patterns are somewhat fictitious. They are abstractions or models that depict the visible realities of everyday life. Social scientists must take care not to become so preoccupied with elegant cartographic and/or statistical descriptions of patterns, that they lose sight of the behavior of the people whose activities produce the pattern. Because men interact in a regularized manner, the identification of patterns is possible. However, *it is the process of interaction* that is the *core concept*, not some elegant method for representing the result. Representation of pattern is a necessary, but incomplete, step for the explanation of spatial distributions created by human behavior.

This warning is appropriate here because, following the next section entitled "Socialization and Interaction," social behavior will be considered in terms of status patterns and patterns of movement. The aim is to demonstrate the effect upon spatial organization of man's attempts to facilitate interaction with those perceived as sharing similar life styles and his avoidance of interaction with those who do not. Despite the apparent emphasis on pattern analysis, *interaction* remains the core concept.

A good illustration of this is the Puerto Rican enclave on Manhattan Island (Fig. 6.1). Almost half a million Puerto Ricans and their American-born descendants live in Manhattan, with the majority concentrated in an eight-to-ten-block area just south of Harlem. Between 40 and 76 percent of all inhabitants of this core area, which is known as Spanish Harlem or el Barrio, are Puerto Ricans or their descendants. Between 1950 and 1960, clustering in El Barrio increased with the retreat from the West Side as Puerto Ricans sought to avoid blacks and urban renewal.

Spanish Harlem is characterized by a youthful, low-income popu-

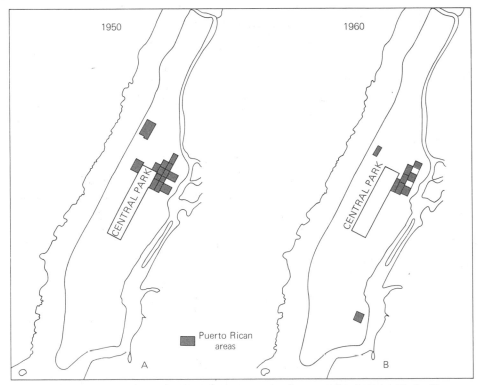

Fig. 6.1 The distribution of Puerto Ricans on Manhattan Island, New York City: (A) The 1950 pattern delimited by Novak; (B) The 1960 pattern delimited by Carey. (Yeates and Garner, *The North American City*, Harper & Row, Publishers, 1971, Fig. 11.2; and reprinted from *The Geographical Review*, vol. 46, 1956, and vol. 56, 1966, copyrighted by the American Geographical Society of New York.)

lation, employed in the garment trades and restaurants. They have an allegiance to Roman Catholicism and occupy unsound and overcrowded housing. These people cluster here because of the (1) availability of low-cost housing; (2) availability of public transit; (3) opportunity for extended families to exist and interaction with friends in Spanish; (4) availability of social services (churches and clubs); and (5) commerce conducted in Spanish.

The first two factors influence the location, but the latter three account for continuance. Because interaction is facilitated by proximity, Puerto Ricans learn to cope within an alien society. Through interpersonal relationships they adjust to their relative deprivation and sense achievement, which makes hardship tolerable.

SOCIALIZATION AND INTERACTION

The social process can be characterized as the reciprocal give and take that molds individual behavior. It is a communicative process (Fig. 6.2). Patterns of individual behavior are formed and transformed through a succession of interactions in which individuals participate. A child is at first socialized within a family through rewards and punishments. Through time he moves beyond the family and learns to respond in a manner that is appropriate to the forces of those people within his reference group.

Individual members of the community dynamically interact with the agents and forces of socialization. The result differentiates a social group from a mere crowd. Through recurrent situations and reciprocating adjustments, a group consensus develops. Approved behavior and objectives result. This coordinates responses to alternative opportunities and provides the capacity for concerted action.

When a similar consensus is developed by groups in different areas, patterns of spatial organization are created. The process leading to the consensus, its change through time, and the patterns it produces stimulate the geographer's research.

"Keeping up with the Joneses" is a familiar illustration of the social process at the neighborhood level. People choose to live among others, whom they perceive as sharing a similar value system and life style, in an area in which a consensus of opinion can be achieved. They also

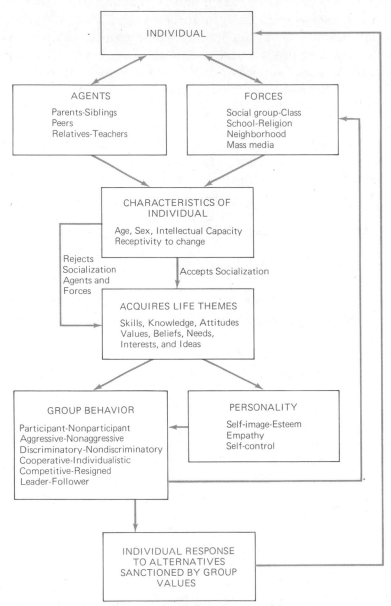

Fig. 6.2 Socialization is a communicative process. Through the system of mutual, reciprocal responses, group values change and transform the agents and forces of socialization themselves.

want to be "good" neighbors. They buy the appropriate car, keep their grounds tidy, adjust family size to the acceptable norm, and chastize their children to maintain the family image in sport, school, and sex. Those who deviate are ostracized. It is a rare community that encourages people to do their own thing.

Neighborhood associations and homeowner organizations are dedicated to enhancing group-approved goals and protecting the area from "undesirable" elements in terms of people, industry, or noxious transportation facilities. Often conversations between neighbors are shallow and seldom delve into profound issues like religion or politics. It is on these issues that attitudes may differ, and conflicting opinions could lead to the development of tension within the group. Neighborhood associations even eliminate such topics by charter, so as to avoid controversial and potentially divisive discussion. Most local governments are nonpartisan for the same reason.

You may be amused by your parents' conformist life style, but your behavior differs only in its manifestations. The length of your hair and the nature of your clothing will differ with the kind of college you attend. It is repeated by similar college groups in other areas. Even the groups on campus that you choose to join or to avoid influence your life style. Where would you place yourself on Fig. 6.2, and what are you doing to change the system?

Interaction: a basic drive

The innate need for interaction with others, and the preference for interaction with those perceived as being similar and familiar are stimulants for social behavior. To facilitate interaction, individuals create formal and informal associations that simultaneously facilitate interchange and constrain behavior by limiting action to that approved by the group. Few of us desire to be alone. Therefore, we accept these social limitations upon alternative courses of action. Families, clubs, sororities, congregations, and associations are some of the groups for whom we modify our behavior in order to be accepted.

The question of legalized abortion is a good example of choice behavior constrained by the social process. Legalization decreases the cost and increases the demand for abortions. However, prevailing social attitudes, including those of some religious groups, are against legalization. Consequently, it is not an alternative for many women. Even within a community, attitudes toward abortion differ. Upper- and lower-income families favor legalization, as do unmarried women, whereas upwardly mobile, middle-income families reserve their approval. Fortunately, social attitudes are changing. But must we await a catastrophic famine to accelerate change in the social attitudes of the exploding populations of the world? Social opinion could be changed by favorable statements from religious and political leaders—agents and forces of socialization— and legal abortion could become a socially and economically feasible alternative to childbirth.

Interaction: a core concept

Interaction implies reciprocal action or influence. It is a core concept in our attempts to understand the *socialization process* whereby a healthy animal is trained to be a conforming adult. Social scientists still do not understand the process. We know that concerted action is possible, and that social organization facilitates interaction and regularizes behavior, but we do not know why socialization fails to guarantee that men will get along. We have reams of empirical studies on socialization failures and hangups—people who reject or overlearn the rules— but simple, general models of how people develop a self-image through interaction amid groups are yet to be developed.

In geography, interaction is a pervasive theme. It is generally associated with the concept of distance and its implied restrictions. In Chapter 5 we used distance as the independent variable in models of agricultural and industrial location, as well as in urban spacing and structure. In each case, distance provided a surrogate for the propensity of individuals in different places to interact for economic objectives.

In social behavior, interaction occurs in overt and covert ways so that the restriction of distance is not as apparent. Social interaction occurs through electronic media, conversation, and body gestures. Language, especially conversation, is the vessel of meaning for man and is vital to the reciprocal give-and-take of individuals who are adjusting to each other.

Movement of people between places (migrating, commuting), or the sending of information and ideas across geographical space (diffusion) are other forms of social interaction. In these, the role of distance is more apparent.

INTERACTION IN EDUCATION AND ARCHITECTURE

Participatory interaction in a seminar is the preferred method of "socializing" students to the mores and customs (concepts and methods) of an academic discipline. Unfortunately, it is not an economically feasible method of instruction in most institutions. Reading a text or merely listening to a lecture is not as effective a learning method, but is less costly. In an attempt to reduce costs of the seminar method, computer-based courses have been developed in which the computer system is used to simulate discussion sessions. Students are seated around a terminal, rather than being in a room with the professor. For example, this text was written to accompany such a computer-based course. But even this strategy has proved too costly for most institutions. Therefore, *Programmed Case Studies in Geography* was written to accompany this text. The case studies approximate an interactive learning environment. They are not as effective as the computer-based dialogues, but they do provide an opportunity for the student to interact with the course material. At least, I have attempted to practice good social science in this respect.

If you reside in a group-living facility, you can observe another application of interaction. Initial friendships are established with students in neighboring rooms with whom interaction is compelled through use of common facilities. Those farther down the hallway, and those on other floors are separated by distance. Your interaction with them is less frequent and they join other friendship groups. Only by joint participation in classes or recreation do you enter other groups. If they are more appealing, you can change your residence so as to facilitate interaction with the groups you prefer.

Architects attempt to allocate space to facilitate personal interaction. The monolithic tower structure with its impersonal halls and endless corridors is being abandoned as campus housing. Clusters of rooms sharing small common facilities are now in vogue. This type of physical arrangement fosters interaction. It assists students to adjust to campus life through interaction with others encountering similar problems.

URBAN DESIGN

New towns in which residences are clustered about neighborhood activity centers are also attempts, through urban design, to facilitate interaction. When families relocate in a new town it is important to assist interaction as a means of developing new acquaintance patterns.

The use of tot-lots (miniparks where mothers can take young children to play), pathways, tennis courts, and swimming pools stimulate interaction. They aid in the development of new friendships. New towns that are built along the lines of the traditional tract development do not foster interaction to the same degree. It is less likely that the residents of these tract homes will coalesce into an active social group. The popularity of the community-oriented housing developments attests to their success in facilitating interaction. Homes within these communities are in demand. The initial investment made by the developers for recreational facilities is more than repaid by the ensuing popularity of the community.

There are numerous other examples of social behavior in space. In fact, they surround you. Think about the division between townspeople and the campus community in a university town like Urbana, Illinois, or the kaleidoscope of social patterns exhibited by students, activists, street people, and businessmen on Telegraph Avenue adjoining the Berkeley campus of the University of California. Skid rows, leafy exclusive suburbs, Cherry Hills, and tenements—each provides examples of social interaction producing distinctive spatial arrangements. These variations will be discussed later in this chapter.

DISTANCE, INTERACTION, AND COMMUNICATION

Physical separation between areas increases the cost of communication and curtails social interaction. Groups with similar life styles in the same city who are separated by areas occupied by other social groups, seldom interact except in business. This is an obstacle in urban policy. An issue may be beneficial to groups occupying different portions of the metropolis, but they seldom develop a common view unless the issue is repeatedly articulated by the mass media. Attempts to increase open space and parks are thwarted in this manner. Support generally comes from middle-class suburbs, but they are only committed to the issue if the park is in their vicinity. If it is across town, they are supportive but unwilling to mobilize their political resources to ensure civic adoption. Consequently, most American metropolitan areas are deficient in parkland. Between 10 and 20 acres of open space per 1000 people is recommended. The average is 4 acres and many areas are below 2 acres.

Even the use of recreational facilities is influenced by distance, as measured in terms of time. People will take advantage of community facilities and activities if they are within five minutes of where they live. If it takes six to eleven minutes to get there, they will hesitate. If it takes more than twelve minutes, they will put it off until a planned excursion.

Human behavior is constructed through the course of interaction with other people. Communication, especially conversation, is essential to this process whereby individuals become socialized to the norms of particular groups. In this manner, common understandings arise and are continually reinforced in a succession of transactions. Communication satisfies an innate human desire to be stimulated by interaction with others. Generally, we prefer this interaction to be with individuals whom we perceive as being our equals or just slightly better. The result of this preference upon residential choice has been to create residential areas that are both status oriented and spatially restricted. And because intervening distance restrains the ability to communicate, similar residential areas—communication networks—develop in different areas of the city.

SOCIALIZATION AND SOCIAL STATUS

There are definite behavioral consequences for individuals occupying different levels in the social system. The style of living, patterns of interaction, attitudes toward life, and the areas in which families choose to live result from an individual's interaction with his family and friends. Geographically, this behavior is apparent in areal differences of family size and composition, socioeconomic characteristics, and the commercial and social services that respond to the desires and needs of separate social neighborhoods.

The values of each culture confer prestige on some occupations and styles of living, whereas others are regarded as being of low status. Those activities that society regards as most important are rewarded by income, power, prestige, and honor. Education and a professional vocation are usually required for high status occupations. Income is less important. In other cultures, religious affiliation, political power, or ancestry are necessary prerequisites.

Social stratifications throughout the world have become more permeable. For this reason, status is used to characterize spatial distributions rather than class or caste distinctions. The latter infers generation-to-generation rigidity. In Asia political change has cut across caste barriers, and in Europe and America inheritance taxes have left society families little else but hereditary titles, directorships of corporations, and membership in the Daughters of the American Revolution. Gradations between open mobility and status rigidity persist and provide a dimension for comparative regional geography. For example, the traditional elite are more influential in Mexican business and politics than the original Spanish landowners in the American Southwest, which was colonized in a similar manner in the sixteenth and seventeenth centuries.

American social structure can be represented as a diamond in which the top and bottom are fairly easily identified. The top by the "jet set" of the wealthy and the political and corporate elite. The bottom by the poor, for whom the avenues of advancement are closed. Working-class also persists, although unionization and specialization in employment has made it difficult to identify by occupation. Between the upper and lower extremes, class distinctions are disappearing. Prestige, power, and economic differentials persist as determinants for social status, but they are no longer a criterion for social class.

Race and ethnicity are no longer important determinants of status. Italian-Americans are no longer street vendors, nor are the Irish always policemen. Blacks who have suffered longest from the connotation of "lower class" have demonstrated avenues of advancement in public service, the professions, and corporate management. No longer is their advancement restricted to the stage or professional athletics. However, because of continued social and employment discrimination and the tragic state of most inner city schools, blacks continue to represent a disproportionate sector of the lowest-status group. In 1970, one-third of all black families lived in poverty.

Status differences begin in childhood. Through interaction with parents, siblings, teachers, and peers, the cues and symbols are learned that define the social environment and reward the appropriate responses. These are the *norms* of behavior that are acceptable to the particular social group to which the child belongs.

From the interactions he experiences, the child develops a self-image that has been reflected back to him by others, and it is upon this basis that his actions and aspirations are developed. The child from a middle-class background learns to compete because he believes that if he is successful it is possible for him to change the environment in which he lives. However, the child from a lower-class home is exposed to a different kind of environment. Generally he is confronted with obstacles that repel his efforts. He learns to cope with the environment through personal adjustment rather than by attempts to change it. If the child from the lower-status family experiences achievement in school, the military, or work this changes his self-esteem. He adopts a new status role that alienates him from his relatives and former friends, and invokes psychological tension, because he is not yet securely a member of the middle class.

Consequences of social status

Systems of social inequality exist in all human societies and there are definite behavioral consequences for different positions in a stratified system. Lower-status people view the social environment as hostile and best left alone. They tend to cluster together and informally control a small section of city "turf," against social workers, police, and outsiders. They are effectively cut off from the urban environment because they do not read newspapers and seldom watch news programs on television. Most of their information comes from friends. Working-class families tend to be more restricted in their patterns of communication than those of upper- and middle-class status. They tend to choose a residence close to relatives and avoid better employment opportunities when migration to new areas would disrupt family interaction. This results in their preference for certain suburbs and the patronage of familiar commercial areas.

Middle- and upper-status persons exhibit a cosmopolitan mobility. They choose friends throughout the metropolitan area, move across town from "mother" or even across the continent. They have been socialized to consider their social environment as fluid. They are active in organizations and capable of utilizing their political resources of time, money, position, and skill should they desire to influence political decisions.

Social structure is not an abstract sociological concept. Rather, it is a concept essential to the understanding of human behavior. The effect upon spatial structure and organization has been emphasized, and, in subsequent sections, information will be provided about the political and economic consequences of socially based behavior for different classes of social status.

Classification of social status

Creating classifications that accurately reflect social behavior is a problem. Labels like "hard hats," "red-necks," "businessmen," "junkies," "civic leaders," "students," and "hippies" are stereotypic titles that imply a specific social attitude and life style. There is wide agreement on their connotation, although the regularity of behavior that the titles confer is misleading. Most social classifications are based upon objective criteria like employment, income, and education, but the intention is to infer a social attitude to life.

Classifications based upon the socioeconomic characteristics of individuals are the most common. Individuals are placed in upper-, middle-, or lower-status groups based upon income, type of employment of the head of the household, and years of education completed. This information is easily obtained from census records where it is generalized for each census tract. However, it does not reliably indicate individual characteristics because household information is averaged.

Socioeconomic status is a *surrogate* measure of doubtful validity in modern *tertiary economies*. In *primary* and *secondary economies* where there is little social differentiation between families occupying the same area, it provides an easily computed index of social status. But even in these societies, social behavior is not reliably indicated by income and education. Employment is a better index, but it is lost by combining households in census areas. Despite the limitations of classifications based upon socioeconomic status, geographers continue to use this system because the data is readily available. However, there is currently considerable interest in classifications based upon differences in attitude.

ATTITUDE STUDIES

Classifications based upon attitude studies provide a more reliable index of social behavior. Gans (1962) attempted to explain why Italian-Americans in Boston's West End did not oppose urban renewal. The renewal plan proposed to destroy the community that they treasured, yet they did not oppose the plan. In order to explain why some individuals became involved while other did not, Gans hypothesized that it could be explained, not by socioeconomic class, but by their orientation to future events.

In a socioeconomic classification, the West End would have been placed as a lower-status, working-class neighborhood. Housing was old, crowded, and deteriorated by urban renewal criteria, but there was an active social structure that preserved family and kin ties, cared for the aged, ill, and unemployed, and supported local stores, churches, and parochial schools. Despite the advantage of the close-knit ethnic neighborhood, most residents refused to become involved in the struggle against urban renewal.

Gans explained their behavior in terms of their orientation to the future. Four categories were distinguished.

1. Present-oriented people, those who lived from day to day and who were either psychologically incapable or unwilling to contemplate and plan for the future.
2. Working-class people who felt that they were dependent upon other organizations like the union, the church, the boss, or city services. They shut out the future by refusing to believe that the city would uproot them.
3. Middle status people who realized the danger, but were able to take care of themselves by selling early and moving, rather than becoming involved in protecting the property of others. In some instances, they stood to gain by selling businesses for which there was little or no community "goodwill."
4. Upper-status people who were future-oriented and realized the danger, and were willing and able to work for beneficial change. This group and some outsiders attempted to resist urban redevelopment, but they failed because of the disinterest of the majority of the residents who were either unwilling or incapable of organizing themselves to resist impending change.

The advantage of the attitude classification over socioeconomic categories for social analysis is obvious. It provides a more reliable index of behavior. Even in lower- and working-class status areas, there are individuals capable of responding to opportunities. They are few in number, but they are future-oriented and do respond. Similarly, affluent neighborhoods are not exclusively upper-status areas. Although there is a positive correlation between income and ability to perceive future outcomes, there are many individuals who, by chance or inheritance, have attained high economic status but are incapable of directing their own lives profitably and are of little assistance to others.

Policy implications of attitude studies

In his provocative book *The Unheavenly City*, Banfield (1970) has utilized the Gans classification to discuss the urban dilemma in America. He suggests that there are two categories of problems: Those that have to do with comfort, convenience, amenity, and business advantage, which can be corrected if we consider them sufficiently important to justify tackling the political and fiscal obstacles to already-known solutions. And, second, serious problems such as poverty, ignorance, and racial injustice, which afflict individuals permanently and impair the good health of society. These are dilemmas that "may cause people to die before their time, to suffer serious impairment of their health or of their powers, to waste their lives, to be deeply unhappy or happy in a way that is less than human. . . ."

Banfield is not encouraging about the prospects of solving problems in the second category. He indicates that they are inherent among those of the lowest social status: a subculture in which people are incapable of imagining a future and of disciplining themselves to sacrifice present enjoyment for future satisfaction. Approximately one-fifth of the nation adheres to this style of living. This is the essence of America's urban problem. Welfare legislation, job retraining, and income supplements all contain provisions to encourage upward mobility of families in this subculture of poverty. However, if these people are incapable or unwilling to become future oriented, short-run supplementary measures are destined for failure. Only a long-term commitment of funds to ensure adequate nourishment and stimulation for the young in the home, and superior child care and elementary schools for inner city children will ensure a free and democratic society.

SOCIAL AREA ANALYSIS

Newton, a suburban new town, is primarily residential with a full-convenience shopping center, two neighborhood commercial areas, schools, churches, and some manufacturing, although most employment is outside the town. There are three types of residential areas.

1. Spacious homes of upper-income families located adjacent to the golf course. The residents are older, their children having departed; they do not participate in civic affairs and seldom interact with neighbors. They cherish their privacy.

2. Single-family, tract homes of middle-income families whose heads of households are professionals, junior executives, or managers. The "joiners" and community leaders come from these areas. Families are young and parents are active in school, church, civic, and service organizations. Family life is frantic; they have moved often and regard their present place as transitional.

3. Small tract home and town house areas of lower-middle income families. The age structure is varied, with grandparents sometimes living within the family. There is little residential mobility as wage earners have several employment opportunities within commuting distance. Boats, trailers, and old cars line the streets. They are active in church groups, but passive about other community activities unless directly affected by them.

Newton represents a microcosm of social areas within a metropolis. People interacting together, or choosing not to do so, establish social patterns which affect spatial organization. In Newton the neighborhoods are small, but in the inner city, huge enclaves of people of different social and ethnic status cluster together in separate areas. The clustering of people is distinctive in itself, but it also affects linguistic, political, and religious patterns, educational and welfare requirements, and provides a delightful variety to commercial and restaurant patterns in the city.

The North American city may be conceptualized as consisting of a series of sectorially arranged social status areas (Fig. 6.3). Upper- and middle-social status areas are to the east and north of the city and the lower-status areas to the west and south. The reason for the orientation is the preference of the more affluent commuter to drive his automobile to and from work with the sun at his back. However, uniform conditions seldom prevail, and the location of the higher-status areas is oriented to view-commanding locations and socially favored areas that are not always to the north and east.

There is some accordance between this idealized model and the sectorial model of urban land use. Sectors of working-class status separate middle-status areas from lower-status areas and the ghetto. These latter neighborhoods are adjacent to the industrial and warehouse zones.

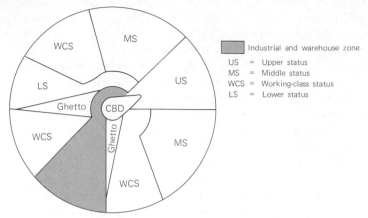

Fig. 6.3 Social status in a hypothetical American city. Sectors of social status radiate from the center. The ghetto differs in that its base is toward the center and the apex penetrates suburbia.

The ghetto sector differs in shape from the other zones: It is a reverse wedge, with its base adjacent to the CBD where black and brown populations cluster in remnant housing. Because the operation of the housing market precludes freedom of choice for black and brown families, they must compete for housing within residential enclaves that owe their identity to race rather than status. And because incomes of black and brown families are lower in America, the black and brown ghettos occupy proportionately more of the deteriorating housing in the central city, and less of the newer, suburban housing. Ghetto areas are based on race, not status, but interaction among people within the ghetto, and their exclusion from participation in mainstream institutions has created territories in which black and Chicano culture is learned, transmitted, and preserved.

The social status of neighborhoods changes through time. A filtering-down process occurs. The grand hotels of the 1920s have become the flophouses and skid rows of the modern metropolis, while the large wooden houses of the former business elite have become tenements. Run-down neighborhood conditions have a negative impact on surrounding properties so that bad housing drives out good. The process continues until such time as either public-sponsored urban renewal or renovation upgrades the neighborhood, or residential use is replaced by warehouses, industry, and freeways.

In the largest metropolitan urban centers, the concentration of low-status people near the center of the city gives a concentric pattern to

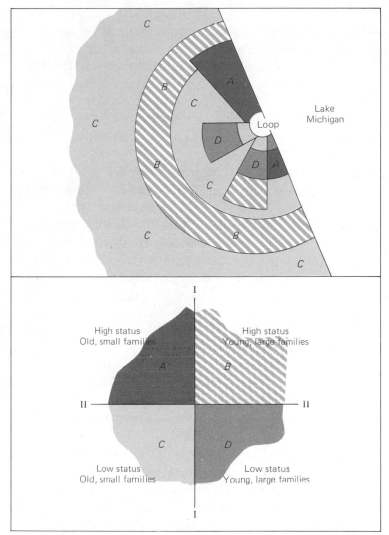

Fig. 6.4 Social areas of the Chicago metropolis. The concentration of low-status people in the oldest, inner city areas creates a concentric pattern. (Rees, 1968; and Brian J. L. Berry and Frank E. Horton, *Geographic Perspectives on Urban Systems: With Integrated Readings*, © 1970, p. 379. Reprinted by permission of Prentice-Hall, Inc., Englewood Cliffs, N.J.)

social status. This is best illustrated by Chicago (Fig. 6.4). A sector of high-status residents extends northward along the lake shore toward Evanston, but elsewhere, lower-status families occupy the inner city with higher-status suburbs on the fringe.

Social behavior and residence

The behavioral basis for the sectorial pattern of social status is the preference by people of similar social status to interact with each other. Migrants to the city seek out neighborhoods occupied by people of similar social status because this facilitates their adjustment. The practices of the real estate profession are another factor. They type neighborhoods in which people of certain status will be accepted. Among other things, this is a covert means of maintaining residential segregation.

Middle- and upper-status families seek out relatively homogeneous areas as a means of reducing social conflict. Where neighbors share similar social values, there is agreement on such issues as home maintenance, noise and traffic control, and child rearing. Those who deviate are subjected to social coercion. Additional controls exist when the community has incorporated as a suburban city. The similarity of views about what constitutes a desirable residential environment enables exclusionist decisions to be reached through a general consensus. The different viewpoints present in larger cities have been excluded through incorporation of only those areas that enjoy similar social status. In relatively homogeneous cities, the average citizen can neglect local affairs because the decisions are made by those whose interests are similar to his own. He closes the garage door on local issues and retires to his television set to become concerned over national issues or sports.

Even residents of the inner city—especially those from working-class and lower-status families—tend to move in an axial direction when they seek new homes. This preserves proximity to family, friends, and known commercial areas. A sectorial pattern of social areas develops with the young large families moving to the fringe of the metropolis while parents and grandparents remain in the older suburbs. This creates a concentric pattern of family status, which overlaps the sector pattern of social status.

Family status

Age and composition of the family are an important determinant in the social structure of metropolitan areas. In the Newton example the difference between the high-status and middle-status families was age. High-status families are older, smaller (because their children have departed), and less involved in local affairs. They are more affluent and cosmopolitan in their interests and activities.

The geographical pattern of family status in urban areas is concentric. The aged persist within, and the young singles gravitate toward, the center of the city where they live in high-density apartments and tenements. The newly marrieds with young children tend to move to the outer suburbs where tract housing provides them with more space for their housing dollar. The older suburbs are occupied by transitional families. If their children live at home, they maintain a single-family residence. If the children are grown, they may renovate their home to facilitate an adult life style, or they may move to a multifamily apartment complex with a private pool and recreational facilities.

The pattern of family status in the Twin Cities of Minneapolis and St. Paul replicates this concentric pattern (Fig. 6.5). Single people and childless married couples cluster in rental quarters near downtown, the university, and along transportation corridors where they occupy urban space with the elderly living on reduced incomes (Fig. 6.5A and B). The outer suburbs are occupied by young middle-status families in tract housing and upper-status families in the more exclusive suburbs where homes are individually designed and custom-built (Fig. 6.5C and D). Working-class families concentrate near the downtown area and in older inexpensive suburban housing (Fig. 6.5E). They share the inner city with lower-status, underemployed families and segregated groups.

In segregated neighborhoods, families of all status groups are clustered together. Distinction is by street rather than by neighborhood. These socially impacted areas are usually dispersed in the least desirable residential locations; alongside skid row, on the other side of the tracks, or amid industrial zones.

Social areas within cities

Social and economic status, family status, and ethnic status create patterns of social homogeneity. These patterns have been criticized as overly simplistic and not empirically verifiable. However, the models assist social scientists to understand the distribution of social status and have enabled the development of more complex models that are assumed to be generally valid for most large industrialized cities within developed nations. Recent empirical studies, utilizing the statistical procedure of

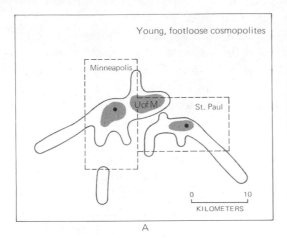

Young, footloose cosmopolites

Minneapolis

U of M

St. Paul

0 10
KILOMETERS

A

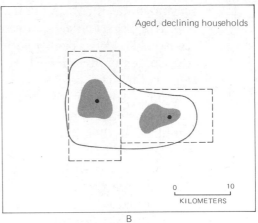

Aged, declining households

0 10
KILOMETERS

B

Rising young families

Suburbs

City of Minneapolis

City of St. Paul

Suburbs

0 10
KILOMETERS

C

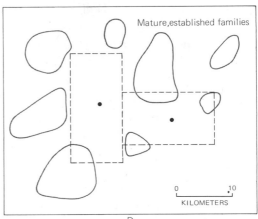

Mature, established families

0 10
KILOMETERS

D

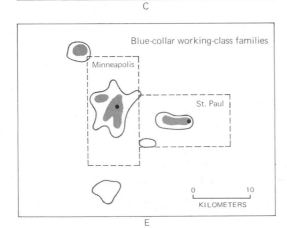

Blue-collar working-class families

Minneapolis

St. Paul

0 10
KILOMETERS

E

factor analysis to define indices of socioeconomic status, family status, and ethnicity from census data, have verified the sector pattern of social status, the concentric pattern of family status, and the nucleated ethnic areas. These geographical patterns are not independent, but complement one another, with each describing a separate aspect of social differentiation within a city.

In a study of metropolitan Toronto, Murdie (1969) hypothesized that the classic models of urban social structure—concentric, sectorial, and multinuclei—were not mutually exclusive, but could be regarded as independent, additive contributors to the social structuring of the city. He conceptualized the problems as patterns of sectorial socioeconomic status, concentric family status, and dispersed "groupings" of ethnic status overlapping within the physical structure of the city (Fig. 6.6). Although the physical structure of Toronto is strongly influenced by Lake Ontario and accessibility along radial transport routes, significantly different areas were revealed. The hypothesis was accepted and social status zones were identified (Fig. 6.7).

Social discrimination is not new. District residential areas were present in the earliest cities when the prestigious families lived near the city center. Improvements in transportation changed this, and affluent families moved to the suburbs. In 1836 Frederich Engels described the conditions of the working-class in Manchester, England, as follows.

In the centre of Manchester there is a fairly large commercial district, which is about half a mile long and half a mile broad. This district is almost entirely given over to offices and warehouses. Nearly the whole of this district has no permanent residents and is deserted at night, when only policemen patrol its dark, narrow thoroughfares with their bull's-

Fig. 6.5 (A–E) Family status in the Twin Cities of Minneapolis–St. Paul. Families of different age groups cluster in separate areas of the metropolis. (A) Young single people and childless married couples—workers and university students—cluster near the downtown areas, the university, and along major transport corridors.
(B) In 1960, the suburban apartment boom was not yet under way. The elderly, living on reduced incomes, concentrated in rental quarters near the downtown areas. (C) Young middle-class families predominate in intermittent tract-housing zones at the fringes of the central cities. (D) In the more exclusive suburbs prosperous middle-aged families predominate. Instead of tract housing, residences usually are designed and constructed individually. (E) Low-income, working-class families concentrate around the downtown areas with additional clusters in older inexpensive suburban housing. (Ronald Abler, John S. Adams, and Peter Gould, *Spatial Organization: The Geographer's View of the World*, © 1971, Fig. 6.29a–e. Reprinted by permission of Prentice-Hall, Inc., Englewood Cliffs, N.J.)

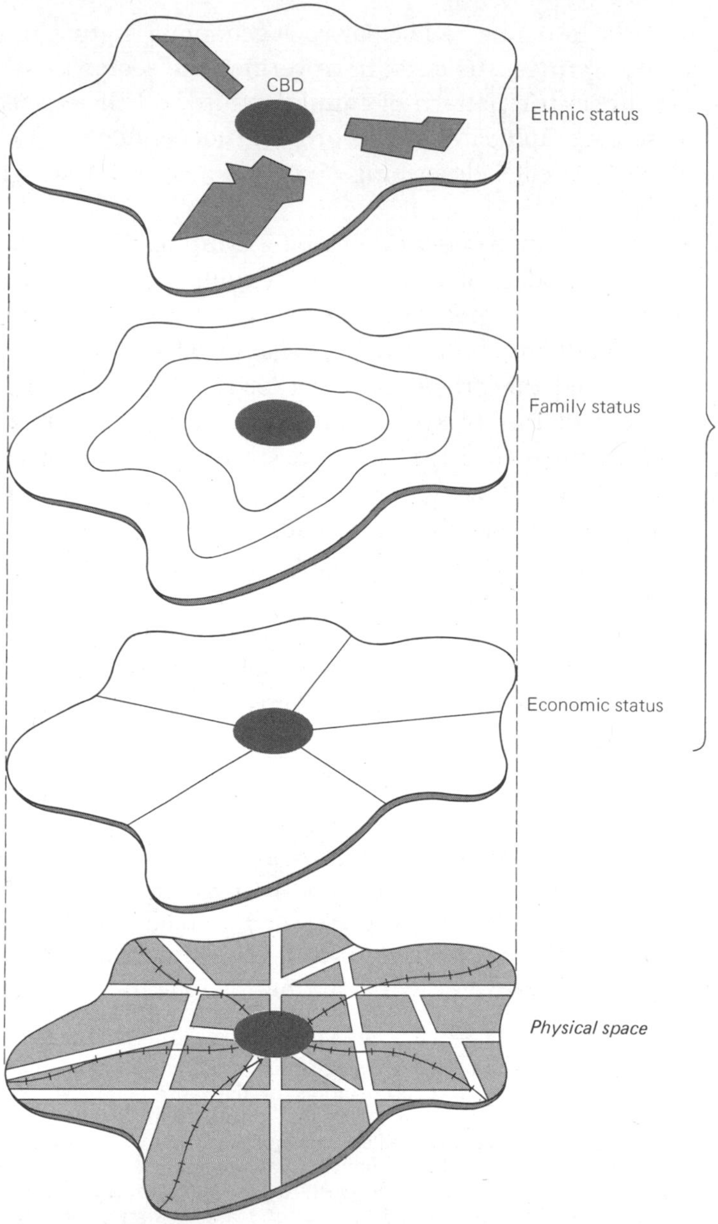

Fig. 6.6 Idealized spatial model of urban social structure. Transportation and other barriers accentuate the sectorial structure of economic status. Each sector is further subdivided by the concentric zones of family status and nuclear areas with distinctive ethnic status. (Murdie, *Factorial Ecology of Metropolitan Toronto*, University of Chicago, Department of Georgraphy, Research Papers, 1969, Fig. 2.)

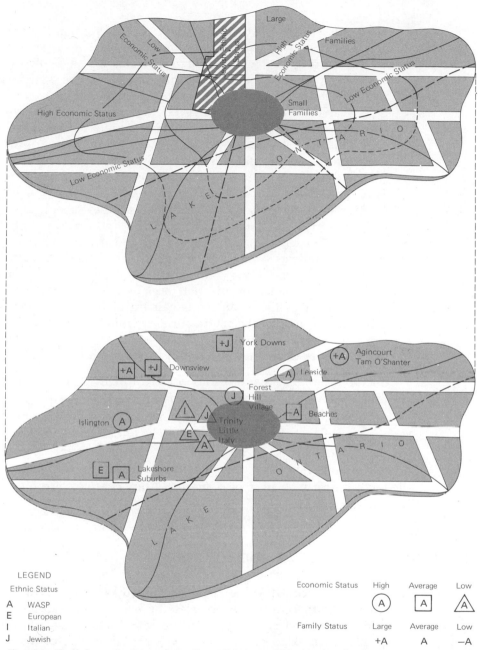

Fig. 6.7 Social areas in metropolitan Toronto. The idealized pattern is curtailed by the lake and distorted by accessibility and view-commanding sites. (Yeates and Garner, *The North American City*, 1971, Fig. 11.3; and after Murdie, *Factorial Ecology of Metropolitan Toronto*, University of Chicago, Department of Geography, Research Papers, 1969, Fig. 29.)

eye lanterns. This district is intersected by certain main streets which carry an enormous volume of traffic. The lower floors of the buildings are occupied by shops of dazzling splendour. A few of the upper stories on these premises are used as dwellings and the streets present a relatively busy appearance until late in the evening. Around this commercial quarter there is a belt of built-up areas on the average one and half miles in width, which is occupied entirely by working-class dwellings. This area of workers' houses includes all Manchester proper, except the center. . . . Beyond this belt of working-class houses or dwellings lie the districts inhabited by the middle classes and the upper classes. The former are to be found in regularly laid out streets near the working-class districts. . . . The villas of the upper classes are surrounded by gardens and lie in the higher and remoter parts. . . . The upper classes enjoy healthy country air and live in luxurious and comfortable dwellings which are linked to the center of Manchester by omnibuses which run every fifteen or thirty minutes. To such an extent has the convenience of the rich been considered in the planning of Manchester that these plutocrats can travel from their homes to their places of business in the centre of the town by the shortest routes, which run entirely through working-class districts, without even realising how close they are to the misery and filth which lie on both sides of the road.[1]

Social area analysis provides a descriptive model of urban social structure. However, the investigation of the processes that create the man-made environment of a neighborhood, or what the French geographer would call the *milieu*, is scarcely understood. Questions regarding how people react to proposals for environmental change in their neighborhood, how they form collective attitudes, and how they view their community as part of a metropolitan complex are challenges for future investigation.

ETHNIC NEIGHBORHOODS AS SOCIAL AREAS

Don is a black aerospace engineer. He works in a suburban plant, but lives in south-central Los Angeles. By occupation and education he is middle-class and could afford to live in an affluent suburb. But because of his black skin, he and his family choose to live in the Cherry Hill section of the Los Angeles ghetto. He could purchase a home in a

[1] From *The Condition of the Working Class in England* (Stanford, Calif.: Stanford University Press, 1958, pp. 54–55).

predominantly white suburb, but feels that he and his wife would be cut off from neighborhood friendships, his children would be chastized at school, and his social life constrained. In central Los Angeles he is active in civic affairs, is influential, and his children enjoy school. The schools are crowded and the quality of instruction leaves much to be desired. Crime rates are higher, insurance coverage is expensive, and food in local supermarkets is both of lower quality and higher cost. These are costs he incurs in order to enjoy friendly social relations within a society in which the majority white population refuses to interact socially with blacks and browns.

America is not unique in its pattern of covert social segregation. In Canada and Australia, the recent immigrants from eastern and southern Europe are discriminated against. In England, it is the West Indian blacks, and in New Zealand the Polynesians. Discrimination on the basis of social status will always be present so long as there are preferences for different life styles. It is inherent in the social process, whereby people choose with whom they prefer to interact. Generally, they choose those whom they perceive as similar. However, discrimination on the basis of skin color or other ethnic characteristics is based upon the *mistaken assumption* that people of black or brown skins (in the case of Chicanos and Polynesians) are lazy, intellectually inferior, and inherently lower-status individuals. The majority confines such groups to the least desirable areas, where they live in crowded ghettos wedged in between undesirable land uses like industry and freeways (Fig. 6.8). Opportunities for normal expansion through migration are obstructed by social convention so that the areas are impacted. The vast majority of blacks, Puerto Ricans, and Chicanos in metropolitan areas reside in such areas where they are dominant.

Ghetto formation

A ghetto is an area from which interaction with the rest of the city is restricted. Originally it referred to a section of a European city in which Jewish people were confined. Jewish families still cluster as an ethnic group near synagogues in many cities, but there is no longer strong social resistance to their interaction within the remaining community. In American cities, ghettos are crowded, deteriorated neighborhoods occupied by members of minority groups who live there because of social and economic pressures. The precise definition of the ghetto

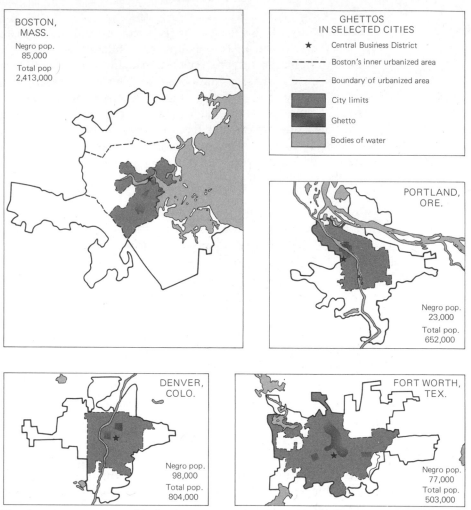

Fig. 6.8 Representative black ghettos in U.S. cities. Most ghettos occupy older housing near the center. The Fort Worth ghetto, however, has become a wedge with its base near the central business district and its apex in suburbia. (Morrill, reprinted from the *Geographical Review*, vol. 55, 1965, Fig. 1, copyrighted by the American Geographical Society of New York.)

depends upon social perspective: White suburbanites may regard all areas occupied by blacks as ghettos, whereas black middle-class residents of the older suburbs regard the ghetto as the deteriorating inner city zones occupied by blacks.

Rose, in *The Black Ghetto* (1971), defines ghettos as areas in which the population equals or exceeds 50 percent black and infers the operation of a social constraint. According to Rose, the ghetto is "the territory which is occupied by black people in American cities and which has evolved out of a system of residential allocation permitting no freedom of choice."

The social process of ghetto formation follows generally that which produced the segregated pattern of social space described previously. Individuals choose residences that reflect their occupation status, income, place of employment, and social preference. However, the refusal of whites to share residential space with minority groups biases residential selection. Whites will not move into neighborhoods when black occupancy exceeds 30 percent, and most blacks are unwilling to contend with the social isolation of life in a white suburb. Therefore, expansion of the ghetto is limited to its fringes as whites abandon areas in order to avoid social interaction with blacks. Expansion encounters less opposition in deteriorating central city neighborhoods with the result that minority groups predominate. This creates the reverse wedge shape of ghetto areas; the base near the CBD and the apex in suburbia.

Within the ghetto, social stratification by area is apparent. Lower-status people, who predominate in minority groups because of previous discrimination, occupy the central portion near the CBD and warehousing zones, with the younger middle-class groups residing in the apex that penetrates suburbia.

Although residential search behavior of minority groups is virtually restricted to the ghetto, social status areas develop within these areas. They differ from the social areas in white communities insofar as the zones are in close proximity, the middle- and upper-status zones are smaller, and all groups share the same commercial facilities.

Concentration of minority groups in the central city continues despite the apparent change in white attitudes. Whereas whites are now showing greater tolerance for integration, the change is occurring when there seem to be declining interest among blacks for integration. Between 1960 and 1970 the proportion of blacks living in suburbia increased by only 1 percent, and they resided primarily in the older suburbs adjoining the central city (Fig. 6.9). Like Don, they recognized the social and political advantage of maintaining the homogeneous characteristic of the ghetto.

The ghetto or barrio represents an expanding residential pattern in all American metropolitan areas. In 1970 almost 19 million black Americans resided in metropolitan areas—74 percent of the total black population—and 95 percent of these resided in the inner city and older suburbs. The black ghetto predominates. Only in New York and Miami

Fig. 6.9 Black migration in the United States (1960–1970)

	1960	1970
Population	18,900,000	22,600,000
Percentage of total	10.5	11.1
Percentage living in:		
Metropolitan areas	68	74
Central cities	53	58
Suburbs	15	16
Rural areas	32	26

Source: U.S. Bureau of the Census, 1971.

do Puerto Ricans cluster in any number, whereas the Chicano barrios are identifiable only in the Southwest. And where the black ghetto and Chicano barrio occur in the same city, as in Los Angeles, they are separated and seldom interact in spite of their common problems.

Commercial areas in the ghetto

The spatial impress of ghetto expansion is noticeable in commercial zones. Although population increases, the purchasing power of families is substantially (as much as 40 percent) lower than that of white families. Convenience and neighborhood centers that had developed in response to the previous residential pattern must either expand the range of their goods to outlying areas (by advertising), or change merchandising strategy (i.e., decrease costs of operations or increase per unit cost). Many stores fail in the process. Owners retire and follow their former patrons to suburbia. Other stores are purchased by new firms offering lower-cost merchandise. Jewelry stores become pawnshops, theaters are remodeled into bowling alleys or pool halls, and the spacious department store becomes a variety store with the upper floors left vacant or temporarily occupied by welfare agencies. Multiple occupancy is common; a hair salon, for example, may offer dry cleaning and real estate services and sell records as well.

Many businesses close when white operators move and new leases are not forthcoming. Boarded-up windows, bankruptcy, clearance sales, and steel window guards, closed at night to discourage theft, convey a drab appearance. Bars provide the action. In contrast to those in white areas (which have subdued exteriors so as to convey the impression of very little going on inside), those in the black ghetto exude action:

music blasting from an open doorway, an offbeat name, and a window cluttered with colors and advertisements. The gay bars in large cities are often located adjacent to the ghetto. Social restrictions have also forced them out of the middle-class white areas.

To only emphasize the dilapidated physical structure of commercial zones overlooks the vitality of ghetto social life. Neighborhoods are closely knit, the inhabitants provide for their own and care for the destitute. Community action, once mobilized, is genuine. Despite the frustration of unemployment and the high cost of living, there is activity and the people exhibit spontaneous happiness. The ghetto is a viable social neighborhood, even though the people are imprisoned by the socially constraining forces of American society.

Employment in the ghetto

Blacks experience more than twice the incidence of unemployment than do whites. In 1971, when white unemployment soared to almost 6 percent, black unemployment exceeded 12 percent, and in the inner sectors of the most distressed cities, it reached 17 percent. Under-employment is even worse for blacks, since discrimination in the job market forces blacks to take positions below their level of skill. The result is that the black median family income is only 62 percent of that of a white median family. Blacks earn less than whites and are more frequently jobless or underemployed.

Attitudes of social avoidance offer a partial explanation for this. A few blacks benefited from the pangs of the white social conscience between 1965 and 1970. They have been promoted to the executive level of companies, and into public service as policemen, firemen, and teachers. However, in the crafts and construction tasks, blacks and other minorities are systematically excluded by exaggerated skill, educational, and experience requirements. In an expanding labor market they get jobs, but when work is slack they are the first to be laid off.

Explanations for unemployment and comparative poverty abound. They utilize one or both of the following themes: race or social status. The choice depends more upon the political philosophy of the researcher than upon sound, behavioral concepts.

Race: The black ghetto is in a similar position to that of the typical underdeveloped nation in that it is exploited by the developed—the commercial and business elite who operate in the CBD and live in the suburbs. Tabb (1970) illustrates the parallel:

> The ghetto also has a relatively low per-capita income and a high birth rate. Its residents are for the most part unskilled. Businesses lack capital and managerial know-how. Local markets are limited. The incidence of credit default is high. Little saving takes place and what is saved is usually not invested locally. Goods and services tend to be "imported" for the most part, only the simplest and the most labor-intensive being produced locally. The ghetto is dependent on one basic export—its unskilled labor power. Aggregate demand for this export does not increase to match the growth of the ghetto labor force, and unemployment is prevalent. As consumer goods are advertised twenty-four hours a day on radio and television, ghetto residents are constantly reminded of the availability of goods and services which they cannot afford to buy. Welfare payments and other governmental transfers are needed to help pay for the ghetto's requirements. Local businesses are owned, in large numbers, by non-residents, many of whom are white. Important jobs in the local public economy (teachers, policemen, and postmen) are held by white outsiders. (P. 22)

Social status: Banfield (1970), in *The Unheavenly City,* emphasizes that most ghetto residents, and many inner city whites as well, are lower-status people. They are "present-oriented" and either socially unwilling, or psychologically incapable, of organizing their lives to take advantage of job retraining, employment opportunities, or more liberal welfare payments. Banfield acknowledges that discrimination and inadequate medical and educational services make the situation worse for minority groups, but sees little prospect for short-run improvement through the plethora of governmental assistance programs. This is a harsh, some even say a racist, interpretation, but the reality of the continuing social malaise lends credibility to his argument.

Regardless of the explanation adopted, all acknowledge the tragic frustration produced by denied opportunities. The cycle of poverty is accepted. It is easier to accept the humiliation of welfare payments than the frustration of attempting to find satisfaction from employment opportunities available to the ghetto dweller. Crime actually pays. The chances of being caught in the inner city are low and, if one is caught, judgment is lenient: The family is even transferred to another welfare category.

When frustrations reach the breaking point, riots occur. They usually involve the younger members of the ghetto community, those for whom the inequities are often most apparent and who will no longer tolerate the injustice. For the youthful gang, rioting is both fun and profitable. Nonresident-owned businesses are generally the target—businesses that often overcharge and take advantage of the ghetto residents. Burning and looting is revenge.

Relocation of industry away from congested city plants to suburban industrial parks hinders employment for ghetto residents. Public transportation is inadequate in most cities and is even worse for those who must reverse-commute from the inner city to the suburbs or across town. It adds to the cost of employment and is especially difficult for those without automobiles. Almost one-half of the unemployed in central cities do not have access to a private automobile for the journey to work.

Dispersing the ghetto

In excess of 300 federal programs were initiated in the United States between 1960 and 1968 in an attempt to improve social life in the city. Many of these granted aid for job-training programs to industry in the central cities. Black leaders benefited through the public participation mandated for those programs and now have greater confidence in their ability to control their own destiny through politics and business. However, these programs merely gilded the real social issue of the ghetto. The ghetto will never be an equal participant in social and economic life until its people can participate freely and equally in the economy of the entire metropolitan area. It appears as if attempts to redevelop the economy and residential areas of the central city are doomed. As soon as families are able, they join the flight to the less crowded suburbs.

Programs that will disperse the ghetto are required, rather than programs that will gild it over. If residential islands (200–500 people) were created in suburban developments to which minority groups could move they would:

1. Preserve the social interaction of neighborhood identity: Parents and their children would not feel ostracized in their immediate home environment and would therefore risk moving from the ghetto.
2. Change social attitudes of black and white children through

interaction in local schools: The island would be sufficiently small so that no one group would dominate any school. Even parents would interact over school policy.

3. Place minority families closer to employment opportunities.
4. Provide an incentive for mobility from the most dilapidated inner city areas so they could be renewed without disrupting neighborhood social ties.

The federal programs that could implement this plan for voluntary relocation are already available, but it would require cooperation by federal, state, and local officials. This is not easily accomplished. However, it is an approach that is consistent with our knowledge of social behavior, for it would facilitate interaction between social groups.

Through interaction, attitudes of both black and white families would change. White families could achieve an appreciation of black culture, a desire for which is currently reflected in school textbooks and the popularity of movies with black cultural themes. And black families would become accustomed to new social opportunities.

The ghetto as an enclave exhibits many features of social behavior because it demonstrates what happens when groups of people are physically and socially isolated. Ethnic difference is the basis of the segregation, but similar effects upon the geography of areas may be observed when people separate or do not interact because of their religious beliefs.

RELIGION AND PATTERNS OF SOCIAL BEHAVIOR

Religious allegiance influences social behavior because it establishes norms and beliefs. Interaction between people sharing common beliefs produces distinct spatial patterns that, together with their symbolic churches and monuments, are the focus for study in the geography of religion. The spatial impress is pronounced in those areas where religious faith determines society's modal value system, so that the cultural landscape becomes an expression of religious belief. Sopher (1967), in his excellent monograph *Geography of Religions*, provides three examples of regions that are the product of religious systems.

The *Amish Mennonite* (Pennsylvania Dutch) communities of southeastern Pennsylvania and Amish communities in Iowa and Ontario are distinguished from surrounding areas by the rejection of social and material traits, and a reliance upon community self-sufficiency. The effect of this religiously based behavior upon patterns of commercial travel was described in Chapter 1 (see Figs. 1.4 and 1.5). The absence of monumental church structures, the lack of finery and display, insistence upon separate education, and a reluctance to use motorized vehicles are based upon religious principles that have influenced the development of an Amish cultural landscape.

The *Mormon* religion also develops social attitudes that have given the Mormon country in Utah and parts of Wyoming, Arizona, and New Mexico a distinctive religious landscape (Fig. 6.10). The core area in

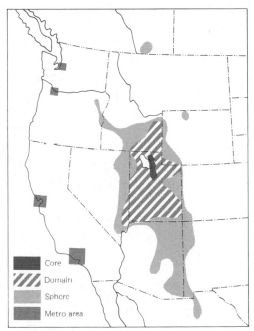

Fig. 6.10 Mormon culture region. The Wasatch Oasis represents the core focus for Mormon society. It contains about 40 percent of the Mormon population. The impact of Mormon culture is apparent throughout the Mormon domain. Outside of this, the Mormon society founded many of the settlements, but their impact on spatial organization is not readily apparent. (Meinig, reproduced by permission from *Annals of the Association of American Geographers*, vol. 55, 1965, Fig. 7.)

the Wasatch Oasis, Utah, contains about 40 percent of the Mormon population and is the focus of organization for Mormon society. Mormon settlements were built as religiously inspired representations of the City of Zion: square blocks, wide streets bordered by irrigation ditches, brick or stone home construction, a compact arrangement of irrigated land around a nuclear settlement, unpainted farm buildings, and fields bordered by Lombardy poplars.

In southwestern Michigan, *Dutch Reformed* adherents have colonized. Over a century and more, choices and decisions based upon firm religious beliefs were applied to the organization and exploitation of the area so that a religiously based landscape has developed. Specialized types of commercial agriculture such as flower and vegetable raising, local industry, and large farm families reflect the doctrinal emphasis upon self-reliance, productive activity, and the agrarian way of life. Nuclear settlements are church oriented. Retail and commercial services are kept to a minimum and deliberately placed on the periphery to reduce their temptation of attraction for the young. Land ownership is exclusive with expansion along borders. Members refuse to sell to non-church members so as to exclude undesirable aspects of non-Calvinist life from the Dutch Reformed living space. The analogy with the exclusive social space of residential neighborhoods is obvious.

Canada has traditionally been more tolerant of exclusive religious beliefs than has America, and the impress of religiously based behavior is apparent in many areas: from the spires of the Roman Catholic churches in the Quebec village to the unique landscape effect of the utopian colonies of the Mennonites in central Ontario and Manitoba, the Hutterites of Saskatchewan, and the Doukhobors in British Columbia. As an inducement for pioneering the Prairie Provinces, reserve lands were given to groups who sought to maintain their cultural traditions and religious freedom. In 1876 the Mennonites from Russia settled in the Red River Valley where they developed a vigorous mixed-farming tradition. French Canadians moved from New England, and reserved lands were also given to groups from England, Scotland, Germany, the Ukraine, Scandinavia, and Iceland (Fig. 6.11).

The effect of religious systems upon the development of cultural landscapes is apparent in many areas. The emphasis in this short section has been on their direct impact, but religious beliefs also influence population dynamics, migration patterns, economic behavior re-

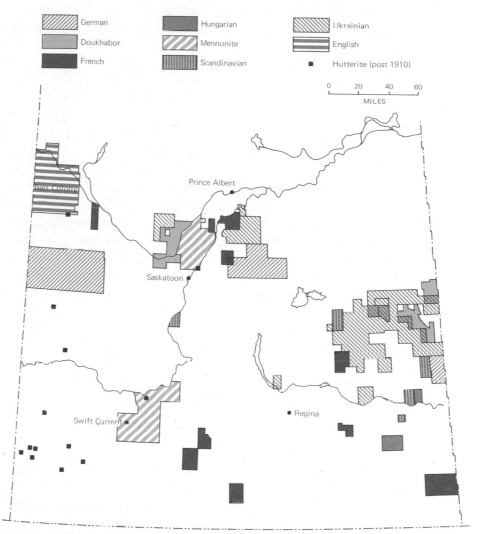

Fig. 6.11 Agricultural group settlements in Saskatchewan, 1870–1910. (Richards, in Warkentin, ed., *Canada: A Geographical Interpretation*, Methuen Publications, Toronto, 1968, Fig. 12.3.)

sulting from religiously based food and commodity preferences, and political allegiance. All these themes are considered in the sources listed in the Bibliography.

Religious behavior is considered an element of social geography because it creates interaction between some people in social groups and the avoidance of others. Like social status, it is a way of life that is learned and continually reinforced, and one that affects man's use of the land.

MOVEMENT AS A SOCIAL PROCESS

Interactions between and within social groups, social areas, and religious associations have been presented as static conditions. This they are not. Interaction takes place within and between these groups through trips, migration, mail, telephone, and news media. Each involves movement: either movement of people between areas or movement of messages and ideas across space. Because of their proximity communications between neighbors and neighborhood facilities is most frequent, but may not be sufficient. For example, shopping at neighborhood centers may be convenient, but satisfaction is derived from driving farther to regional shopping centers, where the range of choice is larger. The likelihood of the individual patronizing local as opposed to the more distant facilities is a function of the individual's desire for a greater range of choice for goods, friends, education, or entertainment, and the cost of overcoming the distance separating the individual and the alternative sources. As in economic behavior, so, too, in social behavior: Distance is an inconvenience with a dollar sign attached.

The role of distance in the social process

The friction of distance—the cost of overcoming intervening space—results in agglomeration of human activities. Our previous illustrations have shown the effect of this behavior on city formation and the arrangement of land uses within cities. In this chapter, it is the cost of maintaining communication across geographical space that has resulted in the development of relatively homogeneous suburbs, and has motivated ethnic and some religious groups to cluster.

Interaction between areas falls off with increasing distance (Fig. 6.12). There is an inverse relationship between interaction and distance. The decline in interaction between places is not linear with distance but is exponential so that the curve is hyperbolic. People do not hesitate to interact frequently at the local level, but they are more hesitant to interact over longer distances. They perceive the distance, or the cost

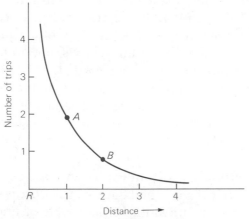

Fig. 6.12   Trips to shopping centers of varying distance from residence.

of overcoming this distance, as increasing exponentially. If shopping center *A* is 1 mile away and center *B* is 2 miles, trips to *A* are more than twice as likely.

Distance and attraction are the two principal variables in determining movement. Together with the transferability of items, the complementarity between areas, and opportunities for interaction, distance, and attraction provide the basis for models geographers create in order to analyze the role of movement in spatial organization. These concepts are usually associated with economic behavior because the movements they induce result in economic patterns. However, they are just as applicable to social behavior.

Transferability: Some goods and people are more readily transferred than others. Bulky, perishable goods are usually produced near markets or processed in rural manufacturing plants before being shipped in semiprocessed form to markets. Similarly, some social groups are more mobile. The label "jet set" infers mobility, whereas lower-status social groups, whose knowledge of other areas is limited, are less prone to migrate. Even their relocation within the metropolitan area is, both socially as well as economically, constrained to familiar areas. Upper-middle income status groups, particularly those employed by international corporations, have become nomadic as a result of corporate policies that encourage mobility. IBM employees joke that the initials denote "I've Been Moved."

Complementarity: Interactions are conducted when a mutually re-warding exchange exists. This might be represented in exchange of goods or money between different areas, or the flow of people and/or messages along pathways. When communication is not mutually re-warding, interaction is unidirectional or nonexistent. Politicians only began to interact with blacks, Chicanos, and students as these minority groups demonstrated their willingness to register and vote. Now the groups have something to exchange. Interaction has occurred with resulting changes in public policy.

Perception of opportunities: Opportunities for interaction are often lost because individuals do not realize the benefits. Advertising attempts to remedy this, but people may be unwilling or incapable of understanding the message. It is extremely difficult to inform people about social welfare programs from which they might benefit, or to advise the unemployed job seeker. They tend to disbelieve information from technical experts whom they perceive negatively; instead, they rely upon rumors from friends and relatives. This distorts patterns of migration from rural to urban areas. Rather than travel to the nearest urban area where employment is available, migrants prefer cities to which friends and relatives have already moved. They perceive such areas as being closer because they have better information. The *psychological distance* differs from linear distance. The reverse of this process also assists in explaining the exponential increase in distance perception (see Fig. 6.12). Individuals are less likely to know about opportunities in distant places; therefore, the propensity to interact with such places decreases exponentially. When knowledge from friends and relatives is available, this distorts individual perception and can affect patterns of movement. Shopping and recreational behavior is also biased. Consumers will travel farther to reach a familiar area than they will to get to an un-familiar area, because familiar areas appear—are perceived to be—closer.

Intervening opportunity: Intervening places affect a person's per-ception of distance. The more opportunities that exist nearby, the less an individual will value distant places. A person living at a beach resort seldom travels to distant beaches despite their superior surf. However, he may travel several hundred miles to a ski resort. In this manner, intervening opportunities restrain interaction across distances. Avoidance and/or placement of intervening opportunities is a strategy food markets play when selecting new sites. The range of goods and service is similar in all markets so the pay-off strategy is to select an area with a sufficient threshold population and to locate so as to intervene in the flow to a competing market.

MODELS OF INTERACTION

The range of variables that can affect the movement of people, goods, and ideas causes geographers to use models that are descriptive summaries of observed regularities rather than predictive models. By selecting variables—usually *surrogates* available from census reports—useful generalizations about the regularity of movement have been achieved through gravity and intervening opportunity models.

The gravity model

The gravity model is the simplest and yet most widely applicable of all interaction models. It postulates that the interaction between any two groups of people or locations increases in proportion to the size of the groups (mass) and decreases with some function of the distance between the groups. Various surrogates for size and distance have been used. Population is the usual measure for size, although employment and income have also been utilized. Distance is normally measured by linear separation, although other measures include driving time and cost of travel. The distance variable is further modified by an exponent so as to represent the different friction of distance for the group or commodity under consideration. For example, movement of upper-status groups involves less friction than that of lower status groups and this is adjusted for by lowering the exponent.

The gravity model is used in store location research to predict interaction between shopping areas and residential neighborhoods within the city. As was shown in Chapter 5, the probability of a consumer traveling from a designated neighborhood to a particular shopping center is assumed to be directly proportional to the size of the shopping center and inversely proportional to (1) the distance between them and (2) competition from other centers. Market studies based upon gravity models identify store-deficient areas without costly consumer interviews.

Despite the relative simplicity of the gravity model and the many factors other than size and distance that can influence consumer behavior, the predicted results are highly correlated with shopping patterns discerned for origin and destination studies. Even for such a specialized function as hospitals, Morrill (1970) has shown that the frequency of trips can be reliably predicted by this model (Fig. 6.13). The farther away a person lives from a hospital, then the lower is the probability that he will visit that hospital. Apparently people choose hospitals on the basis of accessibility, just as they choose supermarkets.

The intervening opportunity model

For some categories of movement—particularly migration—size of, and distance to, attracting cities is not as influential as are intervening opportunities. The more opportunities that exist nearby, the less attractive are distant opportunities. In other words, interaction is directly proportional to the opportunities at that distance but inversely proportional to the number of intervening opportunities. This model in-

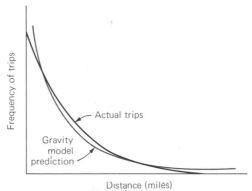

Fig. 6.13 Trips to hospitals and distance. The decline in frequency of trips with increasing distance from Chicago general hospitals is well predicted by the gravity mode. (Richard L. Morrill, *The Spatial Organization of Society*, © 1970 by Wodsworth Publishing Company, Inc., Belmont, Calif., Fig. 7.10.)

corporates psychological considerations—perception of distance and opportunities—more explicitly than does the gravity model, which emphasizes transferability and complementarity.

The distorted shape of many fields of interaction can be accounted for by intervening opportunities. Trade areas on the margins of the cities are pear-shaped, with the apex projected out into rural areas along communication lines. Toward the CBD they are truncated by competition from the larger center. The hinterlands between competing metropolises, such as New York and Boston, are truncated between them but extend farther west where there are no intervening metropolitan opportunities (Fig. 6.14). Trade areas are seldom, if ever, concentric or hexagonal as in the *central place theory.*

PROBLEMS IN MODELS OF MOVEMENT

The movement of people, goods, and messages is a complex behavioral process. Each person evaluates the world about him according to its

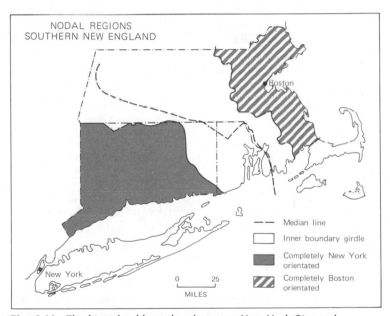

Fig. 6.14   The hinterland boundary between New York City and Boston is based upon the median boundary of railroad coach passengers, newspaper circulation, telephone calls, business addresses of directors of manufacturing firms, and correspondent banks. The extension inland is due to the absence of competition for interaction. (After Green, 1955, Fig. 9.2; and Yeates and Garner. *The North American City*, 1971, Harper & Row, Publishers, Fig. 4.10.)

usefulness in satisfying his demands. Rarely, does he move haphazardly; in fact, each move is planned and in many instances constrained by circumstance. Therefore, it is somewhat surprising that variables like mass, distance, and intervening opportunities are able to reliably predict interaction. The decision to migrate is illustrative of the complex decisions that are involved.

Migration can be conceptualized as a process in which people are encouraged to move, and assisted in adjusting afterward by interaction with others. The process can be divided into two stages (Fig. 6.15), the decision to migrate and assimilation.

The decision to migrate: This is usually caused by dislocation, a change in life style from adolescent to adult or an emergency situation: for example, loss of employment, illness, or good fortune. At this stage the migrant must evaluate the utility of alternative destinations. The media alert people to possibilities. Therefore, closer places have an advantage. Knowledge of more distant places is provided by travel, wartime, or student experience or information received from friends and relatives who have previously relocated. Information from mass media indicates possibilities, but personal contacts are more influential in the final choice. Cost of relocation—distance—is evaluated, but is a secondary consideration because of the alternative means by which it may be compromised. However, distance does affect availability of information and perception of alternative destinations.

Assimilation: Arrival at the new destination does not complete the migration chain. Many migrants are dissatisfied and return to their original place, or move again to a more distant place in a two-step process. The role of friends and relatives is very important in assimilation. If social needs are not fulfilled by mutually rewarding interaction, the immigrant may reject the economic advantage of urban living to return to familiar and friendly areas.

If assimilation is successful, the migrant begins to assist the relocation of others. Return visits to the old home, usually accompanied by exaggerated manifestations of economic success—new car, clothes, and money—encourage others to join the flow.

The mass or population of an area creates opportunities that attract migrants as well as increasing the potential number of pro-

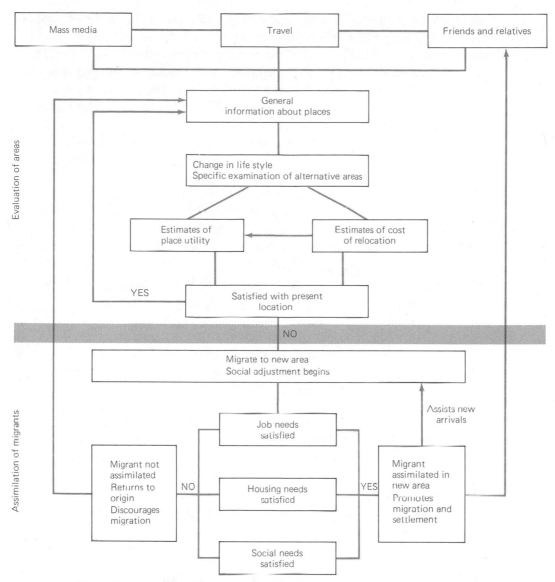

Fig. 6.15 Two-part migration decision: Information from various sources affects an individual's evaluation of the utility of areas. The decision to migrate initiates the second part in which the migrant becomes assimilated or returns.

moters of a particular area's virtues. Distance will affect the flow of this information. Adjacent areas will be better informed, whereas more distant areas will receive competing information from other cities. Mass media are influential because they are produced in the large cities and feature local news. Viewing television and reading the daily newspaper makes it appear that everything exciting happens in the cities.

Population, distance, and intervening opportunities characterize part of the behavioral process that influences the decision to migrate. They cannot capture it all. The gravity and intervening opportunity models are deductive models that seek to describe regularly occurring patterns of human movement. They are helpful because they illuminate something complex that is intellectually intriguing. It is also helpful if this knowledge is associated with how ideas spread since the diffusion of ideas can have a profound effect on movements.

Models of diffusion

Diffusion involves the movement of ideas, innovations, and disease across space and through time. It is similar to models of population movements in that occurrence decays with distance, but it is unlike them in three important aspects:

1. The idea or germ moves between people but there is no loss at the source. The sender continues to contact others as do the recipients of his idea or disease. The number of knowers or carriers increases geometrically until saturation is approached. A logistic (S-shaped) curve represents the process initiated by the innovators and completed by laggards (Fig. 6.16). At first, very few have been contacted, but as the number of carriers increases, the number of new contacts in each time period also increases. Expansion is rapid until only the laggards remain, and the opportunity for new contacts declines.

2. Movement is not constrained to routeways. A wavelike pattern develops which spreads outward from the source. People close to the source are contacted first, whereas those more distant are contacted later in the diffusion process. The analogy of a pebble thrown into a pond is appropriate. A wave develops on impact but is only a ripple when it eventually reaches the edge.

3. Not everybody contacted accepts the idea or becomes contagious. A person may have been inoculated against the disease or a rumor may have little interest for him. Therefore, he is not a carrier since he does not pass it along (Fig. 6.17).

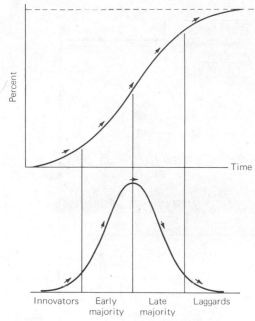

Fig. 6.16 Accumulating the distribution of innovation acceptors. (Gould, reproduced by permission from the Commission on College Geography of the Association of American Geographers Resource Paper No. 4, *Spatial Diffusion*, 1969, Fig. 24.)

These three aspects—logistic increase, wavelike expansion, and the probability of a contact becoming a transmitter—provide the basis for models of the diffusion process. The wavelike analogy is particularly useful. As the crest of the wave moves outward, the zone of most active contact moves with it. However, the probability of acceptance declines with distance from the source. Over time more people will accept an idea, but a crest is reached when somewhat less than all people are contacted.

Diffusion is really a very simple idea that aids our understanding of human behavior. Note the following example:

A college student went to Florida for Easter, had a great time, and returned exhausted to Medville College with mononucleosis. Enjoying a swinger's social life, the student dated ten different people in the following two weeks. Eight of the ten caught the disease and became the

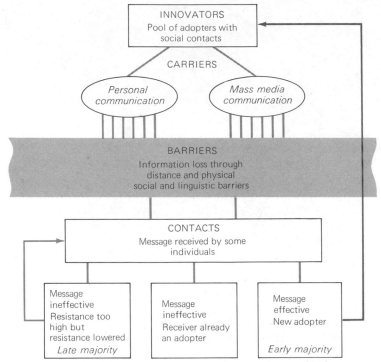

Fig. 6.17 Flow diagram of the diffusion process. Interaction between adopters and potential contacts is obstructed by physical, economic, and social barriers.

instigators of the epidemic. Two were resistant so that expansion in this instance occurred in less than all contacts. The contagious individuals became the early majority who subsequently passed the disease to others. However, the spread was limited to 10 percent of the student body because the dorms were closed by the student health service. A few students, the laggards, became infected after they returned home. Students who did not date (did not interact) were isolated, and those who lived off campus (because of distance) were less likely (i.e., had a lower probability) to become infected. The original student, although a contagious carrier, never became ill and returned home to diffuse the disease among old high school friends.

Epidemiologists learn about the movement of disease through diffusion studies. However, the same approach is applicable to the study of other patterns of movement. For example, modeling the diffusion of agricultural innovations in developing countries and comparing the theoretical results with observed patterns is a contemporary research theme for social scientists who study social and economic change. In these studies, special attention is paid to the *carriers* of, and *barriers* to, the diffusion of innovation because an understanding of their role can accelerate beneficial change.

The diffusion of cooperatives in Northern Tanzania

An area in Northern Tanzania, immediately south of Lake Victoria, experienced a rapid diffusion of cotton-marketing cooperatives over a 15-year period. The diffusion pattern in this instance illustrates the role of physical and human conditions on the diffusion process (Fig. 6.18). The original movement was begun by farmers in the peninsular and island district of Ukerewe. The idea was diffused across the lake by fishermen and dhow traders (carriers) to Mwanza. Two other early-adopting districts were adjacent to the major railway line, and a third was located near Geita. Isolated areas (barriers) were late adopters.

Other factors further complicated the pattern:

1. Cooperatives could not be too close together or they would compete for the same hinterland. Each required a threshold of suppliers.
2. Cooperatives were an effective channel for political organization. The British Trusteeship Administration tried to control the spread for both political and financial reasons, whereas TANU, the party that led Tanzania to independence, sought to expand cooperatives. Political allegiance was both a barrier and carrier of the cooperative idea.
3. The cooperative movement, like union organization, afforded prestige to officeholders. Ambitious men often saw their opportunity through organizing rival cooperatives or by accelerating adoption in the eastern portions of the region where new cotton lands were developed.

A *hierarchical* pattern of diffusion is apparent. From Mwanza the idea "jumped" to areas near the marketing places of Geita and Shinyanga. There is more contact between these places than between intervening areas so that the probability of adoption is higher. The idea spread from these centers of innovation by *contagion*. A concentric pattern about the early nodes (indicated by the *arrows* on Fig. 6.18)

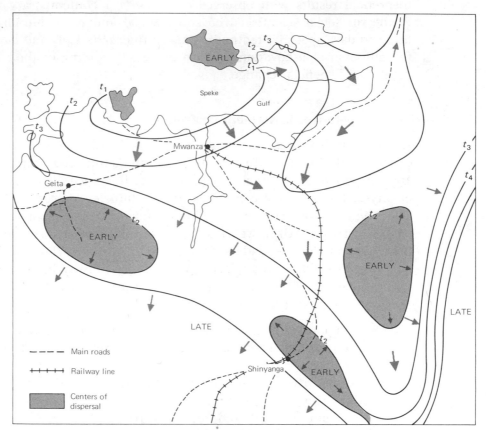

Fig. 6.18 Diffusion of cotton cooperatives in Lake Province, Tanzania. (After Gould, reproduced by permission from the Commission on College Geography of the Association of American Geographers Resource Paper No. 4, *Spatial Diffusion*, 1969, Fig. 53.)

occurred as farmers in adjoining areas observed the benefits achieved by joining a cooperative. It is common in the diffusion of innovations to observe a pattern that consists of a hierarchical spread through urban nodes followed by a secondary contagion of adjoining areas. Urban areas were the nodes of innovation from which the idea spread by contagion to surrounding areas.

Diffusion is a rich and challenging field for geographical research. It combines theory building about human behavior with the opportunity for testing in all geographical realms. This example has been based upon a study by Gould (1969). He concludes his Tanzanian example with the following summary of the effects of innovation upon modernization.

When institutions of this sort diffuse through an area, we must not forget the tremendous changes they can bring in their wake. The cooperative movement stopped unscrupulous buying practices by former cotton agents, and it provided a system of nodes from which new seeds and cultivation practices could be transmitted to the farmers. Incomes rose sharply in the area, although most of the money went for immediate consumption rather than long-term, capital investment. Similar cases can be found all over the underdeveloped world. During the 1940's in eastern Nigeria, for example, small palm oil presses diffused like a forest fire through the area, and by 1953 over 3,000 were in operation. Later Pioneer Oil Mills spread equally quickly, and handled large quantities of kernels extremely efficiently. Pressed yields quadrupled the old, inefficient way of extracting oil by boiling, and the quality was also raised. Incomes went up accordingly. But the innovation had an impact far beyond the economic. Young men became rich, and tensions between generations became severe as a new class of entrepreneurs challenged the traditional bases of obedience. The women's traditional right to the hard kernels was lost when these were cracked and pressed by the mechanized mills, and many women rioted in response to the disruption in extended family organization. Thus, waves of innovation may leave behind them eddies of social change, disruption, and conflict that continue to swirl for a long time after the excitement of the initial impact is past. (P. 50)

Because Gould's description emphasizes the ramifications of the interaction concept, it is an appropriate conclusion to both the study of diffusion and models of interaction. Additional information on diffusion is provided in the *Programmed Case Studies in Geography.* The steps for simulating the diffusion of a rumor using the Monte Carlo method in an urban area are outlined. Students with computer systems can grapple with the problems of simulating human behavior themselves. Those without such systems will be able to observe and interpret the results of previous simulations in terms of the content of this chapter.

The interaction theme provides continuity for the entire chapter. Human behavior is not as individualistic as was inferred previously in Chapter 5. Groups form and their members interact in such a way as to modify individual behavior into acceptable patterns of social behavior. Communication in common languages is an important aspect of the socialization process: so, too, are relatives, friends, family, schools, and religion. They structure collective behavior that creates the spatial patterns geographers seek to understand. The models of interaction serve to illuminate the role of variables such as distance, mass, transferability, and complementarity, but much remains to be discovered about the process of interaction and the dynamics of human behavior, which seek to maintain patterns of favorable interaction. Social grouping by neighborhood and social segregation are static manifestations of this process. Patterns of migration and of spatial diffusion are movements that can be explained by the differing interaction among people.

Social interaction is essential to human development and the creation of tolerable environments. The need for interaction and the results therefrom are inherent in many contemporary policy issues, but their import is seldom appreciated.

INTERACTION AND URBAN POLICY

Although economic opportunities in cities exert the greatest pull on migrants, they are reinforced by the social advantages of life in the city. The superiority of urban education, the availability of cultural facilities, and the health care available in metropolitan centers are especially attractive to middle-income families. It is from these families that technologically oriented industries and administrative organizations draw their key personnel, so metropolitan areas have become increasingly attractive to this expanding sector of the economy. Growth creates additional employment opportunities for new migrants and accelerates urbanization, which creates problems for urban and rural areas alike.

In America, 96 percent of the population lives in an urban sphere (Fig. 6.19). Only 4 percent of Americans are rural inhabitants. Extensive agricultural regions in southern, western, and midwestern America, once the home of an integrated rural society, have been depopulated. Stores and schools have closed. Even landowners have moved to town where they can organize farm operations through agricultural contractors. The lack of economic opportunity in rural areas has pushed out people who were ill-prepared for the competitiveness and anonymity of the urban areas toward which they were pulled. The new migrants have augmented the urban malaise of unemployment, congestion, crime, and pollution. Many are dissatisfied with urban life. They indicate a preference for a rural, or at least a suburban, way of life, but economic necessity confines them to the inner city and older suburbs.

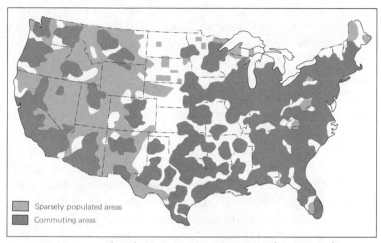

Fig. 6.19 Areas within daily commuting distance of a metropolitan center, 1960. Eighty-seven percent of the population was located in the dark areas. If areas within commuting distance of cities of 30,000 or more are included, then 96 percent of the American population would be included. (After Brian J. L. Berry and Frank E. Horton, *Geographic Perspectives on Urban Systems: With Integrated Readings*, © 1970, p. 42. Reprinted by permission of Prentice-Hall, Inc., Englewood Cliffs, N.J.)

Alternatives to urbanization

Various suggestions have been made to curtail urbanization and assist the return of migrants. Such programs are sponsored by elected representatives from rural areas. Decentralization of industry is a usual theme, but the experience of the British government in assisting development of industry outside the London metropolis is not encouraging. Industry moves to rural locations in automated, governmentally subsidized plants, but management, in which there are expanding employment opportunities, remains in the metropolis.

Governmental schemes for rural development neglect the social factor. They focus on the economic incentive. This is not sufficient to attract the assimilated city dweller away from accustomed interaction with family, friends, and recreational opportunities. Opinion polls indicate a preference for the rural way of life, but assimilated urban residents also wish to preserve social interactions enjoyed in the city. Happiness would seemingly consist of a low-density suburban environment with access to a cheap, clean, and efficient rapid transit system to facilitate interaction with the city. The Japanese and Scandinavian new town developments emphasize this kind of social interaction.

New developments beyond the commuting range of the metropolis are not attractive. They rely on specialized employment opportunities and seldom offer a range of social and recreational possibilities. Viable alternatives are: *Research and administrational complexes* located in rural areas within commuting distance of smaller cities. The governmental and corporate development of the research triangle between Durham, Raleigh, and Chapel Hill in North Carolina is an example, or a *linear city* in which development is extended along an arterial transportation route. Industry, commerce, and apartment housing is located adjacent to the artery with space-consuming, single-family residences, schools, and recreational areas extending into rural settings. Urban development could be contiguous or separated as nodes. A star-shaped adaptation of the linear city has been suggested for Washington, D.C., with the interstitial areas preserved as open space (Fig. 6.20).

The advantage of these plans is that they decentralize population. Yet through superior public transportation, they enable business and industry to enjoy the economies of agglomeration. For people, they provide ease of social interaction. Perhaps the rewards that these opportunities could provide would condition people to accept a more cooperative way of life, one that is less independent and more responsive to the ecological conditions of the world that we all share.

Attitudes toward the environment

If people were more aware of the interdependency of our life styles, then perhaps they would be willing to seek cooperative solutions to environmental problems. For example, we are concerned about air pollution and seek to enforce control through modification of automobile engines. Yet modifications required to meet the 1970 Clean Air Act will increase gasoline consumption by 15 percent per annum. At the same time petroleum reserves are being depleted.

Thus, the air pollution problem must also be resolved from the standpoint of energy conservation. The question of whether the environment would be better served by policies designed to reduce automobile use by expanding mass transit should be carefully examined. Rather than enforcing strict emissions control for automobiles, which decreases engine efficiency, more cooperative solutions should encourage the use of transit systems, which use only one-fourth the energy to move people an equivalent distance.

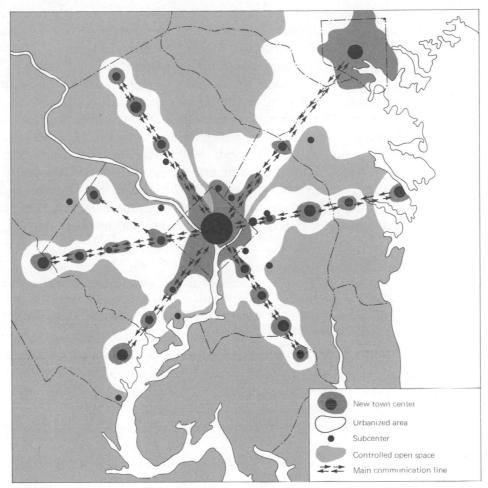

Legend:
- New town center
- Urbanized area
- Subcenter
- Controlled open space
- Main communication line

Fig. 6.20 The suggested radial corridor plan for Washington, D.C. (Maryland-National Capital Park and Planning Commission, 1964, p. 20; and Yeates and Garner, *The North American City*, Harper & Row, Publishers, 1971, Fig. 18.4.)

Although a mass transit policy was a wartime necessity it has not been a popular alternative in peacetime. But the world faces both pollution and energy crises, and a nation that is willing to adopt innovative solutions could change the course of environmental conservation. The technology is available: All that is lacking is the public commitment to a cooperative solution. Unfortunately, too many people would rather retain their cars and pay the additional cost for the reduction of automobile emissions, than interact with unfamiliar people each day in public transit systems.

Discussions of policy issues have been appended as a conclusion to emphasize the importance of the social process when attempting to outline beneficial solutions to contemporary dilemmas. The tradition of individual initiative and competitiveness is insufficient in the contemporary world, where the dangers of self-interest are evident in warfare, crime, and environmental devastation. Cooperation is urgently needed to solve such vexing questions as segregation barriers, equitable schooling, and population redistribution if we are to preserve a humane life. A more socialized social policy is required rather than policies that reward individual competitiveness. A similar theme is emphasized by Skinner (1971a) in *Beyond Freedom and Dignity*. In addition, by his comments on the design of culture (1971b), he provides a warning for Americans that ought to be read by all developed nations:

> Our culture has produced the science and technology it needs to save itself. It has the wealth it needs for effective action. It has, to a considerable extent, a concern for its own future. But if it continues to value freedom and dignity rather than its own survival as its principal value, then possibly some other culture will make a greater contribution to the future. (P. 75)

Political behavior is also a manifestation of the social process. Political units strive to maintain internal interaction and limit external interaction. However, political behavior has such a profound influence on spatial organization that it warrants a separate discussion in Chapter 7.

SUGGESTED READINGS

There are two approaches to further study of the social process; reading of textbooks or novels. Many excellent novels that explore social behavior are available. The black urban experience is outlined in the following:

Frazier, E. Franklin. *The Negro Family in the United States*. Chicago: University of Chicago Press, 1966. This is a revised and abridged edition of Frazier's 1939 edition. Of particular importance is chap. 13, "Roving Men and Homeless Women"; chap. 20, "The Brown Middle Class"; and chap. 21, "The Black Proletariat."

Green, Constance McLaughlin. *The Secret City*. Princeton, N.J.: Princeton University Press, 1967. A noted black historian describes the black experience throughout the history of Washington, D.C. She refers to

Washington as a "secret city" in the sense that the white Washingtonians are never really aware of the black middle class, which has all the characteristics of any ethnic middle class but cannot realize their aspirations because of a segregated city.

Liebow, Elliot. *Tally's Corner.* Boston: Little, Brown, 1967. Liebow is an anthropologist who did a study of the street-corner blacks in Washington, D.C. It is an honest and compassionate study of men who are likely to become losers but have not "abdicated completely their quest for dignity."

Among geography texts of interest to the student, Wagner's emphasizes cultural and social themes:

Wagner, Philip. *The Human Use of the Earth.* New York: Free Press, 1960.

From sociologists and psychologists there have been several texts that students will find useful:

Gans, Herbert J. *The Urban Villagers.* New York: Free Press, 1960.

Shibutani, Tamotsu. *Society and Personality.* Englewood Cliffs, N.J.: Prentice-Hall, 1961.

Skinner, B. F. *Beyond Freedom and Dignity.* New York: Knopf, 1971a.

Skinner, B. F. "Beyond Freedom and Dignity: Pre-publication Summa." *Psychology Today* 5(1971b):37–80.

Smelser, Neal J. *Theory of Collective Behavior.* New York: Free Press, 1963.

An attempt to integrate social status with policy is provided in the following controversial book:

Banfield, Edward G. *The Unheavenly City.* Boston: Little, Brown, 1970.

Geography texts that deal with special aspects of social behavior are listed below. The Resource Papers, published by the Commission on College Geography, provide summaries designed for undergraduate students.

Movement

Gould, Peter R. *Spatial Diffusion.* Resource Paper no. 4. Washington, D.C.: Association of American Geographers, Commission on College Geography, 1969. Also reprinted in Ronald Abler, John S. Adams, and Peter R. Gould, *Spatial Organization: The Geographer's View of the World*, (Englewood Cliffs, N.Y.: Prentice-Hall, 1971.

Morrill, Richard L. "Interaction: Movements of People and Ideas." *The Spatial Organization of Society.* Belmont, Calif.: Wadsworth, 1970, chap. 7.

Yeates, Maurice H., and Garner, Barry J. "Settlements and Interactions." *The North American City.* New York: Harper & Row, 1971, chap. 4.

Religion

Sopher, David D. *Geography of Religions*. Englewood Cliffs, N.J.: Prentice-Hall, 1967.

Social areas and social status

Abler, Ronald; Adams, John S.; and Gould, Peter R. "Classification" and "The Bases for Spatial Interaction." *Spatial Organization: The Geographer's View of the World*. Englewood Cliffs, N.J.: Prentice-Hall, 1971, chaps. 6 and 7.

Berry, Brian J. L., and Horton, Frank E. "Concepts in Social Space." *Geographical Perspectives on Urban Systems*. Englewood Cliffs, N.J.: Prentice-Hall, 1970, chap. 10.

Rose, Harold M. *Social Process in the City: Race and Urban Residential Choice*. Resource Paper no. 6. Washington, D.C.: Association of American Geographers, Commission on College Geography, 1969.

Rose, Harold M. *The Black Ghetto: A Spatial Behavioral Perspective*. New York: McGraw-Hill, 1971.

CHAPTER 7
THE POLITICAL PROCESS

THE POLITICAL PROCESS can be characterized as a series of actions that serve to establish or maintain political systems. Its purpose is to integrate individuals and groups into an effective political entity. Competition among groups is regulated to a tolerable level, and allegiance is sought by promoting symbols such as the flag, royalty, ceremonies, public buildings, and national heroes. Communication is encouraged within, and curtailed between, rival units, and the integration achieved through communication enables collective action for the mutual interest.

The dynamics and spatial impress of these political processes can be studied at the local, state, or national level. As a systematic field it is known as political geography. However, the purpose of this chapter is not to summarize political geography, but rather to explore how the interaction within and between political units can explain spatial distributions.

The areal context of the political process is direct. All areas are subject to political control and all control applies to an exclusive area. A distinction is made between local, state, or provincial, and national governments. Each has an areal limitation and a separate administrative organization, and the discontinuity of authority along border zones creates changes in human activities. For this reason, border zones are often chosen as illustrations of the differential effects of the political process. These contrasts are apparent even within metropolitan areas.

The political process in metropolitan areas

The myriad political authorities within metropolitan areas enable the observation of contrasts within a relatively small area. Cities normally retain the right to control land use within their territory. This control reflects the desires—that is, the political culture—of the city. In Los Angeles County, where there are seventy-seven independent cities, and in adjoining Orange County where there are twenty-six, contrasts resulting from independent political behavior are noticeable (Fig. 7.1). Cities like Vernon, Commerce, Industry, and Santa Fe Springs are industrial suburbs with their own local governments. A more amusing example was provided by Dairy Valley, Dairyland, and Cypress: cities designed to keep people out and to preserve dairy farming as islands within the urban complex. All land was zoned exclusively for agricultural use by the farmer-councilmen. Their aim was to eliminate complaints about flies and farm odors, as well as to curtail property tax assessments, until such time as the land had appreciated to a level where it was profitable to sell. Today only remnants of agricultural land use survive. Dairyland is now La Palma and Dairy Valley has changed to Cerritos ("rolling hills"), more attractive titles for real estate speculation.

In the 1950s the majority of voters in these three cities decided it was in the "public interest" to preserve the land for dairying. The

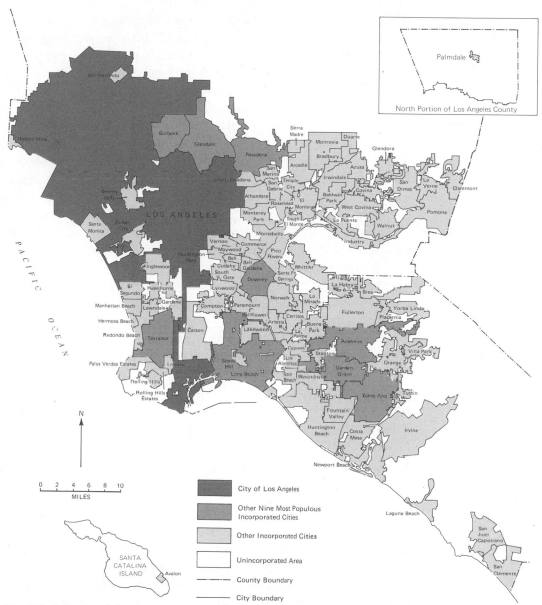

Fig. 7.1 Incorporated cities in Los Angeles and Orange counties. Policies of each city reflect local political sentiment. These policies affect spatial organization and often provide amusing examples of urban political geography. (Los Angeles County Regional Planning Commission and Local Agency Formation Commission, Orange County.)

dairying interest group was opposed by a minority who desired speculative activity and who resented the agricultural zoning ordinances
imposed by the city councils. Opposition continued, and during the subsequent ten years attitudes changed. Many of the original supporters
of restrictive zoning wished to retire or relocate to modernized dairies
in the San Joaquin Valley, and they now desired financial gain. Their
political philosophy had changed, and legislative action to liberalize
land-use zoning in the mid-1960s reflects this new "public interest."

The term *public interest* is set off by quotation marks because it
is used in a special way. Elected officials often say their decisions are
in the public interest when they mean the *majority* interest. Seldom is
there widespread agreement on issues; rather, there are many different
interest groups, each with their own view on the issue. As a result of
competition between groups or the lack thereof, these interests are
articulated. The legislation enacted is usually a compromise and in
this way the "public (majority) interest" is established.

At the municipal level these decisions may have a profound effect
on spatial distributions. Decisions on land-use zoning or the location of
a freeway are examples of this. And often these decisions are made
because a small but politically effective group has been able to persuade
elected officials that their private interest is in fact the "public interest."

One can easily become negative about decisions influenced by an
effective minority. However, one of the achievements of democratic
governments is the ease with which individuals and groups may participate in decision making. If the issue is of sufficient importance,
groups can influence the final decision, and it is by facilitating individual and group participation that democratic societies earn allegiance.

Interaction and the political process

Participation affords an opportunity for interaction within a political
system, so that the individual achieves the allegiance that makes collective action possible. As emphasized in Chapter 6, political behavior is
an aspect of social behavior. Some duplication of ideas occurs because
interaction is used as the core concept in both social and political behavior. Families, churches, and neighborhoods, as well as the economic
system, regulate behavior through interaction. The modern political
system encompasses all of these because it is the ultimate source of

enforcement. In this respect, it also coordinates economic and social activities so that the impress of the political process is apparent in most areas.

In the following sections the individual's acceptance of collective authority and its effect upon spatial organization will be explored. This is followed by a discussion of how legislation, whose aim it is to avoid conflict and promote interaction within political units, results in geographical distributions. A final section is devoted to political boundaries as barriers to interaction.

COLLECTIVE AUTHORITY

Man is both a competitive and cooperative individual. Where his security is threatened he readily cooperates in order to facilitate collective action. When the danger passes, or when he feels secure as a member of a powerful state, the pendulum swings to a more competitive way of life. Specialization in activity occurs, and there is freedom of choice. Because this latter condition is preferred to the constant vigilance necessary when every family is responsible for its own protection, a tradition of collective authority has developed. Wherever man has gathered in groups, some system of collective decision making, with power of enforcement, has been created

Security is one of the most valued benefits derived through the creation of a central authority. For this reason, political units have traditionally sought to increase security through defense and to provide institutions to prevent or resolve internal conflict.

From the earliest period of history men have aggregated their families into tribal associations that afforded protection, opportunity for specialization, and more effective exploitation of resources. Members married within groups or between acceptable groups, while outsiders were feared and hunted. Glorification of *we* and denigration of *they* was a method for bolstering group identity. Exhibitions of strength were paraded before potential aggressors. At ceremonial events lavish gift-giving was a means of demonstrating strength. Modern nations continue this tradition and even encourage military attachés in foreign embassies to ensure that displays of strength by the host nation are not missed.

Maintaining authority

Stability of any society is based largely upon political organization, which establishes order within the occupied territory. In traditional societies, where human interaction is limited and cooperation is essential, custom, taboos, and respect for elders maintain authority. Much the same system remains in small rural communities where families are interdependent and regulations are directed against outsiders. Running the rebels out of town is still common, but now they have "hot wheels" rather than a "loose gun."

In larger political units, and particularly in metropolitan societies where man is independent and largely anonymous, man's inhumanity to man increases. Cooperative behavior gives way to competitive behavior in the city, and this necessitates external regulation. Laws and codes of discipline are enforced to help maintain acceptable forms of social conduct. A professional police force is supported collectively, and elaborate private security measures are sought in the form of doormen, walled communities, guard dogs, and burglar alarms.

The urban situation is stressful and competitive. Life is circumscribed, not by custom, but by regulation enforced by governments created in the tradition of collective authority. Despite its turmoil and regulation, urban life is exciting. It seems to energize man's insatiable curiosity, his inventiveness, and his intellectual capabilities. Individuals living in an urban complex suffer from noise, polluted air and water, crowding, congestion, overstimulation, and paradoxically, for some, isolation. Yet, they also enjoy novelty, sustained innovation, and freedom from conformity. They are also better paid, better informed, enjoy varied activities, and have superior medical facilities and police protection.

The search for security

Man's innate desire for security—a drive developed in infancy—is manifested by laws and regulations that safeguard life, family, property, and economic investment. To achieve security, people sacrifice the independence of solitary pleasure and abide by the restrictions of a collective authority. Security, or the lack thereof, is the explanation for many spatial patterns. Strategic sites were chosen for cities and many were originally enclosed by walls. The clustered farm villages of Europe and

Asia, as opposed to the dispersed pattern of farmhouses in Canada, the United States, and Australia, are examples of a collective form of defense.

The single-family, detached tract home that is open to the road, is a consequence of security. It is the ultimate residential expression of security after generations of protection. With rising crime rates and the use of "law and order" as a campaign issue, families are beginning to reconsider that security. High fences are appearing in suburbia. The enclosed patio and the walled community patrolled by a security force are the housing market's response to this concern for safety. The apartment tower and the block of town houses surrounding private recreational facilities are yet another spatial expression of the desire for security and community.

The choice of residence in a relatively homogeneous suburb is a further manifestation of this search for security. Neighbors of similar life styles and residences increase the likelihood of similar responses to threatening situations, and afford an opportunity for children to socialize with others possessing similar social values. Respite from urban stress is one thing a family seeks in its search for a residence.

For similar social reasons, few black families, irrespective of their incomes, choose to live in white suburbs. They prefer the better localities within black communities. This will not change until social attitudes toward race are transformed. Islands of black or Chicano residences within suburbia would provide security, as well as facilitate interaction between adults in local associations. Interaction would promote attitudinal change toward racial stereotypes and strengthen political entities by enhancing integration. Federal and state governments, through their control of banking and mortgage finance, could require such a policy in new suburban development; but they have not used their political power to achieve this social objective.

Changing the rules

Laws help to maintain acceptable codes of social conduct. But as codes of conduct change, so must the law. The government is the institution that implements change, but motivation for change comes from the demands of groups living within the society. Labor, business, professional people, and many other groups attempt to persuade the government to create laws that will protect their interests. The governmental process moves slowly. Who gets what, when, and how is usually decided only after protracted debate, but in this manner government is able to accommodate diverse interests. Acceptable forms of conduct are usually maintained, the state survives, and people are able to live and work together in tranquility.

The political process originates from this desire for security. It was exhibited in man's initial aggregation into tribal associations, and is manifested today by the way individuals attempt to protect their own interests by competing for advantage in local, state, and national governments. The outcome of this competition has a profound effect upon the manner in which man uses land. Where and how he builds houses and factories, the location chosen for freeways, and the crops grown in response to agricultural programs are all the outcome of political decisions.

INTERACTION AND INTEGRATION

The concept of interaction is a convenient way in which to explain the political process. Whereas the quest for security leads to the creation of political authority, interaction within the political unit is the means by which the unit survives and sustains its power. National units provide the best example, although similar processes operate at the local level.

A political unit is strengthened by pursuit of the following objectives:

1. The peaceful solution of disputes
2. Legitimizing authority through ceremonies
3. Protection against external aggression (armed forces) and internal revolution (police and armed forces)

Interaction in the form of communication is essential to the achievement of the first two objectives. A national language and effective communication systems aid integration by facilitating the exchange of goods and ideas throughout the political unit. However, they are seldom uniformly available, even in technologically advanced nations. Different linguistic regions within the same political unit and areas where communications are poorly developed curtail interaction and weaken allegiance to the state. Core areas of national identity, in which there is much interaction, can be differentiated from isolated areas where communication is obstructed by language, socioeconomic, or physical barriers. The capital region and major metropolitan complexes are usually well integrated through frequent interaction, but rural areas—especially those where the economy is self-sufficient—are not integrated and weaken the state.

South Vietnam is a tragic example of our failure to realize the importance of interaction. The lowland areas about Saigon and the Mekong Delta were socially and psychologically oriented to the Vietnamese way of life. In these areas there is a common language and Vietnamese (Animite and Annamese) people predominate (Fig. 7.2). If protected against the Viet Cong and modernized through land reform and improvement of communications, these lowland areas would have provided the foundation for a democratic state whose cohesion and economic success could have been an obstacle to Communist expansion. By contrast, the hill country of central Vietnam is dominated by non-assimilated minority groups that represent defeated aborigines and refugees from other areas. They are a fiercely independent people who speak many languages. Three-quarters of Vietnam is occupied by these hill-country ethnic groups, though they constitute only 12 percent of the population. They have never identified with either the North or the South and have preserved their independence by playing one side against the other. They resented protection if it implied allegiance, because they were incorporated into these nations without their consent. Lack of allegiance, coupled with the chaotic arrangement of hill and valley terrain, made their defense impossible.

The importance of security and effective communication to political integration is tragically apparent. Effective protection of lowland South Vietnam was not possible simultaneously with the hill-country campaigns, and the people of the lowlands lost confidence in their government's ability to afford them security.

To provide coherence within political units, governments foster policies that encourage interaction within the unit and avoid interaction outside. Some of the more obvious examples are policies that encourage the development of a collective identity and education.

Collective identity

Identity is sought in a common heritage which is celebrated in the form of parades, national holidays, anthems, flags, and rituals whose true

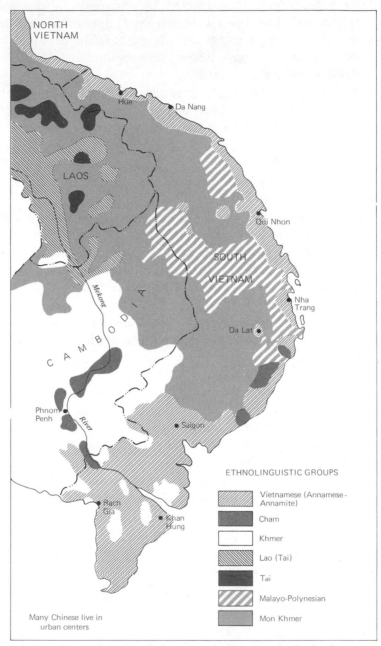

Fig. 7.2 Ethnolinguistic groups in South Vietnam: The lowland areas are predominately Annamese whereas in the highlands a variety of language groups can be identified.

meanings are often subverted as a means of promoting integration. Public monuments in the form of buildings and national parks are preserved and widely publicized. The purpose is to provide for the experience of a common history so that complementary habits and facilities for communication develop.

Capital cities are the most lavish examples of political symbolism. Canberra, Washington, Brasília, and Islamabad (in Pakistan) are political fiat cities and beneficiaries of art, architecture, and superior communications. Even the executive, legislative, and administrative sections of Ottawa, London, and Tokyo are distinctive by their spaciousness and bureaucratic architecture. They have been designed to capture the imagination of the nation and create a perception of common identity.

The same process is exhibited at state and local seats of government. Many are imitations of national capitals, such as the domed state capitals of the United States. Even the courthouse squares of the county seat in the Midwest and the town and green in New England have a symbolic form which, despite uniformity in design, are not without charm when properly maintained.

At the city level, symbolism is frequently attached to prominent features. San Francisco's Golden Gate Bridge, Saint Louis' Gateway Arch, and New York's Statue of Liberty are proud manifestations of a city's aspirations. Superlatives like "The Sugarbeet Capital," "The Hub City," or "The Birthplace of . . ." are used by smaller cities as symbols with which citizens might identify.

Integration through education

Education also plays an important role in political integration and, for the most part, it is publicly controlled. Educational institutions—particularly those at the elementary level—along with the family transmit social values and allegiance to the young. Schools also develop the skills of communication which are essential to interaction. Through education, individuals are socialized to accept the operating political system. Teachers and parents regard it as their moral responsibility to encourage acceptance of national goals and allegiance to institutions. They perform their task with little incentive and without close supervision.

By promoting the national language and developing the skills of communication, schools foster collective identity. Tolerance for bilingual education is increasing, but many school authorities continue to suppress the language of the home in favor of the state language although such repressive policies are not supported by theories of learning. A Chicano or Puerto Rican child who has learned to think in Spanish faces an enormous hurdle when expected to think and converse in English. Bilingual education would benefit such children, but few educational systems provide for it. The state language is insisted upon for patriotic rather than for educational reasons.

Education is an almost ubiquitous activity in technologically advanced nations. Schools, colleges, and universities are major occupiers of urban space, and even in remote areas where there is no store, seldom a church, and not even a gas station, a school will be located and supported by public funds. Schools fulfill a political objective by developing allegiance through the skills of communication. Other governmental institutions seek to limit such interaction.

Restraining interaction

Simultaneously with the promotion of internal communication, a state also attempts to control interaction with rival political units. Passports, health, trade, and agricultural restrictions, radio censorship, and broadcast jamming are common. This behavior, pronounced at the national level, is even practiced at the local level. Restrictions on the interstate shipment of fruit and vegetables, and limitations on milk shipments from dairies not inspected by city sanitation inspectors are examples of this.

The original purpose of such restrictions was to reinforce identity and protect against insects and disease. However, groups frequently utilize this motive to provide security against outside competition. Tariff barriers between nations are the most common means of restricting outside competition, although the reverse of this policy is exhibited by governments who offer tax incentives to promote industrial investment by foreign companies.

The influence of political decisions upon economic behavior is so pervasive that no explanation of the location of industry or agriculture is complete without attention to the role of the political process. The distribution of sugar is a good example.

Sugar is produced most economically from cane in the developing nations of the humid tropics, land and labor are cheap and the partially refined product can be shipped in bulk to consumption areas for finishing. Yet developing nations face difficulty in marketing their own crop. Tariff barriers exclude cheap sugar from many countries as a means of subsidizing domestic beet sugar production. The additional cost is paid by the consumers. In the United States, for example, both the cane producers of Hawaii and Louisiana, and the sugar beet growers in western states have benefited from the exclusion of Cuban sugar. Nationalism is promoted by protecting domestic commerce, and international cooperation is thwarted.

The political process is behavior that results from political decisions. It is a series of actions that serve to strengthen a political unit: to increase allegiance in order to make collective action possible. Integration of individuals and groups through interaction is the paramount theme. Conflict is minimized to a tolerable level; communication within is encouraged and controlled between political units. Allegiance is sought through education, symbols, national monuments, and propaganda. Each activity affects human behavior, because government is the ultimate source of authority and can enforce its decisions upon various areas.

RESOLUTION OF CONFLICT

People might live together in harmony if there could be common agreement on ends and means. But this does not happen for two reasons: first, because of conflicting aims and, second, competition between men, even between friends, is usual. The government's dilemma is to preserve competition and yet keep such conflict within bounds so that it does not destroy the system.

The creation of institutions that encourage consultation provides a means for the peaceful resolution of conflict. The judiciary explains laws, hears disputes, and ensures that the rights of law-abiding minorities are not abridged by the majority. Commissions, authorities, and special committees created by legislatures are nominally independent and serve similar functions. They are intended to be administrative bodies that will hear individuals and groups who desire to influence or avoid the restrictions of public policy. Like the courts, these institutions seek to clarify different points of view and achieve acceptable compromises within the law. When a negotiated agreement cannot be reached, the ultimate authority of the state is used to impose settlement. The use of political action to maintain social equilibrium has a profound effect upon man's utilization of land.

The choice between alternative courses of action in matters of public concern is the essence of politics. Of central importance is who gets what, when, and how; the outcome of which affects urban expansion, the location of commercial and industrial areas, and the selection of sites for airports, expressways, or universities. Economic and social elements are taken into account, but the ultimate decision is political. It represents an attempt to reconcile different interest groups who strive to influence the outcome in their favor.

Political activities leave their impress upon spatial distributions in many ways. A distinction between actions that *regulate* spatial behavior, as opposed to those that *redistribute* resources within the political unit, is useful. A further distinction between *areal* decisions that apply to the entire unit and *sectional* decisions is also appropriate in geography.

Regulative policies

As life becomes more complex, laws, rather than customs, regulate human affairs. Traffic and criminal codes, labor legislation, health regulations, tariff protection, and land-survey systems are examples of regulatory activities applicable to the entire community. These represent areal policy. Building codes and land-use zoning vary within each area. These are sectional policies.

Zoning ordinances regulate the amount of land allocated to various uses within the metropolitan area. Only a small proportion—normally 4 to 5 percent—of urban land is utilized for commerce, and seldom is all land suitable for commercial use zoned for this purpose. Local governments attempt to restrict expansion so as to avoid complaints about noise and traffic from adjoining homeowners. Because availability of land for commercial activities is restricted, commercially zoned land is three times as valuable as similar land zoned for single-family residences. Spirited political competition arises between land developers, who seek to have residential land rezoned into commercial property for banks, gas stations or markets, and adjoining homeowners who will suffer increased traffic without commensurate gain.

In the rural-urban fringe, various regulatory techniques have been employed to curtail urban expansion onto prime agricultural land. Both the nature of agriculture and land values are affected by these policies. When not restricted, agricultural land in the rural-urban fringe acquires a higher value, because land can be used for either agricultural or urban activities. A speculative value is also added because of the potential for urban activities as the city expands. The Von Thünen graph represents this additional value within the concept of economic rent (Fig. 7.3). Regulations that mandate exclusive agricultural use, such as the British Greenbelt proposals or the Stopline legislation in Northern Ireland, depress the speculative value and increase agricultural value. The inherent productivity of the land is the same, but the politically regulated use has changed. Restriction affects both land use and value.

TARIFFS AND TRADE

Canadian tariffs against American-assembled automobiles are also an attempt to regulate competition. The purpose is to safeguard investment and employment in Canadian automobile plants from plants benefiting from greater economies of scale. Also, money spent within Canada primes local enterprise rather than draining foreign funds. The result is apparent in the industrial geography (Fig. 7.4); duplicates of American assembly and machinery plants have been established in Windsor and several other Ontario communities that owe their continuance to preferential tariffs. Prior to 1968 the duty on American assembled cars was 17 percent, but this has been reduced in favor of preferential marketing agreements with American companies, in which Canadian plants specialize in certain models for the entire North American market.

There is another tariff benefit. Automobiles and automotive parts manufactured in Canada, as opposed to their American counterparts, receive preferential tariff treatment in Commonwealth countries. Britain, Australia, and New Zealand prefer to import Canadian models for this reason.

If trade across the border were not regulated by tariff and import restrictions the industrial geography of Ontario would be different. The type and distribution of industry would probably reflect, to a much greater extent, the superiority of this northern zone for the processing of mineral lumber resources. Industry would be more like the primary or extractive activities in Wisconsin, Minnesota, and upper peninsular Michigan than a replica of the secondary processing found in southeastern Michigan and northern Ohio.

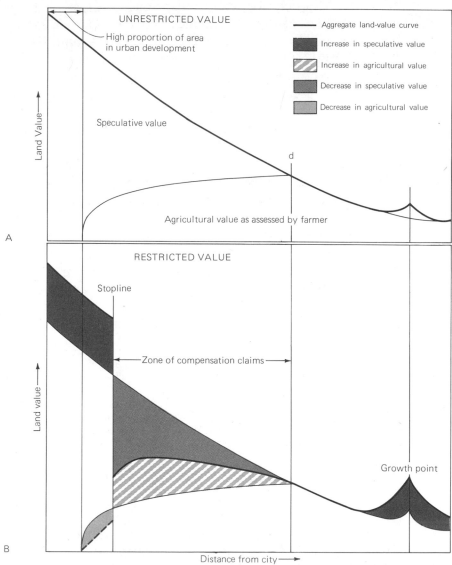

Fig. 7.3 Value of land in the rural-urban fringe before (unrestricted value) and after (restricted value) curtailment of urban expansion. Land values beyond the stopline of urban growth decline precipitously, reflecting the political limitation of land uses. Compensation was paid to land owners whose land declined in value. (Boal, reproduced by permission from *The Professional Geographer*, vol. 22, 1970, Fig. 1).

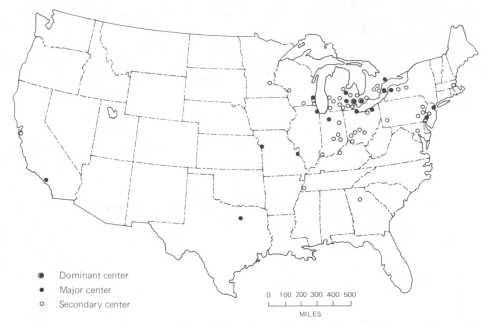

Fig. 7.4 Distribution of the automobile industry in the United States and Canada. Duplication of plants on the Canadian side of the border is a reflection of tariff and marketing agreements.

LAND SURVEY

In order to minimize conflict over property rights, states have created systems of land survey and procedures for property registration. Because the survey system is reflected in the pattern of roads and farms, it is a prominent feature of the geographical landscape. In 1784 the U.S. Government established the rectangular method of survey for new territory. The checkerboard pattern of land use and rectangular road network of the American Midwest and West is the result. Only where settlement had preceded the Northwest Ordinance, east of Ohio and in the French settlement of Louisiana, is the *metes and bounds* system used (Fig. 7.5).

The Spanish rancheros of California and the Southwest established rectangular survey systems, but these were not oriented in a north-south, east-west direction. The effect of different systems is apparent in many California cities, where roads that follow the survey lines intersect at acute angles (Fig. 7.6).

SEGREGATION AS A SECTIONAL POLICY

Segregation of people by social class and skin color persists. In most countries it is maintained by the social processes described in Chapter 6,

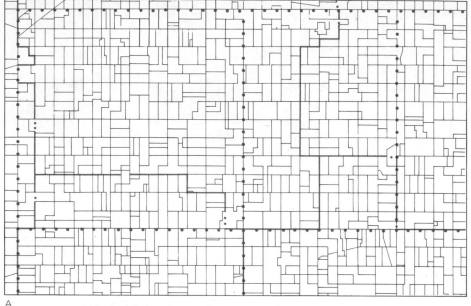

A

──────────── Public school district and property line coincident, c. 1955

• • • • • • Public school district and property line not coincident, c. 1955

● ● ● ● ● Civil division boundary (county or township)

──────────── Property lines, c. 1955

(Combinations denote more than one function.)

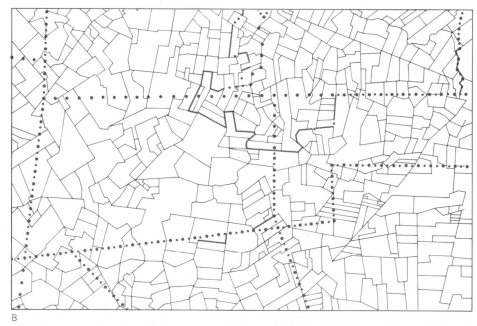

B

Fig. 7.5 Contrasting landscapes in central Ohio. Pattern of roads, and the boundaries of property and minor civil divisions differ in the two almost-similar areas. Area (A) was surveyed in a systematic rectangular manner whereas (B) is from the unsystematically surveyed Virginia Military District. Different political control after the Revolutionary War resulted in patterns of subdivision which persist. (Thrower, reproduced by permission of the Association of American Geographers, from *Original Survey and Land Subdivision*, Monograph No. 4, 1966, Fig. 22a and b.)

Fig. 7.6 Street pattern in downtown San Francisco. Note acute intersection between North-South, East-West streets based upon the U. S. Land Survey System and those surveyed under Spanish land grants in the older southern portion.

but in others it is also sanctioned by political authority. Because it applies only to designated groups within an area, it is a sectional policy.

Among the many reasons given for official segregation is the prevention of conflict. It is presumed that by restricting residential choice and employment, competition and conflict will be minimized. However, the denial of freedom by segregation, as the United States has learned, can only be maintained by escalating conflict.

Apartheid in South Africa is an example of sectional restriction. It is a policy of racial discrimination that aims to restrict the numerically large, but politically weak, Bantu, colored, and Asiatic "minorities." It is manifest, not only in the regional pattern of White Republic and Bantu Reserves, but also in every city, in every factory, and on every farm. Enforcement has been relaxed somewhat, but the regulations remain. The pattern is the result of a political attitude shaped and enforced by conservative Afrikaners. The geographical patterns that have resulted from this political process have been described by Sabbagh

(1968). The following paragraphs have been abstracted from his description and evaluation:

The Bantu Reserves, some 260 fragmented areas, occupy 13 percent of the land area of the country [Fig. 7.7]. During the past century the overpopulated Reserves have survived economically through absenteeism —work in, and migrations to, the Republic. The land is impoverished and overcrowded with people and livestock; practically no economic development has taken place, and the primitive subsistence agriculture

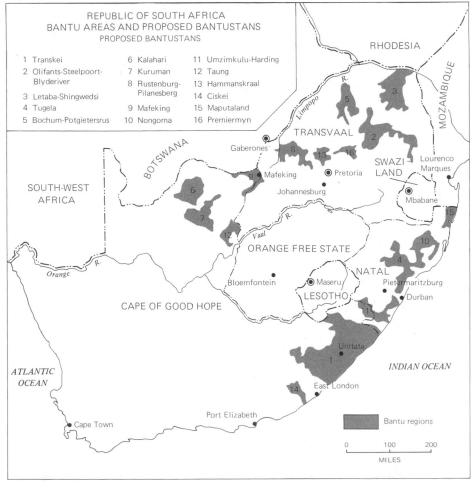

REPUBLIC OF SOUTH AFRICA
BANTU AREAS AND PROPOSED BANTUSTANS
PROPOSED BANTUSTANS

1 Transkei
2 Olifants-Steelpoort-Blyderiver
3 Letaba-Shingwedsi
4 Tugela
5 Bochum-Potgietersrus
6 Kalahari
7 Kuruman
8 Rustenburg-Pilanesberg
9 Mafeking
10 Nongoma
11 Umzimkulu-Harding
12 Taung
13 Hammanskraal
14 Ciskei
15 Maputaland
16 Premiermyn

Fig. 7.7 Bantu areas and proposed Bantustans in South Africa. Contrasting landscapes result from politically imposed resettlement. (Sabbagh, reprinted from the *Geographical Review*, vol. 58, 1968, Fig. 1.)

cannot at present support even the small proportion of resident Bantu; there are almost no mineral resources and no industry; and the population has acquired neither skills nor capital. The Republic, on the other hand, has survived a precariously lopsided economic beginning, has been sustained largely by Bantu labor, and has evolved into one of the world's most thriving technologically advanced economies, based on industry, mining, manufacturing, and agriculture.

In the last ten years the policy of apartheid has entered its final stage—"Separate Development." The crux of this phase is the development of the Bantu Reserves to support, not only their present population of 4.5 million but, eventually, the 6.5 million Bantu presently residing in white areas, and also to provide for the rapid increase in the Bantu population. As the first step, the government has embarked on a program to develop the present Reserves into economically viable units. Sixteen ethnic blocks have been delimited, from which will emerge seven "Bantustans," or Bantu states. The first Bantustan was established in 1963 in the Transkei, a region probably settled by the Bantu about four centuries ago [Fig. 7.7].

This scheme of Separate Development is an immense undertaking, beset by seemingly insurmountable social and economic problems. The economic problems by themselves are formidable. The thriving white mining-manufacturing-industrial economy has had for more than a hundred years—and will continue to have in the foreseeable future—an unbalanced dependence on Bantu labor. Present indications are that no concessions are intended with regard to the Republic's economy and that the prospective economic development of the Reserves will be hampered by political attitudes and economic prejudices.

The policy of Separate Development is basically an attempt at transformation. It is an attempt to transform a system of stratified integration which has evolved over more than a century and which is evident not only in the morphological geographical landscape but also in the whole complex functioning of South Africa as a geographical entity. Moreover, the stratified integration is the result of a long-continuing trend that has intensified during the last decade, when efforts at regional separation have ostensibly been made.

In summary, then, pluralism has reached a stage of evolution where an attempt, guided by the political policy of apartheid, is being made to reverse a well-established growth pattern. The transformation represents a radical change in attitudes toward plural development.

The Bantu Reserves are not densely populated: Relocation of population will be necessary, and this will not be achieved without hardship.

Despite the regulations designed to dissuade permanent black residency in urban areas, increasing migration has occurred in response to economic opportunity.

Bantu are allowed in the cities only by permit. They cannot own land, join trade unions or political groups, and they must reside in specified locations or in small structures a designated distance from the living quarters of their employers. The Bantu rely upon the whites for employment and the white economy is dependent upon the cheap Bantu labor. Some Bantu have been trained for specialized tasks by the government, but the vast majority are day laborers.

It is not intended for this situation to change. However, because white South Africans (one-fifth of the 16 million population) have become alarmed at the dangers of growing urban Bantu population, the policy of resettlement has begun. Bantu families will live on reservations, and workers under a permit system will be contracted for urban employment. When an individual becomes militant, his permit is canceled and he is returned to a reservation.

Redistributive policies

Redistributive policies seek to share a nation's wealth among the people. Reallocation may take the form of grants-in-aid for public works, supplementary payments, provision of public services and tax incentives for development. In all but the latter category, states use their power of taxation to reallocate financial benefit. The objective is to prevent individuals, groups, and areas from becoming so economically depressed that they are alienated and potentially disruptive to the system. The problem is economic but the motivation and implementation are political.

Health care and education are examples of areal redistributive policies: Their effect upon geography is both direct and indirect. The location and magnitude of these institutions have direct impress. As service activities, a hierarchical structure of organization is often exhibited similar to that described for commercial locations in Chapter 5. Variations in the pattern, discordant with demand, are a challenge to geographical investigation (see Fig. 7.8).

The indirect effect of superior health care and educational facilities can be observed in differential regional growth. They provide an area with a competitive advantage, and higher than average population

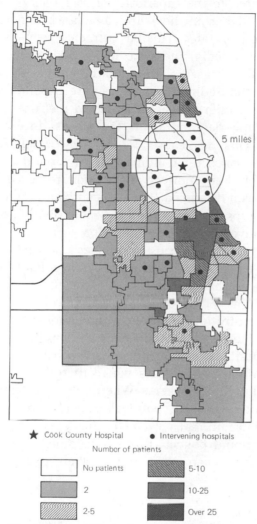

★ Cook County Hospital   ● Intervening hospitals

Number of patients

☐ No patients   ▨ 5-10

▨ 2   ▧ 10-25

▨ 2-5   ■ Over 25

Fig. 7.8 Inequality in the distribution of hospital services in Chicago. Most poor patients are forced to travel beyond closer intervening hospitals, which they cannot afford, to Cook County Hospital. Movements originating in the southeastern sector are indicative of the concentration of low-income families in this sector of the city. (Morrill, 1970, Fig. 10.1.)

growth results from migration to these areas. In market-oriented, tertiary economies, this results in economic growth and additional tax revenue for reinvestment in public services. In part, the attraction of urban areas for rural families is related to the superiority of social services.

California provides higher medical and assistance benefits to the disabled than do many other states. This has attracted people in the 40–60-year age group. Undoubtedly, the state has benefited economically from the expenditure of savings that migrants brought with them, but whether it has equaled the additional state welfare expenditure is not known. However, as most migrants have settled in metropolitan areas, they have accelerated the demand upon the state's air, water, and recreational resources. This has caused voters, who might otherwise have supported welfare issues upon humanitarian grounds, to oppose these policies because of their indirect effect upon resources. A new-residency tax has even been discussed as a disincentive to migration.

Powerful interest groups seek to control the redistribution of welfare programs in order to divert areal programs for sectional benefit. In South Carolina, for example, numerous techniques are used to obstruct black families from receiving federal welfare assistance. Paulson (1969) has shown that, given established levels of need, the more political power concentrated in the hands of an elite, the lower the level of welfare assistance. Concentration of power in the hands of a few at the county level effectively blocks application of federal welfare programs. The only consistently positive relationship observed between need and welfare assistance was in those counties where there was a high proportion of unemployed white workers. Where black voters are not organized as a competitive base of political power, traditional white preferences continue. A traditional power elite has survived, and areal policies can become sectional policies through administrational discretion. Political influence is even pronounced when redistribution is intentionally sectional.

THE SECTIONAL REDISTRIBUTIVE POLICY

The advantage that areas receive from sectional redistributive policy attracts geographical interest because of the contrasting spatial distributions that selective financial assistance is able to produce. As funds for redistribution are limited, areas and groups vie with each other for benefits. Relative influence and the skill with which this influence is used determines who will get what, when, and how.

Because of the traditional bias in favor of representation from rural areas, agriculture has been a special beneficiary of governmental assistance. Demand for agricultural produce is more elastic than supply because farmers lack the capital and knowledge to accomplish change in accord with consumer preference. Therefore, farmer organizations in most nations have sought and obtained supplementary payments to offset declining farm incomes. More often than not, this has resulted in the continuance of undesired production and embarrassing surpluses that cannot be released without undermining prices in international markets. Nevertheless, subsidized prices continue and are a major determinant of crop patterns. In Texas, for example, the two most important factors that affect farm incomes are rainfall and the level of federal support payments. Without subsidies and tariff protection there would be little cotton or sugar beet production in the United States. Even wheat production would be drastically reduced since Canadian growers produce superior wheat at less cost (Fig. 7.9). To counteract this, American farmers have replaced wheat with barley and raise more sheep. This produces contrasting crop and livestock associations in the vicinity of the border. The avowed purpose of these programs is to encourage local production and avoid dependence on foreign suppliers. However, subsidies are sought by farmers as a means of maintaining their income to offset the harsh reality of changing demand in an industry that is slow to modernize. Subsidies are pacifiers that help keep voters happy during economic transition.

The allocation of cotton acreage provides an excellent example of sectional redistributive policy. Commercial surplus of grain and fiber crops in the mid-1920s, coupled with the Great Depression were ruinous for many farmers, especially for the small cotton growers of the Old South. They lobbied for federal assistance and even threatened to riot. Various legislative proposals were made in response to the demands from agricultural interest groups, which culminated in the Agricultural Adjustment Act of 1933. Under provisions of the act, hundreds of cotton farmers entered into contracts to reduce the acreage planted to cotton in return for benefit payments.

Cotton was a way of life in the Old South, and there was widespread local support for the reallocation of federal funds from the more affluent Northeast. Southern congressmen used their seniority advantages and skill to maintain financial assistance. However, the Old South was not the principal beneficiary. Subsidy payments through

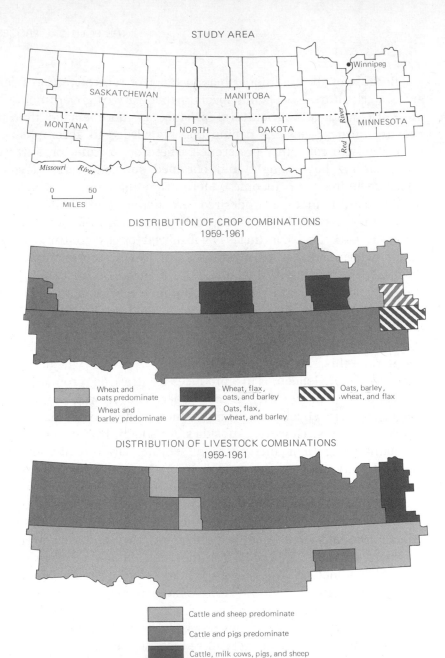

STUDY AREA

SASKATCHEWAN

MANITOBA

• Winnipeg

MONTANA

NORTH DAKOTA

MINNESOTA

Red River

Missouri River

0   50
   MILES

DISTRIBUTION OF CROP COMBINATIONS
1959-1961

Wheat and
oats predominate

Wheat, flax,
oats, and barley

Oats, barley,
wheat, and flax

Wheat and
barley predominate

Oats, flax,
wheat, and barley

DISTRIBUTION OF LIVESTOCK COMBINATIONS
1959-1961

Cattle and sheep predominate

Cattle and pigs predominate

Cattle, milk cows, pigs, and sheep

Fig. 7.9 Contrasting crop and livestock associations along the U.S.–
Canadian border. These contrasts result from differing governmental
policies. Because of the wheat allotment program in the United States,
much of the former wheat land was transferred to barley. For similar
reasons, sheep are more important on American farms. The National Wool
Act of 1954 encourages farmers to raise sheep by paying a guaranteed
"incentive" price for wool. This incentive is not available to Canadian
farmers who find it more profitable to raise pigs as they are protected
by tariffs from American competition. (Reitsma, reproduced by permission
from *The Professional Geographer*, vol. 23, 1971, Figs. 1, 3, and 5.)

governmentally supported prices were available to all American farmers. Ranchers in the irrigated areas of West Texas, California, and other parts of the Southwest could grow superior cotton at lower prices. It became their most profitable cash crop on irrigated land and a new system of acreage limitation had to be introduced to curtail surplus production and yet give the Southern small farmer a satisfactory income.

In 1954 acreage allotments in cotton were automatically applied because the production in the previous year had exceeded demand. The acreage in cotton was to be reduced by 5.5 million acres (22 percent) over that planted in 1953. In order to protect the older producing areas, the reduction formula was based upon average production over a long period of years. Counties within states that had only recently commenced cotton production were to suffer disproportionately. Counties within the Old South were reduced to 75 percent of their 1953 acreage, whereas in the Southwest, farmers were reduced to 65 percent.

It is easy to be cynical about political influence in agriculture without considering the benefits of such influence. Supplementary payments have assisted adjustment to new economic conditions in the South and ensured that adequate domestic cotton was available during peak wartime demand. Aggregation of smaller properties and mechanization, both made possible by artificial prices, reduced farm population and the voting power of the cotton lobby. As military and urban programs have loomed large, support for agricultural assistance has waned. And in the fall of 1970, limitations were placed upon the dollar amount any farm could receive for a subsidized crop. As interest-group strength has shifted to other sectors, new redistributive programs benefit from federal largesse.

Agriculture is not the sole beneficiary. In the United States, traditional industries like footwear in the Northeast and textiles in the Southeast are recipients of indirect aid through tariff protection. Tax incentives are the most popular method governments use to assist industry. Additional depreciation allowances and special deductions are offered as incentives to industries in economically depressed areas. Exemption from state and local taxation is even granted by some localities in their drive to attract industry as a base for economic development.

Many hypotheses to explain locations for industries and public facilities can be advanced if students are aware of the role of the political process in decision-making. Seldom is the optimal economic location chosen: Either the personal desires of management or some political incentive tends to be influential.

THE LOCATION OF PUBLIC FACILITIES

Political influence is even more apparent in the location of public facilities. Because of their effect upon economic development, areas compete for the location of highways, river and harbor projects, irrigation schemes, government offices, and universities. The reverse occurs when localities seek to avoid the noxious effects of freeways, airports, and sanitary schemes; these are more likely to be located in politically weak areas.

Geographical literature provides many examples of the impress of political influence upon location decisions. In *Programmed Case Studies in Geography*, the adoption of a freeway is used to illustrate this process at the local level. The Suggested Readings at the end of this chapter offer additional illustrations.

Another relevant example of such political influence is the selection of a site for a state university. Most new universities have been located on parklike campuses in affluent suburbs. The futuristic cement towers of the University of Illinois' Chicago Circle campus within the inner city are a tribute to both the power of the City of Chicago and the skill with which Mayor Daley intervened against suburban interests. The struggle for the location reveals the interplay of geography and politics in decision making on a controversial issue. The result has had a profound effect upon the geography of the entire neighborhood. Kasperson (1965) described what occurred during the site selection as follows:

Miller Meadows, a county forest preserve in a western suburb, was one of the earliest sites under serious consideration. Strongly recommended by a real estate research organization which had been hired to recommend sites, its chief advantages were that it was inexpensive ($.29 per foot with a total cost of $3 million) and had a reasonable accessibility (55.4 percent of the potential students were only an hour away by public transportation). Furthermore, Miller Meadows boasted the added attraction of scenic beauty. On June 27, 1956, in the face of powerful opposition from the Advisory Committee of the Board of Forest Preserve Commissioners, the Board of Trustees of the University of Illinois selected Miller Meadows as the site for the new campus.

Legal difficulties and political opposition persistently hamstrung plans for this location, however, so that in early 1959 the Board of Trustees concluded that the adjacent Riverside Golf Club should be the site. At this juncture, Mayor Daley intervened. At a meeting of the Board of Trustees on February 23, 1959, he announced that the City of Chicago would defray any extraordinary cost arising out of the selection of alternative sites in Chicago as compared with the cost of the Riverside Golf Club location. In effect, this action allowed for a large number of alternative sites which were formerly economically unfeasible. A proposal to use Meigs Field was rejected because the city wanted to retain its services as an airport. When the Board of Trustees selected Garfield Park, Mayor Daley again countered with a successful proposal to locate the campus on Chicago's near west side.

In terms of political benefits, the near west side location possessed several important advantages. Strong support for this site was provided by local business interests, such as Sears-Roebuck Company, whose main plant was threatened by neighborhood deterioration. Second, inhabitants of the core area and inner zone gained the advantage of a sizeable new source of employment and ease of accessibility for attending the University. Finally, the approved plan pleased many voters in the frontier zone of competition and the outer zone, because the plan included an extensive urban renewal and conservation plan which would eliminate the city's worst slum district and supplant it with an intellectual center. Moreover, two-thirds of the financing necessary for the project would be provided by federal sources.

Mayor Daley's adroit political maneuverings serve to illustrate the effectiveness of the politician's tools. To obtain a favorable decision on his proposal of the near west side site, his administration took the following actions. First, the city arranged for the University to secure more than twice the amount of frontage along the Congress Expressway than was originally planned. In addition, elimination of a portion of the site originally proposed prevented the campus from being split by a major thoroughfare. Second, the city administration and the Chicago and Clearance Commission pledged a new urban renewal program for the provision of new private apartment buildings in the area. Third, Mayor Daley guaranteed that city housing agencies would "push" a large community conservation program to the west of the campus. Finally, Mayor Daley's proposal conveniently received support when prominent business and civic groups announced that the city would contest the legality of the alternative area (Garfield Park). A visible grain of truth can be found in the angry remark of Sam K. Lenin, President of the Garfield Park Chamber of Commerce. "Our Garfield Park site has been overpowered by the downtown money interests and outmaneuvered by the Chicago politicians."

The campus, the expressways that run along two sides, and the adjoining urban renewal program all result from government expenditure. Not all sections of the political community can benefit simultaneously, because public funds are limited. Those with power and influence are able to determine who will benefit and the resentment on the part of the losers is understandable.

POWER AND POLITICAL INFLUENCE

It is easy to become cynical over the importance of politics in societal decisions. But outcomes are determined as much by lack of interest as they are by the participation of those who have a stake in the outcome. About two-thirds of the population is apolitical. Participation, if any, is limited to voting, and in local affairs many do not even exercise this option.

Political influence is, therefore, distributed unevenly. Those who participate regularly are more effective. However, one of the great strengths of the democratic system lies in the ability of individuals and groups to mobilize their political resources and to compete in decisions in which they have interest. For a large corporation, these resources might be money and legal skill. For students, they consist primarily of time. Each has a place and, if used skillfully, can influence the outcome of political decisions.

When explaining the outcome of political decisions such as the selection of a university site or freeway route, geographers utilize the concept of *political power* as developed by political scientists. It provides a means of estimating the power of any individual or group relative to the power of all other groups who choose to participate.

The political power of an interest group is dependent upon its cohesiveness: the more cohesive a group, the greater its power. This gives an advantage to corporations who can dictate company interest and mobilize resources in support. Special-purpose groups, such as dental and medical associations and unions, have a similar advantage, although the range of their effective influence is limited to specific issues. On other issues they are ineffective.

Although cohesiveness is important, the effective power of a group is an aggregate. The resources (money and time), position (offices and roles held) and political skills(ability to debate, negotiate, and arrange allies) that members possess constitute group power. These attributes can be estimated relative to other groups who choose to participate. This is the *power quotient* for the group.

Power in and of itself is not sufficient to determine policy. Groups must be prepared to utilize their power in order to influence decisions. Frequently, the most powerful are disinterested or preoccupied with other problems. The billionaire industrialist is potentially far more powerful than his chauffeur, but the latter, who has ample spare time and is president of the local Democratic Club, may have more influence than his employer on issues such as where the new hospital will be located or whether urban renewal is initiated.

A model of political power

In an attempt to clarify the difference between power and influence, March (1966) distinguished between potential power and committed power. He hypothesized that the outcome of an event would be determined by the ratio of one group's power to the power of all other groups participating in the decision. The power of the group on a specific issue would be a function of total group power and the proportion of that *potential* power a group was willing to commit to that issue. In *Programmed Case Studies in Geography*, you will have the opportunity to use this model to analyze an urban policy issue.

The advantage of this approach lies in its avoidance of the fallacious assumption of a *power elite*. Too much influence over decisions is usually ascribed to elected and appointed governmental officials: They and their circle of friends are reputed to control what happens. When individual decisions are analyzed by observing who participated and to what extent they became committed, a pluralistic interpretation is usual. Many groups participate in public decision making. Sometimes one group may gain control of a particular sector, but it is virtually impossible for them to control all sectors simultaneously. Negotiated settlements are observed much more frequently. Only where decisions are made without competition is an unfair advantage achieved. This latter circumstance occurs most frequently in small nonpartisan cities, rather than in metropolitan, state, and federal affairs.

The political game

Politics is a game in which rival groups participate to influence outcomes. The stakes are high, and competition is vigorous, but generally legal. Insofar as government is able to resolve conflict peacefully, it is essential to human endeavor. Where there is no common agreement as to social objectives, political decisions are required so that economic and social life may continue. Fair competition between groups and the various institutions of government is the essence of democracy.

The very diversity of political life limits coercion. It is impossible under the democratic system to control the game in all spheres for very long. It is more like a tournament than a game, with events occurring simultaneously in several arenas. Groups participate according to their interests, and through such competition the public interest is established. In this way, locational decisions are made for universities, freeways, and airports, as well as those concerning legislative decisions on tariffs, subsidies, and tax inducements. All have a profound effect upon the way man chooses to use land. Through the interaction of groups within political systems, decisions are made and new geographical patterns emerge. Communication between the groups is essential because issues can then be resolved peacefully.

COMMUNICATION AND POLITICAL INTEGRATION

Communication is characteristic of, and basic to, human behavior. It develops faculties for thinking, controls how people think, and determines whom they perceive as thinking similarly. Language and gestures are the vessel of meaning for man and are vital to social order. Therefore, governments seek to extend and control education and communication systems as a means of strengthening allegiance.

There are four types of communication that affect political integration:

1. Verbal communication, in which issues can be discussed person to person, person to group, or what is most familiar in contemporary politics, person to mass.
2. Symbolic communication, used to emphasize or supplant verbal communication, is achieved through movements of the body. Hands, arms, and even fingers are used symbolically. Facial expressions, movements of eyes, and direction of attention all hold meaning. Even distance between communicants is a silent language which differs between cultures. The Englishman moves back but the Frenchman moves in to clarify a contended point.

3. Visual communication that enhances allegiance by enabling individuals to identify with their leaders, and with the state through ceremonies, public buildings, and monuments. The towering presence of the cathedrals in West European cities helps to create psychological communities. Imposing capitol buildings and city halls are designed to achieve shared allegiance.
4. Communication through the movement of goods that results in exchange between areas. Through the reciprocity of other goods or money, transportation stimulates interaction.

Without an adequate communications network democratic government cannot be sustained. Communication strengthens government by creating a culture in which political goals are shared. It also enables leaders to rule by consent rather than coercion. Where communication is impeded by linguistic and physical barriers, as in South Vietnam, the state idea is not shared. Integration is achieved only where there exists complementary facilities for communication: radio and television, a national language, and extensive transportation systems. Each is an example of communication systems supported by governments to achieve political integration. Each deserves separate attention, but because of the importance of transportation in geography, illustrations will be chosen from this type of communication.

Facilitating communication

Constructing highways and railroads by means of governmental assistance programs has been a primary method used to integrate political units. Railroads served this purpose well in the nineteenth century, and in the twentieth century road building and airport construction have been important.

The Interstate Highway System linking the metropolitan centers of the coterminous United States demonstrates the influential role of government (Fig. 7.10). Initiated in 1957 for defense reasons, the system has transformed the American way of life and reshaped land-use patterns. Within two decades the Interstate System and other freeways have suburbanized the cities and metropolitanized rural America. Few areas are now beyond the daily influence of metropolitan life as 96 percent of the population are now within commuting time of an urban center of 30 thousand people or more (Fig. 6.19). The cleavage be-

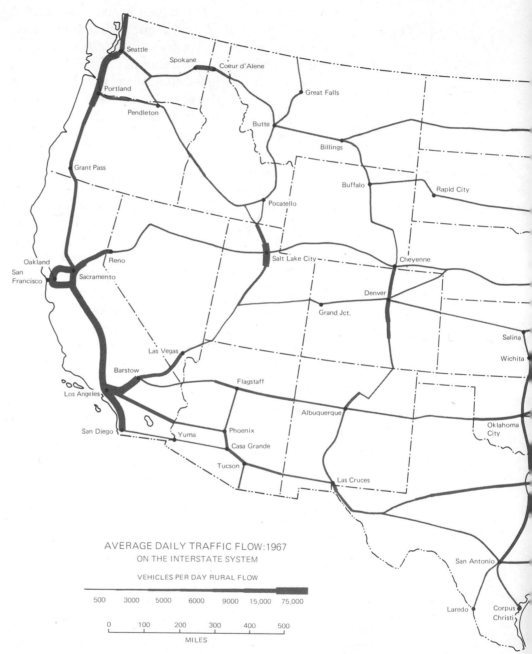

AVERAGE DAILY TRAFFIC FLOW:1967
ON THE INTERSTATE SYSTEM

VEHICLES PER DAY RURAL FLOW

500   3000   5000   6000   9000   15,000   75,000

0   100   200   300   400   500
MILES

Fig. 7.10 The Interstate Highway System. Highway construction has placed 96 percent of the American people within daily commuting range of urban centers. Only

mountainous and arid areas, together with the sparsely populated farmland of the High Plains, remain rural. (After *The National Atlas of the United States*, p. 227.)

tween urban and rural America has been reduced by metropolitanization: a process accelerated by freeways, built by state highway departments and funded primarily by the federal government with money acquired by taxing sales of gasoline, automobiles, and accessories. As a result of the increased interaction between urban and rural areas, the nation is more cohesive in attitude, even if less stimulating because of its homogenization.

In the mid-nineteenth century, railroads acted as a cohesive force in new nations. In Europe, Germany best exemplified the role that rails could play in creating a national state and, as the Canadian nation came into being at almost the same time, railroads were suggested as a means of stimulating nation building through interaction.

When the confederation of the British North American colonies into one dominion was suggested, the Maritime Provinces made it a condition for their joining that the Intercolonial Railway linking Montreal, Quebec, and St. John, New Brunswick be built (Fig. 7.11). The condition was met and the Confederation came to pass in 1867.

Even the location of the route was decided politically. It was to be an all-Canadian route and for defense reasons, as far removed from the American border as possible rather than cutting across Maine as does the present Canadian Pacific Railway. The railway was an economic failure. Its reason for existence and its location were political.

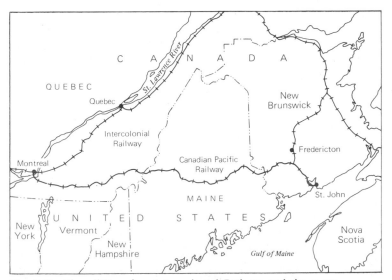

Fig. 7.11 The all-Canadian Intercolonial Railway and the more recently constructed Canadian Pacific Railway. (Wolfe, 1963, Fig. 4.)

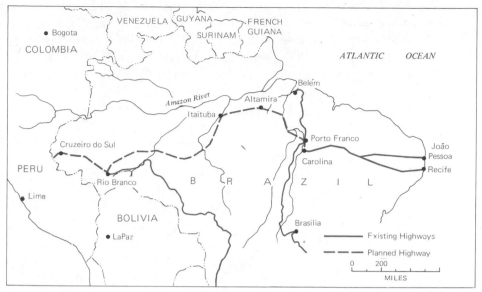

Fig. 7.12 The Amazonian Highway. The proposed route bisects Brazil's tropical interior and facilitates interaction between the isolated western provinces and the economically advancing Atlantic provinces.

However, its economic failure was more than compensated for by its political success.

Brazil has adopted a similar policy of territorial integration, but roads replace rails. The Amazon Basin has always been marginal to Brazilian economic life and the sovereignty of western territories has been disputed with Peru and Bolivia. The Trans-Amazon Highway now under construction is an attempt to nationalize the Amazon Basin through interaction. A monumental 2480 miles are to be carved through the tropical rain forest, with its rampant revegetation, seasonal flooding, tropical diseases, and sometimes-hostile Indians (Fig. 7.12). Economic rationalizations have been advanced, and 6 miles on either side have been reserved for state-sponsored settlement schemes, yet political integration is the primary motivation.

Restricting communication

For reasons of political allegiance, interaction between political units is restricted. This is most obvious between adjoining nations, but also occurs between states and municipalities.

Development of the Australian railways reflects the former independence of each state. Until federation in 1901, Australian states owed more allegiance to Britain than to each other. In order to obstruct interaction between states, rail gauges were established at different widths (Fig. 7.13). Goods from interior New South Wales could not be sent to Port Melbourne, Victoria, without transshipment at border railway stations. Since federation, many of the older lines have been replaced by standard-gauge lines.

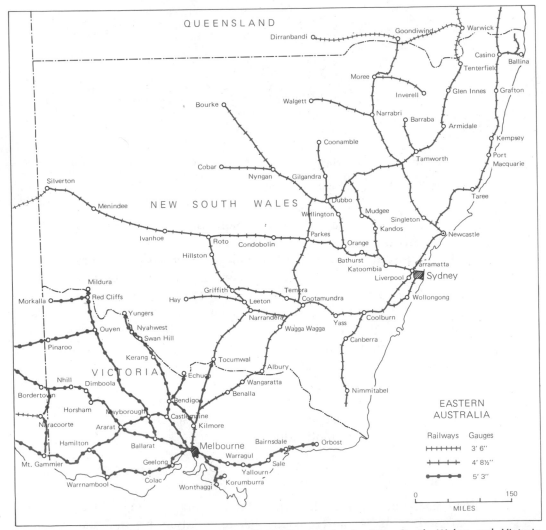

Fig. 7.13 Railway networks and railway gauges in New South Wales and Victoria, Australia. The focus upon Sydney and Melbourne persists although the major lines have been changed to standard gauge. (After *Oxford Atlas for New Zealand*, 1960, p. 21. Reproduced by permission of Oxford University Press.)

Australia has outgrown colonial attitudes, but the separation resulting from these attitudes persists. Towns that originated as border transshipment centers survive as market towns. Intrastate transactions in commerce are preferred and reinforced by state-controlled education, utilities, and the marketing of some agricultural products.

Differences in railroad gauges within connecting routes are common throughout the world, although obstruction of interaction is only one of the reasons. The distance between rails on a standard-gauge railroad track is 4′ 8½″ but there are no fewer than thirty-nine different railroad gauges in use today. The diversity is a result of many factors: inability during earlier stages to see that railroads would be linked; technical disagreement as to the best gauge; shortage of capital; the desire to prevent competition; and military strategy. The military advantage was illustrated in World War II when the advancing Russian troops could not use the German railroads because the retreating army destroyed the rolling stock and the Russian equipment was built to operate on a different gauge.

Human decisions are the result of a variety of causes, some acting separately and others simultaneously. The emphasis given to the political process in this chapter is not intended to preclude other influences. Rather, it is intended to clarify understanding of the political process as *one* of the multivariate factors influencing spatial distribution of phenomena.

COMMUNICATION THEORY

Geographers have long been concerned with the viability of political units: the components that tend to integrate a political region (*centripetal*), and those that are disruptive (*centrifugal*).

Because of the concern for areal differentiation, emphasis in political geography has been focused upon those structural features of the state that affect its ability to function as a politically organized space. Capital cities, communication lines, trade, linguistic divisions, and physical barriers are featured in these studies. This tradition continues, but the analysis of *transactional flow* between areas has offered geographers a fresh perspective on the fundamental processes that bind people together as cohesive political organizations.

A *transaction* is defined as an exchange between units that involves the communication of information or transfer of people, goods, or services. Transaction is a synonym for interaction. The measurement of transactions completed is used as an index for estimating the degree to which people are connected with each other. However, integration between areas need not be positively correlated with high levels of transaction. Many other factors also affect *salience*, or mutual awareness. Salience can lead to positive or negative reaction, to cohesiveness as well as conflict, depending on the kinds of information exchanged. Therefore, transactions leading to positive reaction (mutually rewarding) are distinguished from those that are threatening (mutually depriving).

Soja (1968a) has illustrated the integrative role of communication in East Africa. By analyzing telephone traffic in East Africa before and after Kenya, Uganda, and Tanganyika achieved independence he obtained a surrogate for interaction (Fig. 7.14). Because communication is vital to political integration, Soja hypothesized that the density of transaction between areas provides an indicator of changing patterns

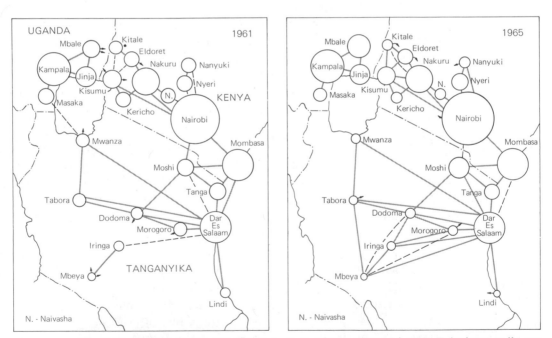

Fig. 7.14 Salient transaction flows in East Africa, 1961 and 1965. Telephone calls are used as a surrogate for interaction. Size of circle is proportionate to all trunk calls between all centers in each time period. The linkages between the three colonies were interrupted after independence except for the coastal link. (Soja, 1968b, Figs. 1 and 2.)

of mutual awareness (salience). The positive or negative content of the messages was not considered.

A variant of the gravity model is used to determine salience. The model presumes that the number of transactions from area *A* to area *B* will reflect the relative attractiveness of *B* within the entire system to which *A* may send or receive messages. Attractiveness is determined by a common measure of magnitude, such as the proportion of all messages in the system originating and received by *A*.

Many forces affect the pattern of communication, such as the friction of distance, political boundaries, and cultural and economic differences. By establishing where deviations from the expected value occur, geographers are able to focus upon these other variables utilizing multivariate analysis to establish relationships.

Soja recognizes many limitations in his pioneer study. However, it does demonstrate the utility of transactional flow analysis as a measure of territorial integration. His conclusions, as they pertain to the political geography of East Africa, may be summarized as follows:

1. The primary factor shaping the patterns of salient relationships between areas was the existence of international boundaries.
2. The repelling effect of boundaries increased after independence as a result of each nation's striving to achieve political identity and win allegiance from people in frontier zones. The original bright prospects for East African federation soon disappeared.
3. The most isolated of the three former colonies was Uganda, where political boundaries constitute formidable barriers to interaction with adjacent areas in Kenya and Tanzania.
4. In contrast to communication between states, physical proximity was the most important variable affecting intrastate communications. The population mass and friction of distance are more reliable predictors of communication flow when international influence is removed.
5. Internal communication in Kenya is further split into two networks, one focusing on Nairobi and the other on Nakuru. This reflects ethnic and political divisions that could develop into a disintegrative form of regionalism.

The application of transactional flow analysis to telephone traffic in East Africa yields conclusions pertinent to the spatial impact of political behavior. Leaders of Kenya are well aware of the need to curb regional isolationism by extending communications. Priority has been given to the improvement of road links. The use of television has been extended to the coast and the "Voice of Kenya" and the Kenya News Agency have been created to stimulate the diffusion of national information. Vast programs of agricultural resettlement and industrial development in outlying areas have also been undertaken to deemphasize the concentration of economic activities in the former White Highlands about Nairobi. However, even in government-sponsored development, the function of communications is apparent: The accessible areas, those within or adjacent to urban centers, receive the most aid.

In a more detailed study entitled *The Geography of Modernization in Kenya*, Soja (1968b) has demonstrated the uneven pattern of economic development (see Fig. 1.7). Proximity and accessibility to the major urban nodes, and communications lines between these nodes, is cited as the most important variable affecting the spread of modernization. Nairobi is clearly the major nucleus for diffusion and the generator for the entire system.

State-sponsored railways have played a vital role in modernization. To a very great extent they have created the urban system, provided the backbone for the development of the White Highlands, stimulated the spread of Asian traders, hastened the development of African education, and established Nairobi as the focal point of social and economic communication. Political influence is apparent in all phases of economic life. This is characteristic of developing nations.

Geographers have always carefully analyzed the role of areas that have dominated the economic, social, and political life of nations. This is normally the function of the capital city, but in cases like the United States, Brazil, and to some extent Canada, where the seat of government has been moved from the largest cities, dominance is shared. Attention has also been focused upon areas that strategically control interaction between nations.

GEOPOLITICS

The occupation of strategic areas controlling land and sea communication has been for centuries the aim of ambitious rulers. British hegemony of the Mediterranean and Suez Canal in the nineteenth century and

Napoleon's and Hitler's attempts to subjugate Eastern Europe are examples. This strategy is known as geopolitics.

Several geopolitical models of world power have been proposed. They produce an over-simplistic view of world power and are dangerous because of their popular appearance and frequent misinterpretation. Such models tend to underestimate technological changes in communications and weaponry and overestimate the strategic advantage of land masses that formerly controlled interaction between peripheral areas.

The Heartland theory is probably the best known geopolitical theory (Fig. 7.15). It regards the vast Asian landmass as a power core, strategically located for mobility yet secure from maritime attack. This pivotal area was named the "Heartland," around which lay an "Inner Crescent" of partly continental, partly maritime lands and an "Outer Crescent" of oceanic powers.

H. J. Mackinder outlined the Heartland theory during the first two decades of this century. He recognized the pivotal advantage of Asia, yet he regarded the nation states of Europe as too powerful to allow the Heartland to dominate. Mackinder therefore proposed his famous dictim: "Who rules Eastern Europe commands the Heartland, Who rules

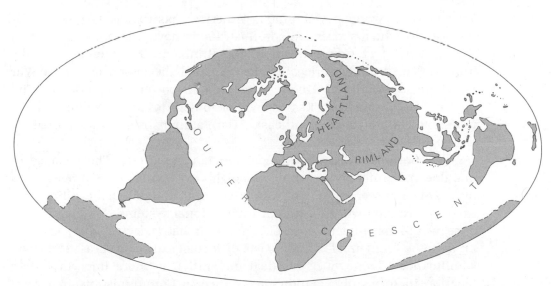

Fig. 7.15 Geopolitical map of the world. Strategic areas in land-based models of world power: The Heartland, Rimland, and Outer Crescent.

the Heartland commands the Whole Island, Who rules the World Island commands the World."

The Heartland theory continues to be popular. However, it overlooked the obstacles of language to political unification, the importance of sea and air power in national strategy, and the competition for world power among nations in the "Outer Crescent."

Spykman (1944) criticized the land-based thesis of power and called attention to the "Inner Crescent," which formed the buffer between sea and land powers. He called this zone the Rimland and advanced the hypothesis that: "Who controls the Rimland rules Eurasia; Who rules Eurasia controls the destinies of the World."

Variations of these untested models of world power persist as national strategy. As competition has developed between the Heartland (USSR and China) and the Outer Crescent (Canada, the United States, and Australia), nations of the Inner Crescent (Rimland) have become strategically more important. Competition for influence and outright conflict have developed as a result in Central Europe, Southwest, Southern and especially Southeast Asia.

American foreign policy

This view of world power among American politicians is reflected by the way in which successive administrations have attempted to contain the expansion of Communism in the Rimland. Overemphasis on the importance of strategic location has negated the lesson of World War II, where superiority of American sea and air power, as opposed to land power, was proved. It has also contributed to an unwillingness to assess the viability of Southeast Asian administrations supported by U.S. policy.

The nations of Southeast Asia are not dominoes. The collapse of one does not infer the crash of its neighbors. Control of Southeast Asia by a single power is unlikely since cultural and linguistic differences favor interaction within different international systems. American influence would have been more effective if it had selected allies and the areas to be "contained" on the basis of ideological, as well as territorial, significance. The level of political integration is more important than location in terms of a nation's resistance to Communist-inspired revolution.

Proximity is but one variable in communication. Control of strategic areas by force alone is an advantage, but is not a durable source of power as two European wars have demonstrated. Domination produces one-way communication. Effective political integration necessitates reciprocal interaction. Boundaries between adjoining nations are established to obstruct any interaction that might lead to a transference of allegiance.

BOUNDARY STUDIES

Because of their relevance to the organization of political areas, boundaries have been traditionally recognized as structural features in political geography. They are the areal expression of the limits of political jurisdiction. However, the contrasting landscapes along frontier zones assume new meaning when interpreted as the result of political curtailment of interaction between adjacent areas. The geographical impact of this process has been described in reference to transactional flow in East Africa and land-use contrasts between cities in the Los Angeles metropolitan area. There are numerous other examples.

Even between friendly nations, the boundary is marked by customs and immigration facilities designed to monitor interaction. Between unfriendly nations, defensive barriers are constructed and frontier towns become military garrisons. On either side the impress of contrasting culture and political organization is visibly apparent. Anyone who has stood in Calexico or El Paso and looked into Mexicali or Juarez, or between a divided Berlin or Jerusalem before 1967, will recognize the spatial impact that is inferred.

Appreciating the landscape differences on either side of a political boundary is an enjoyable experience for the perceptive observer. Upon crossing into Canada from the United States, differences are readily apparent. The prominence of the post office, the imperial gallon of benzene, and the new and different crops grown under a similar physical environment delight travelers and present a challenge to geographical research.

Lösch (1954) demonstrated the effect of a boundary upon commodity flow by comparing El Paso's financial hinterland on either side of the U.S.-Mexican boundary (Fig. 7.16). The difference in areal extent was explained by the dislocation by the boundary. Lösch transformed the barrier factor into a distance value and expressed the rela-

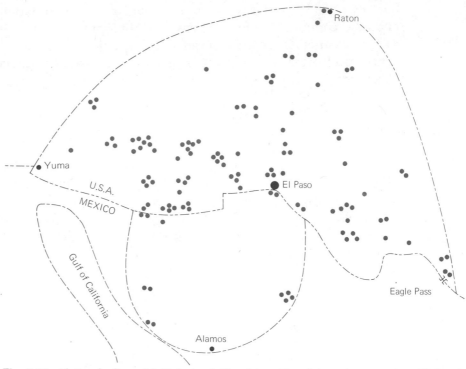

Fig. 7.16 El Paso's financial hinterland. The international boundary restricts El Paso's influence to the south. (After the *Location of Reserve Districts in the United States*, 63rd Congress, Second Session, Senate Document 485, Washington, 1914, p. 149; and after Yeates and Garner, *The North American City*, Harper & Row, Publishers, 1971, Fig. 4.7.)

tionship between boundaries and spatial organization of commodity flow as a graphic model (Fig. 7.17).

Boundaries are even more effective barriers to social exchange than to commercial interaction. Migration, marriage partners, and religious affiliation have all been shown to have been influenced by deflection of interaction away from political boundaries. Telephone traffic, as you have seen, is one means of observing the interaction, but there are others. People in Vancouver, for example, are more likely to marry partners from Toronto or Winnipeg than from Seattle, Tacoma, or Bellingham, despite the proximity of single people in the latter group.

The hierarchy of political authority as exhibited in the boundary zones is also a focus for study. In this respect the concern is over structure and its effect on the way man uses resources. Usually the political boundary of a national unit is also the boundary of provincial

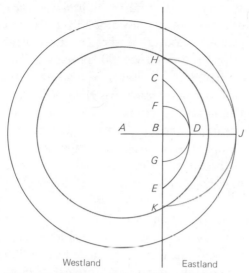

Westland   Eastland

Fig. 7.17 Reduction of market areas by a
tariff. If Eastland collects duties of a height
DJ, the market of *A* in Eastland would be
bounded by *CDE* if deliveries can be marked
directly to every point, and by *FDG*, if only
through the customhouse *B*. (After Lösch,
1954, Fig. 60.)

and local governmental units. Jurisdictional problems arise from this
multiplicity of control. These, in turn, stimulate research. This is
especially true in attempts to control pollution and develop shared
resources.

Metropolitan government

In an era of modern communications, interregional trade and environmental consequences of technological progress that spill over traditional
boundaries, there is an urgent need to develop new and more flexible
administrative systems to deal with the urban crisis. Yet the inertia of
tradition in local government is strong. Cities incorporated in previous
generations, and water and sanitation districts created to collect local
sewerage and dump it almost raw in the local river are unwilling to
submit to metropolitan, or even statewide, control. The tenacity of
local control and the inability of local government to manage the conflict arising out of any program of beneficial change is at the heart of
the urban crisis.

From the observation deck of the Los Angeles City Hall on a clear day, if such an event should ever occur again, you look over a metropolis of 7 million people. Los Angeles County contains 233 local governments, all but 8 of which have property-taxing power. Of these units, 76 are municipalities and 16 have populations over 50 thousand. There are 95 school districts, 29 water districts, 9 natural resource districts for irrigation and soil conservation, 5 cemetery districts, 4 health districts, 4 park districts, 2 hospital districts, 2 housing and urban renewal districts, 2 library districts, 1 transit district, 1 sewer district, and 3 multi-purpose districts. In addition, the county operates 239 subordinate special taxing areas and there are numerous private companies providing contract services like trash collection and hospitals for public agencies.

It is, therefore, little wonder Los Angeles has failed to control transportation, which is the basis of the smog problem, or to prevent private companies and even local authorities from polluting flood control channels and the ocean. New administrative systems that can cope with the magnitude of the issue are required, but federal and state governments are hesitant to preempt local authority. Even when legislation exists, enforcement is uncoordinated.

Los Angeles is not unique. The New York metropolis with 3 states, 500 autonomous governments, and about 1000 additional units is ungovernable. In fact, American metropolitan areas in general, consist of a bewildering maze of overlapping jurisdictions, which obstruct beneficial programs whether they be plans to reduce pollution, reorganize the police force, create a housing authority, build a new airport, or renovate structurally unsafe schools.

Geography offers many examples of political boundaries obstructing sound policies. Three examples from air pollution, water pollution, and resource development will serve to illustrate the obstruction of boundaries.

AIR POLLUTION

Air pollution does not respect political boundaries, yet the methods of its regulation are political. The difficulty is increased in the United States where regulation, usually as an element of land-use control, is delegated to counties and cities, the lowest levels of effective authority.

Although central cities control stationary sources of pollution, chiefly factories and refineries, it is not unusual to find that counties adjoining the metropolitan area remain permissive in their control. "Polluteries" choose locations outside the city and discharge their waste into the body of air shared by the entire metropolitan area. Regional control is warranted but seldom present.

Action by the federal government has been required to correct this alarming situation. Under the 1970 Air Quality Act the federal government requires each state to establish regional airsheds and to designate appropriate controls. Where different interests of political units cannot be accommodated, federal authorities have been given the power to intercede and establish standards for clean air. In 1973 the Federal Environmental Protection Agency said that California had failed to comply, and recommended a program of gasoline rationing and mass transit. Public transit was to be subsidized by a tax on parking. However, the cities objected to federal control: They would rather suffer polluted air than curtail business by increasing the cost of operating automobiles!

WATER POLLUTION

An even more tragic situation is apparent in water pollution (Fig. 7.18). The Hudson and Delaware rivers are transformed from sparkling trout streams to open sewers within their comparatively short courses. Methods of pollution control are available, but the political obstacles cannot be resolved among the many political units that control use of the river within their boundaries.

The Delaware River extends 360 miles from its source in New York's Catskill Mountains to its estuary. For the first 200 miles the water quality is excellent. But after the industrial town of Easton, the Delaware is increasingly fouled by swill and pollutants. The 70 miles between Trenton, New Jersey, and Wilmington, Delaware, is the worst stretch. This includes the cities and factories of Philadelphia, Bristol, Camden, Chester, and Marcus Hook, which draw their water from, and return their partially treated sewage to, the river.

For instance, the city of Philadelphia (with a population of 2 million) has three major waste-treatment plants, but only one is of the secondary type in which the sewerage is chlorinated to kill bacteria. The other two, so-called improved primary plants, still rely on the mere settling of larger solids before they release effluent into the river. Detergent foam and fecal bacteria are left in the river for the next downstream community to treat.

On the lower estuarine reaches of the river there are more than a hundred factories and refineries that regularly dump oil and hydrocarbons into the river after the minimum filtration process. The result,

Estimated Prevalence of Water Pollution, by Drainage Basin, 1970

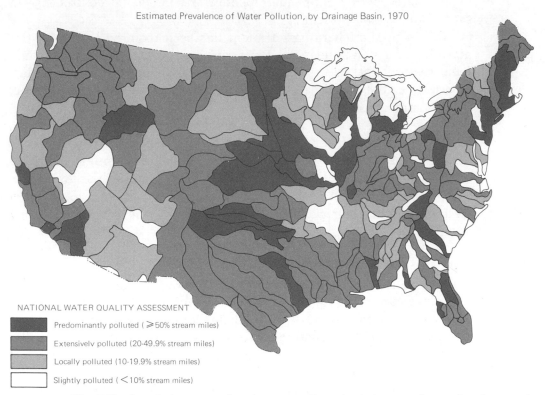

NATIONAL WATER QUALITY ASSESSMENT

Predominantly polluted (≥50% stream miles)

Extensively polluted (20-49.9% stream miles)

Locally polluted (10-19.9% stream miles)

Slightly polluted (<10% stream miles)

Fig. 7.18 America's most polluted streams. Even rivers in sparsely populated mountain areas are polluted with effluent from mining operations. Rivers through metropolitan areas in the East and portions of the Midwest are virtual open sewers. (U.S. Environmental Quality Council, 1971, Fig. 3.)

a tidal estuary filthy and foul beyond belief. The water has an oily, bluish sheen and bubbles of gas pop to the surface from decomposing matter on the slimy river bottom.

A four-state Delaware River Basin Commission has been created to enforce water quality regulations upon companies and cities. However, it will take years of political activity to correct the damage resulting from failure of communities to act responsibly in the past.

RESOURCE DEVELOPMENT

The St. Lawrence Seaway Project, a joint, U.S.-Canadian proposal that enables oceangoing vessels to travel inland to Chicago, was stalled for many years by opposition from American railroad interests. The boundary was an obstacle to participation. Only when Canada threatened to proceed alone did Congress agree to American participation.

In the West, development of the hydroelectric power resources of the Columbia River, which traverses the boundaries of three states and British Columbia, is indicative of how shared jurisdictional control can exaggerate local conflict. Washington State residents, who opposed the construction of new dams because they believed them to be responsible for the declining salmon catch, obtained support from groups outside of Washington who opposed water diversion. Their strategy was to broaden the issue and obtain allies. Mutually acceptable solutions for the power-fishing conflict were feasible at the local level, but fishing interests would not compromise. The conflict has been prolonged by the injection of interstate and international loyalties and development has been stalled. The election of a new provincial government in British Columbia has further complicated the issue, because the new administration has suggested cancellation of agreements signed by the previous one. The dams have not been built and, what is worse, the fishing is no better.

CONCLUSION

The political process exerts a pervasive influence upon the spatial distributions studied by geographers. Few aspects of human endeavor are independent of political influence. Even the development of physical resources, such as oil, coal, minerals, and forests, are politically manipulated to suit national requirements.

The desire for security provides the basic drive to collective behavior and acceptance of political restraint. As De Tocqueville explained, an individual obeys society "because he acknowledges the utility of an association with his fellow men and he knows no association can exist without a regulating force."

Security is enhanced in communities in which there is reciprocal communication between individuals, groups, and areas, and in which institutions are provided for the peaceful resolution of conflict. When security falters, a political unit is at the mercy of more powerful external aggressors and revolutionaries. Although it may continue to exist, the political unit is no longer effective, because the ultimate source of power has been usurped and it cannot enforce its regulations.

City governments within major metropolitan areas suffer this malaise. Because they are not able to solve the problems of crime, pollution, and transportation at the local level, responsibility is passed to higher levels of political authority. Cities are ceasing to function as effective political units. By force of tradition they persist, but their existence is always threatened by the more effective county authorities and special-purpose metropolitan agencies.

SUGGESTED READINGS

General

Dahl, Robert A. *Modern Political Analysis*. Englewood Cliffs, N.J.: Prentice-Hall, 1963.

Jackson, W. A. Douglas. *Politics and Geographic Relationships*. Englewood Cliffs, N.J.: Prentice-Hall, 1964.

Kasperson, R. E., and Minghi, J. V., eds. *The Structure of Political Geography*. Chicago: Aldine, 1969.

Interaction and integration

Deutsch, Karl W. *Politics and Government*. Boston: Houghton Mifflin, 1970, chap. 6.

Prescott, J. R. V. *The Geography of Frontiers and Boundaries*. London: Hutchinson, 1965.

Soja, Edward W. *The Geography of Modernization in Kenya*. Syracuse, N.Y.: Syracuse University Press, 1968.

Soja, Edward W. *The Political Organization of Space*. Resource Paper No. 8. Washington, D.C.: Association of American Geographers, Commission on College Geography, 1971.

Wolfe, Roy I. *Transportation and Politics*. Princeton, N.J.: Van Nostrand Searchlight Book No. 18, 1963.

Conflict resolution and power

Coleman, James. *Community Conflict*. Glencoe, Ill.: Free Press, 1957.

Kasperson, Roger E. "Towards a Geography of Urban Politics: Chicago, a Case Study." *Economic Geography* 11(1965):95–107.

March, James G. "The Power of Power." In *Varieties of Political Power*, edited by David Easton. Englewood Cliffs, N.J.: Prentice-Hall, 1966, pp. 39–70.

Sabbagh, J. E. "Some Geographical Aspects of a Plural Society: Apartheid in South Africa." *Geographical Review* 58(1968):1–28.

Wolpert, Julian; Mumphrey, Anthony; and Seley, John. *Metropolitan Neighborhoods: Participation and Conflict over Change*. Resource Paper No. 16. Washington, D.C.: Association of American Geographers, Commission on College Geography, 1972.

CHAPTER 8

THE PSYCHOLOGICAL PROCESS

They told me that my neighborhood was a slum. I'd always thought that it was home.

Comment of a Ghetto Child

T HE BASIS OF ALL behavior is psychological. Although it has been convenient to consider economic, social, and political behavior separately, they are intimately related, and all originate in the minds of men. Behavior is affected by the way each person perceives situations and remembers them; the way each learns and thinks about alternative courses of actions, and decides to act.

The four terms, *perception, cognition, memory,* and *decision making* will be used throughout this chapter and ought to be explained at the outset. *Perception* is the ability of the mind to apprehend objects through the senses of sight, hearing, smell, and touch. *Cognition* is the thinking about the perceptions in terms of an individual's previous experience. The cognitive process may entail recall of previous experience (*memory*) or more thorough evaluation of the object perceived. *Decision making* also involves a cognitive (thinking) process. After evaluation of a perceived object or event an individual may decide to act or not. In most instances he does not act. He ignores the perceived object. And, even if the individual does decide to act, he seldom acts in a way that will achieve an optimal solution because the very perception of the object is affected by the individual's previous experience and values.

The comment from the ghetto child captures the importance and complexity of the psychological basis of behavior. Change occurs when a person becomes disenchanted with a neighborhood. If he can, he moves and creates a migration pattern. If he cannot move, he becomes alienated and even resentful. In contrast is the behavior of the industrialist who sees (perceives) an ideal industrial site in a ghetto area, but who decides not to buy the site because he remembers crime statistics and social issues that he associates with ghetto life. The entire geography of urban areas is affected by such perceptions, memories, and the decisions that result.

Perception of and reaction to the physical elements of the environment are equally as important as is the perception of the human conditions. In any area, survival is dependent upon man's ability to perceive and learn about the physical environment. Failure to learn how to perceive and adapt to situations results in tragedy. Nowhere is this more apparent than in catastrophic flooding.

PERCEPTION OF FLOOD DANGER

After highway accidents, floods are the most common form of accidental death. Losses are highest in developing nations where population crowds onto gently sloping and inherently fertile floodplains. However, losses of life and property are also common in nations with well-developed flood-control programs.

Despite the billions of dollars that have been spent on flood control in the United States, annual losses from floods continue. Two-thirds of all states of emergency declared by state and federal agencies result from floods. Whole river basins like the Missouri have been controlled with dams and levees, and this has encouraged man to develop areas that remain hazardous when abnormal floods occur. Areas are perceived to be safe because some protection has been achieved, but people appear unwilling to remember that abnormal floods have caused tragedy in the past.

Flood control is based upon the "normal" 30-year flood; that is, the flood likely to occur at least once every 30 years. However, floods of greater magnitude—the 100-year flood—do occur. They exceed capacities of dams and channelized rivers and spill over onto land presumed to be safe. Engineers warn developers and local officials of the potential dangers, but subdivisions and trailer parks are approved. If they have good luck, and severe storms do not follow one another, they may escape damage for many years. However, occupants of these hazard zones are playing a game with nature. Residents incorrectly perceive their location as safe, but when it floods their property losses are disastrous.

The situation in developing nations is much worse than in North America. Floodplains are at a premium for food production, and farmers are willing to risk danger. In addition, dams and stopbanks are weak and communications poorly developed. Catastrophic damage results because structures collapse and people cannot be warned of impending danger. In excess of 300,000 lives were lost as a result of the cyclone-induced flooding that swept coastal Bangladesh in 1970 and again in 1971.

When hazardous events like floods are rare, memories are short-lived, and few people make adequate preparation. They fail to perceive the threat of nature because of their reluctance to face unpleasant realities. People forget the physical aspects of the accidental danger, preferring to remember the usual or unflooded years. They conjure a pleasant view of the future in which flooding is unlikely to reoccur, whereas climatologically it is anticipated. Generally, people cannot tolerate the potential threat, so psychologically they tend to minimize the probability that it will occur: They become satisfied with their present existence. Strategies that might avoid loss are neglected, or floods are assumed to be "acts of God" and beyond human control.

Empirical studies

Although there is no adequate explanation of why people misperceive hazardous situations, empirical studies have documented the divergence between perception of the problem and historical experience. Studies of the perception of floods have been conducted by Kates (1962) and White (1964), and of droughts in the Great Plains by Saarinen (1966). Some of their conclusions were:

1. When the hazardous event is rare, people's memories appear to be short and little is done to alleviate the problem. For instance, in LaFollette, Tennessee, flooding is likely to occur at least once every five years, yet only 25 percent of those endangered have made protective adjustments (Fig. 8.1).

2. Long-term residents of an area perceive the risk more realistically and are better prepared than are more recent arrivals. Repeated losses have impressed upon them the necessity for protective measures.

3. Individuals who are highly motivated toward achievement tend to be better prepared than those with low-achievement aspirations. Apparently, they are better able to perceive the danger, to think about alternative protective strategies, and then to implement their decisions.

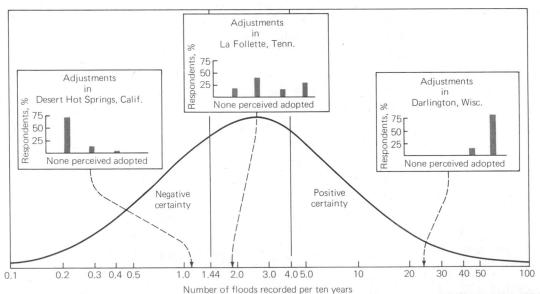

Fig. 8.1 Perception of flood hazard. Diagram relates the frequency of floods to perception and adjustment in 496 urban places. Insets show perception and adjustments at three sites. (Kates, 1962, Fig. 9.)

Potential studies

Perception or awareness of environmental hazards and the adoption of control strategies is an exciting theme for geographical research. Many hypotheses can be developed from this concept that may explain spatial organization. Students must combine their knowledge of the physical environment together with our developing knowledge of why people perceive hazards unrealistically. Two current themes for your consideration would be air pollution and earthquakes.

Why do people minimize the effect of air pollutants upon health? Why are they not willing to pay the cost of cleansing the air? The controls are known, and innovations in public transportation are available. All we lack is the commitment to implement them.

And why do we choose to neglect earthquake damage in those areas known to be subject to earth movement? The San Fernando, California, earthquake of 1971 destroyed at least three schools and damaged many others. Fortunately, the largest shocks came early in the morning, before children had arrived. More than a hundred school structures in the Los Angeles Basin are known to be unsafe. Yet, within eight months of the San Fernando quake, a school tax issue designed to provide funds to replace the unsafe schools failed to obtain the two-thirds voting majority necessary to pass the bond issue! Consequently, children still utilize these structurally unsound buildings. How should the issue be presented so that voters could perceive the danger?

Man need not be subject to these natural hazards. If he perceives the problem accurately, he has the ability to adopt control strategies that will minimize the potential dangers. He is not subject to environmental control, but can adapt the environment or his own behavior to reduce, or even eliminate, risk.

ADAPTATION

Man changes the areas he occupies through adaptation. He builds bridges, constructs houses, develops new crops and equipment in order to adapt the resources of an area for his use. Usually, those areas in which the environment is too harsh are neglected. But over most of the land surface man has adapted areas to his beneficial use through a trial and error process.

Two paradigms are utilized to conceptualize the learning process: stimulus response (S-R) and stimulus-mediated-response (S-M-R). Psychologists continue to debate the relationship of each paradigm to learning, but we will not become involved in this controversy. S-R behavior is illustrated by blinking or by our reaction to touching hot or cold. It is action that is not premeditated.

In S-M-Rs we perceive a stimulus and consider it before responding. Most of our spatial behavior falls into this category. We consider our action against previous experience and in terms of our needs and objectives before responding.

Consider for a moment your own spatial behavior in choosing a bank. Normally you have a choice, but choose the location that is most convenient. Assessment of convenience is a mediated response, because it has required a review of your own behavior to decide convenience and the assessment of banks in terms of your need for security. You remain, so long as service is satisfactory, but should they muddle the accounting or prematurely bounce your check, you may decide to change by activating a search procedure.

Searching for a new residence

The decision to search for a new residence is a mediated response to existing situations. It also involves adaptation, because an optimal residential location is seldom found, and the family must adjust life styles to suit the neighborhood. Moore (1972) has presented the decision to move as a sequential process (Fig. 8.2). The values of the individual or family create a set of expectations regarding life style and dwelling conditions. The present residence (stimulus) is evaluated (mediated) against these values and expectations, and a decision (response) is made as to whether to seek a new residence. Questions about ownership or rental, length of residence, and social ties enter into this decision. Even as the search proceeds, the individual continues to evaluate his present residential situation. A decision to remain and modify the existing structure or to readapt his life style and expectations are as likely as the decision to seek a new residence. The optimal solution has not been achieved, but the individual resolves the decision by adjusting to a satisfactory solution.

Most of our knowledge on the search for new residences comes from the files of agencies who compel relocation because of development. The movements compelled by the developments of the Boston

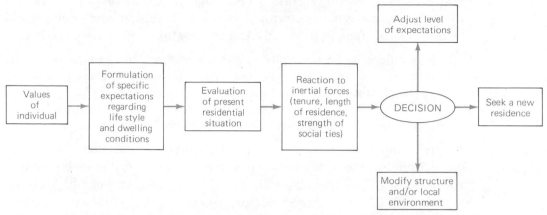

Fig. 8.2 Searching for a new residence. Individuals constrain the search by establishing criteria of need and status. Once vacant opportunities are located, they are evaluated against the existing dwelling. The stimulus is mediated before the response is formulated. (Moore, reproduced by permission of the Commission on College Geography of the Association of American Geographers, Resource Paper 13, *Residential Mobility in the City*, 1972, Fig. 5.)

West End have produced classic studies by Gans (1962) and Fried (1963). These studies reveal the degree of personal association between lower-income individuals and the neighborhoods in which they live. Real grief is expressed when such residents are compelled to move. However, among lower-income groups there are some individuals and families who value social advancement and welcome the opportunity to move out of the central city. These upwardly mobile people would probably have moved voluntarily had not relocation assistance been available. The psychological motivation was present. They were more successful in adapting to their new suburban neighborhood, and they did not grieve for their lost homes.

Environmental determinism

Failure to recognize man's ability to mediate his perceptions of the environment invalidated the environmental determinist approach, which dominated geographical thought in America during the 1920s and 1930s. Environmental determinists sought causal influences on human behavior, but they chose to view the physical environment rather than human capability as the determinant. Man's behavior was erroneously ascribed to the physical conditions under which he lived.

The determinism thesis made man a mere creature of his environment, predestined to civilization or savagery, wealth or poverty by the physical conditions within which he lived. Tradition and culture and the free will of man was denied. As Lewthwaite (1966) remarked:

> Yes, gentlemen, give me the map of a country, its configurations, its climate, its waters, its winds, and all its physical geography; give me its natural productions, its flora, its zoology, and I pledge myself to tell you, *a priori*, what role the man of that country will play in history, not by accident, but of necessity; not at one epoch, but in all epochs.

Environmental determinists adopted the S-R paradigm; that the physical environment provides the stimulus and man responds. Four to five decades ago the centers of learning and business were in Western Europe and Eastern United States, where the climate was seasonal rather than uniformly warm. The abilities of people living elsewhere were little known and their skills unappreciated. The presumed superiority of seasonal climate regimes for intellectual activity appeared justified.

As a result of anthropological research we have achieved an understanding of the complex strategy which people in tropical lands have developed to utilize resources of the lands they occupy. A sophisticated S-M-R learning process has enabled men to achieve a delicate balance between man and the land where resources are scarce. By playing games with nature, tropical farmers have selected crop rotations suited to the low-nutrient soils and unreliable rainfall. The failure of midlatitude farmers to observe these strategies against nature when they have attempted to develop tropical land has led to such widely publicized failures as the British ground nut scheme in East Africa and the American factory-farmers in Northern Queensland. In both instances, corporations attempted to develop tropical land by mechanized farming. They failed because mechanical equipment compacted the soil, and even when crops did mature they were harvested by wildlife that could not be fenced out of large fields.

LEARNING ABOUT THE ENVIRONMENT

We have limited knowledge of the complex process by which people sense and respond to their environment. The process may be portrayed schematically, but the diagram must be viewed as a simplification of a highly complex situation (Fig. 8.3).

Although our senses include vision, hearing, smell, touch, and

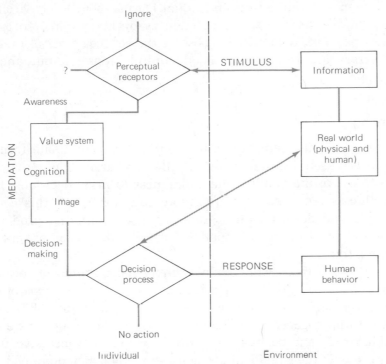

Fig. 8.3 Environmental perception and response. Perceptual receptors are continually receiving stimuli. A few stimuli result in a behavioral response. Most are lost in mediation. (After Downs, 1970, Fig. 8.)

temperature perception, most of us receive about 90 percent of our information through sight. The following sections concentrate upon criteria that relate to visual stimuli and awareness.

Adaptation of an individual to an environment involves three processes: awareness of the stimulus, thinking or meditating about the stimulus, and the decision or response. The source of information is the real world, of which individuals become aware through receiving stimuli. This information is thought about by the individual in terms of the individual's knowledge, ability, and value system. Information passed through these "filters" enables the individual to construct his image of the real world. This is a perceptual image, rather than an exact replica, because perception is affected by an individual's knowledge and values.

On the basis of this image an individual decides to act or not, or to search the real world or his own memory before acting. The decision to act is the observed behavior and the very act itself changes the environment, creating feedback as new information. Additional decisions and behavior may result as the individual learns about his environment by acting and observing the consequences of his action. Unfortunately, too few people take the time to observe the consequences of their actions and errors are repeated in flood control, conservation, and foreign policy.

Values and learning

Decisions and the behavior resulting from them originate from a complex process. Individuals differ in their awareness of environmental stimuli and in their ability and willingness to make decisions. However, the value system among men is more consistent. It is this consistency of needs and desires within groups and societies that produces regularity in the patterns of spatial behavior that geographers seek to comprehend.

In Chapter 6 you were made *aware* of the existence of social groups. It should now be possible for you to conceptualize an *image* of this type of behavior and to *decide* how it explains the clustering of families into relatively homogeneous residential areas. These groups have acquired similar needs and desires. The way in which they perceive the urban environment, their residential choice, and their neighborhood behavior reflects the consistency their value systems produce.

Segregation behavior on the basis of skin color is learned from friends or relatives. The stereotype behavior anticipated for people of white, black, or brown skin preexists in the value system and warps the manner in which individuals perceive the behavior of others. There is no causal relation between skin color and behavior. Yet millions of people erroneously behave as if there were. Segregation behavior is a fantasy which men and women develop in their attempt to organize the baffling situations of life to their own advantage. The patterns of residential segregation that were described as a response to the social process are also influenced by phychological behavior.

Judging those of a different race on the basis of their skin color is one way of relegating them to an inferior status in order to elevate oneself: This is understandable behavior, but one with inhuman consequences. The results of this behavior can be seen in the denigrating quality of life in the American urban ghetto. The nation could afford to improve these areas. However, the warped perception of the majority white population makes genuine solutions politically unacceptable.

Obstacles to learning

Downs (1970) has compared the psychological process to a communication channel. Stimuli provide the information and responses are the output. But there is rarely exact correspondence between input and output. The deviation is due to two sets of factors:

1. Noise: the irrelevant stimuli that are received from the environment in addition to the desired information. The stimulus is obscured, perception of relevant information becomes difficult, and thinking is confused.
2. Information within the organism (memories and value systems) modifies, even distorts, the stimuli before they are decoded. This information also affects the awareness process because it alerts individuals to information relevant to the value system. Cultural bias, ethnocentricity, racial biases and attitudes are manifestations of the operation of this factor upon behavior.

The analogy with the communication channel revives themes enunciated in Chapter 4. The value system that an individual acquires through language and learned traditions affects the way in which he not only perceives the world, but also the way in which he behaves.

The United States and the world face an energy crisis of major proportion because of the shortage of fossil fuels. European governments have been aware of the possible shortage for several years, and because they share a value system that implies conservation, it has been possible for them to develop strategies that have alleviated shortages. However, in the United States the consumer ethic prevails and restrictions on consumption are distasteful. In addition messages about the impending shortage were obscured by "noise" information about the vast petroleum reserves in Alaska and offshore that could be developed if the government would only provide tax incentives for exploitation and override the objections of the ecologists.

The long-range projection for mineral resources is as gloomy as the petroleum forecasts. Society cannot sustain the current rate of population and industrial growth if we remain dependent upon the known resources. Short-range technological fixes might give some relief, but a genuine conservation ethic is required if the affluent society is to survive. But progress toward a more conservationist way of life cannot be achieved if people fail to perceive the problem accurately.

The first step should be to face up to the consequences of the in-fatuation with the automobile, but the apathetic American public would not believe that there is an energy supply problem until gas stations closed and the cost per gallon doubled. Viable solutions exist through land-use controls and development of rapid transit. However, in the smoggy Los Angeles Basin, where motorists manage to burn up 8.5 million gallons of gas daily, no one is willing to assume leadership in transportation planning and resolve the political and institutional prob-lems that prevent the development of rapid transit.

PERCEPTION OF AREAS

Consciousness sets man apart from nature: It enables him to perceive the world that surrounds him and to organize it to reflect his own values and aspirations. Often the mental image that man creates is inaccurate because it is tinged by experience and warped by the opinions of friends and relatives. The patterns of agricultural, industrial, and commercial location, and the social and political processes that have been presented are affected by the psychological process. Our under-standing of both the patterns and the process will be fragmentary and superficial without some knowledge of how spatial patterns are associ-ated with conceptual images.

Through his system of values, man is able to discriminate between the welter of stimuli he receives and to organize them into sensible patterns. The values he acquires differ with his culture and within cultures by social group and geographical areas. These different value systems—more appropriately labeled in geography as views of the world —will affect appraisal of areas and resources, migration behavior, and appropriate environmental designs.

Appraisals of areas

People develop their own systems of categorizing information about places. These systems differ, not only in content, but also in complexity and rigidity. *Mental* or *cognitive maps* are terms used to describe these images.

If you are traveling in foreign countries and attempt to ask direc-tions you will quickly realize the cultural effect upon mental maps.

American and most English-speaking people tend to organize their perception of urban areas about landmarks and pathways oriented to an approximate north-south, east-west grid. But if you ask directions of a Mexican citizen in your best Spanish, he will attempt to give directions in reference to a central plaza rather than in reference to your present location. In Japan, the same problem is even more confusing for the foreigner. Even Japanese geographers become lost traversing the urban area. The urban area is organized about nodes or localities rather than pathways. Details of each node are known intimately, but the relationship between nodes is unclear.

Information about areas is inversely related to distance. Neighboring areas are known in detail, whereas information about distant areas is frequently inaccurate. The New Yorker's view of the United States (see Fig. 1.3) illustrates this perceptual distortion. Familiar areas are exaggerated, and the unfamiliar are reduced, omitted, or misplaced. Mass media further distort the image. Hollywood and Florida are prominent for just this reason.

Migration behavior

Perceptions of areas also affect migration behavior. Americans are mobile people. One-fifth of them change residences annually. This has profound effects upon spatial distributions, not only of people, but also of the functions that serve them. The most mobile groups are between fifteen and twenty-five; the period when new life styles are established. As was indicated in Chapter 6, distance and interactions with friends and relatives in potential receiving areas influence an individual's decision to migrate. However, perception of areas is also a factor.

In a study of the perception of areas by college students by Gould, it was found that perceptions differed between students in different regions (Ronald Abler et al., 1971). Local areas were preferred over distant, but certain states like California, New York, Florida, and Colorado—areas of higher income, social welfare, and recreational amenities—tend to be appraised as more desirable by students in all areas except the South (Fig. 8.4A–D). Upon graduation, students are more likely to seek employment in and migrate to those areas that they perceive as desirable.

Migration is one of the primary means used to achieve equilibrium

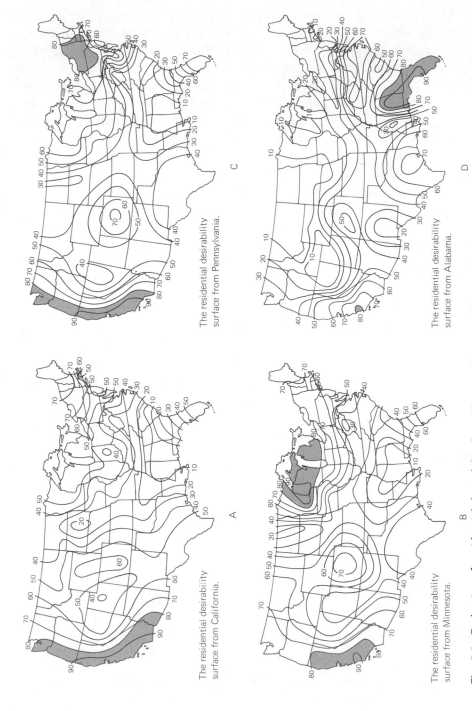

Fig. 8.4 Evaluation of residential desirability by college students at different locations. Distance, amenities, and reputation affect appraisals of potential locations. (Ronald Abler, John S. Adams, and Peter Gould, *Spatial Organization: The Geographers View of the World*, © 1971, Figs. 13.31–13.34. Reprinted by permission of Prentice-Hall, Inc., Englewood Cliffs, N.J.)

The residential desirability surface from Pennsylvania.

The residential desirability surface from Alabama.

The residential desirability surface from California.

The residential desirability surface from Minnesota.

in society. As the economy changes, people must move to new areas that have greater productivity and that they perceive as providing more opportunities. Geographers have sought to understand how this process affects international and interregional migration, rural to urban migration, and, more recently, intraurban moves. Novelists like John Steinbeck in *Grapes of Wrath*, Erskine Caldwell in *Tobacco Road*, and Sinclair Lewis in *Main Street* explore similar behavior and describe the social consequences of the move and the psychological problems inherent in adjustment.

Caldwell recognizes the social and psychological aspects of the way in which people perceive opportunities. In the preface to the 1940 Edition of *Tobacco Road*, Caldwell writes:

> It is good after ten years to look backward and to be able to see clearly how a novel had its beginning.
>
> My recollection of how *Tobacco Road* had its beginning is stark and vivid.
>
> It was in the heat of midsummer in Georgia, below the Piedmont, and I was walking along a dusty, weed-bordered, wagon-rutted road.
>
> Here I was in my own country, among eroded clay ridges and barren sand hills, a land I had known all my life.
>
> All around me were clusters of stunted, scrawny, scraggly cotton plants trying vainly to exist in the depleted soil.
>
> The land was desolate.
>
> Not far away across the fields were several tenant houses, shabby and dilapidated, two-room shacks with sagging joists and roofs. Around the buildings were groups of human beings. The children were playing in the sand. The young men and women were leaning against the sides of the houses. The old people were merely sitting. Every one of them was waiting for the cotton to mature. They believed in cotton. They believed in it as some men believe in God. They had faith in the earth and in the plants that grew in the earth. Even though they had been fooled the year before, and for many years before that, they were certain the fields would soon be showered with tumbling, bursting bolls of glistening white cotton.
>
> But I had walked along that same road and had stopped and gazed upon those same fields the previous autumn, and I did not know how many autumns before that, and I had never seen any man gather enough cotton from those stunted plants to provide himself with food and clothing.
>
> It was not difficult to survive in summer when it was warm and balmy, and when there was the vision of cotton to look forward to in

the autumn. One could always find blackberries and wild onions and, sometimes, rabbits.

But when it was fall and winter and early spring it was a different matter.

I had walked along the road in midwinter and had seen hungry people wrapped in rags, going nowhere and coming from nowhere, searching for food and warmth, wanting to know if anywhere in the world such things still existed.

They asked for only enough food to keep them alive until spring so they could plant next year's cotton.

They had so much faith in nature, in the earth, and in the plants that grew in the earth, that they could not understand how the earth could fail them.

But it had failed them, and there they were waiting in another summer for an autumn harvest that would never come.

It all had happened once before.

Not to these same people, but to their forefathers.

Their forefathers had seen tobacco come and flourish on these same plots of earth.

But after its season it would no longer grow in the depleted soil.

The fields lay fallow for many years.

Then came cotton.

Cotton thrived in abundance for several generations, and then it, too, depleted the soil of its energy until it would no longer grow.

First, tobacco, and then cotton; they both had come and gone.

But the people, and their faith, remained.[1]

Specialization is an efficient way of utilizing resources. However, the basis of specialization is continually changing. Areas that were once perceived positively because they offered opportunity and attracted migrants can become negatively perceived as resources are depleted or as new and more efficient centers of production emerge. The experience of forced relocation from rural to urban areas, which Steinbeck and Caldwell have so enduringly re-created, are classic examples of this changing perception of areas in a dynamic economy. Families were pushed out of rural areas by mechanized farming and attracted to urban areas and life styles for which they were unprepared.

The decline of central cities is a contemporary example of a similar problem. Residential areas adjoining the central city were once perceived positively because they provided accessibility to urban attractions.

---

[1] From Erskine Caldwell, *Tobacco Road*, by permission of Little, Brown and Co. Copyright 1932, 1940, by Erskine Caldwell.

The automobile changed this and provided accessibility from newer and lower-cost residential areas. The blight and decay of the central city residential areas result from the continued negative appraisal of these areas.

But who should pay for the consequences of these changing appraisals? Should the older cities pay the full cost for redevelopment that is necessitated by the relocation of the affluent population to the suburbs and that has been made possible by automobiles using freeways constructed by state and federal funds? And on the regional scale, should industrial areas based upon older coalfields be allowed to lose population because of their obsolescence? Or does the government have an obligation to intervene so as to ease the economic adjustment that results from the changing perceptions of areas?

Governmental intervention

The United Kingdom has faced two problems arising out of the changing perception of areas. Older industrial regions like southern Wales and northern England are perceived negatively because of obsolescent industries, unemployment and out-migration. In contrast southeastern England, and Greater London in particular, are perceived positively, and the urban areas are receiving more immigrants than they can accommodate.

In order to stimulate redevelopment in the "distressed" areas and to curtail population growth in southeastern England, a series of governmental programs have been introduced to alleviate the stress and modify the perceptions of areas that the changing economy has created. Haggett (1972) has summarized a four-level system of governmental assistance as follows: (1) areas of rapid growth and high prosperity, subjected to negative controls on further expansion (e.g., Greater London); (2) "normal" areas with neither positive nor negative intervention (e.g., most of southern England); (3) areas with moderate economic difficulties (e.g., Plymouth); and (4) depressed areas (e.g., South Wales) receiving the full range of government assistance. France has a similar five-stage series of zones, with metropolitan Paris and rural Brittany at opposite ends of the scale.

Vast sums of money have been spent on various programs that have included investments in public works, inducements to private companies, and incentive payments to individuals and families. However, their success has been limited, and out-migration to southeastern England has not ceased. The new factories built in the distressed areas are automated and provide few employment opportunities. Most of the new employment opportunities have occurred in the administrative and service activities of each company, and these activities tend to cluster in the favorably perceived metropolitan areas of southeastern England.

Similar migration patterns have emerged in developing nations where metropolitan areas are more favorably perceived than rural areas. In Nigeria, the young, professionally trained elite, whose experience as teachers, doctors, and agricultural development officers is desperately needed in the rural villages of their origin, prefer the urban activity nodes upon graduation (Fig. 8.5). A period of country service is a requirement in most governmental agencies in order to counter this urban preference.

Perceptual images of areas are formed through personal experience and information from numerous sources. These images, which change with age and circumstance, control the way individuals conceptualize the world and make decisions.

PERCEPTION OF THE CITY

As the Los Angeles Department of City Planning reported in 1971:

> People are angry about their environment. They are sick and tired of smog, sign-cluttered streets, the lack of sufficient parks and landscaped open space, the intrusion of unsightly uses in residential neighborhoods, and the absence of amenities for the pedestrian in shopping and business centers. Finally, the public is expressing itself and demanding that Government do something to erase the environmental problems our City faces.

Genuine solutions to these problems are obstructed by the differing perceptions of both the city and the issues. Citizens conceptualize the city from different perspectives: from the social groups to which they belong and from the area that they occupy. It is difficult, therefore, to attain a sufficient level of support for any controversial program of civic improvement. Articulate minorities, by raising dubious questions, can obstruct programs that would provide more parks, better schools, and drastically reduce air pollution. They succeed because there is no unified image of the city against which issues can be decided.

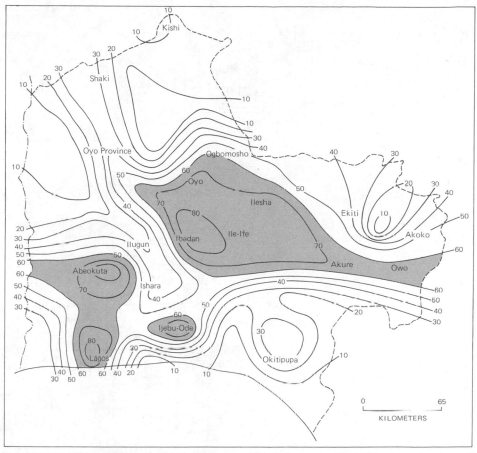

Fig. 8.5 Residential desirability for 23-year-old students in Oyo, Western Region of Nigeria. The urban nodes of Ibudan, Abeokuta, and Lagos are preferred over the rural areas from whence many of the students have come. (Ronald Abler, John S. Adams, and Peter Gould, *Spatial Organization: The Geographers View of the World*, © 1971, Fig. 13.45. Reproduced by permission of Prentice-Hall, Inc., Englewood Cliffs, N.J.; and after Daniel Ola.)

Image of the city

An image of the city is a bag of memories. It consists of paths, edges, nodes, districts, and landmarks (Figs. 8.6 and 8.7).

1. *Paths* are routes of frequent travel that are shared by many citizens. Freeways, boulevards, highways, and mass transit corridors are examples.

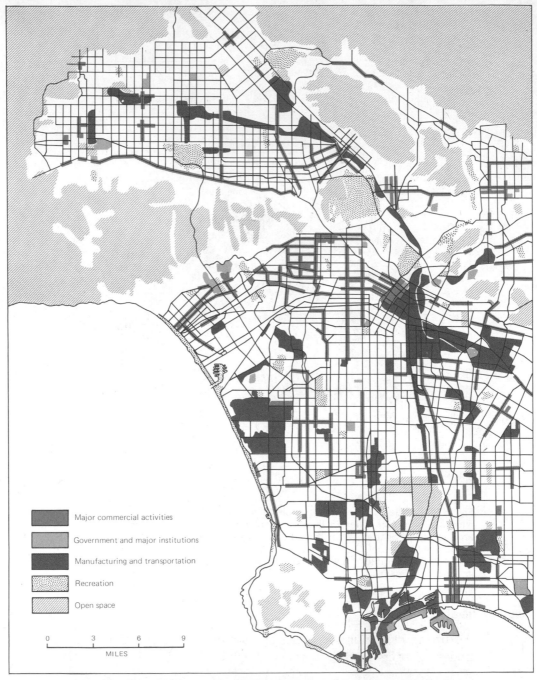

Fig. 8.6 Physical form and land utilization in Los Angeles. Los Angeles is a
low-density urban area which can be divided into five sectors by terrain and location
in reference to downtown: Central; Western, including the coastal communities;
Southern, containing the harbors; the San Gabriel Valley to the northeast; and the
San Fernando Valley to the northwest. (After Los Angeles Department of City
Planning, 1971, Fig. 1.)

Legend:
- Major commercial activities
- Government and major institutions
- Manufacturing and transportation
- Recreation
- Open space

0 3 6 9
MILES

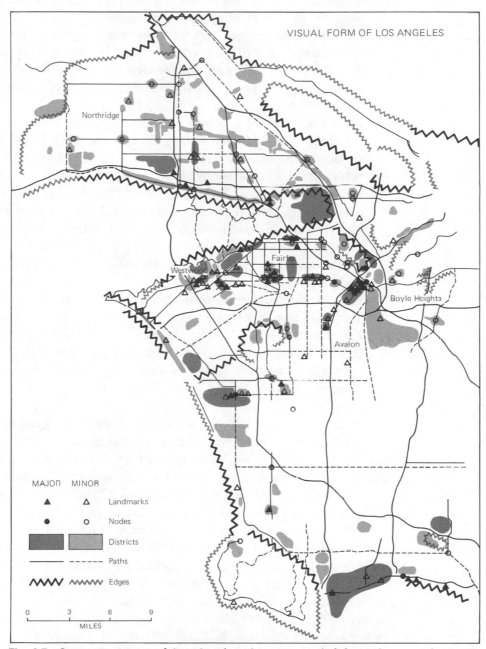

VISUAL FORM OF LOS ANGELES

Northridge

Fairfax

Westwood

Boyle Heights

Avalon

MAJOR MINOR

▲   △   Landmarks

●   ○   Nodes

    Districts

——— - - - - Paths

ᘜᘜᘜ ᨆᨆᨆ Edges

0   3   6   9

MILES

Fig. 8.7 Composite image of Los Angeles. A map compiled from the mental images described by residents. It differs from the physical form shown in Fig. 8.6. (After Los Angeles Department of City Planning, 1971, Fig. 2.)

2. *Edges* are boundaries between different areas. In a metropolitan area these are often physical features like mountains, rivers, and the shoreline. Streets are also used to mark the perceived boundaries for well-known districts. In planned communities greenbelts are designed to provoke the image of a boundary: to create perceptual breaks between relatively homogeneous areas.

3. *Nodes* are strategic points of urban interest. Monuments, civic buildings like the city hall, museum, or library, or the intersection of prominent pathways like "1st and Main" are nodes of reference shared by many citizens.

4. *Districts* are areas having some recognized common identity. They are regions that have coherence in terms of special uses like universities or automobile and restaurant rows. Some residential areas like Westwood and Northridge are districts because of the social cohesion that distinguishes them from adjoining residential areas.

5. *Landmarks* are similar to nodes. They are objects that stand out because of their height, color, or construction. City Hall in Los Angeles, the Eiffel Tower, the Pan Am Building in New York, the St. Louis Arch, and San Francisco's Golden Gate Bridge are examples. They are locations that help individuals to structure a mental map of their surroundings.

If similar images of the city were shared by all, a good deal of the conflict that develops over proposed beneficial changes would be eliminated. However, each group develops its own image. Even the image of similar groups in different parts of the city will be in conflict. Urban plans that are proposed for the community's benefit often violate the image held by one group and opposition is voiced.

The development of mass transit systems is obstructed in this manner. Four buses carry the equivalent of a mile of four-lane freeway at a fraction of the horsepower and resultant air pollution. But buses on local streets, before they reach the freeway, are offensive: They obstruct traffic, are noisy, eliminate curbside parking, and are not esthetically attractive. There is no doubt that increased bus service could reduce air pollutants immediately, but bus systems receive little support. The citizens would much rather think about high-speed monorails or guidance systems for personal rapid transit. These latter systems are futuristic in design. They appeal to our imagination, but they cost $15 million a mile to build, and it will be many years before they can provide the solutions to traffic congestion and air pollution that we need now.

Image from different points of view

Groups differ in their ability to perceive the future and the ways in which they organize their lives to take advantage of anticipated changes. Although high-status groups are not necessarily future-oriented, there is a positive, though not necessarily causal, correlation between them. High-status people are mobile and are familiar with different parts of the city. Since their friendships are not limited to their own residential neighborhoods social interaction acquaints high-status individuals with various districts. Home, work, and friends are scattered to form a network that Webber (1964) has called a "community without propinquity." Middle- and lower-status people are less mobile.

A similar distinction can be observed between the image of the city as perceived by higher- and lower-status groups. Higher-status groups have a more comprehensive image of their city, whereas the image of citizens from lower-status districts is restricted primarily to immediate neighborhoods. In part, this may be related to their economic ability to experience distant areas of the city.

In a remarkable series of maps designed to emphasize planning problems in Los Angeles, the city planning department has portrayed these different images of the city. Each map is a composite of maps drawn by many people in each area.

Westwood and Northridge are upper-status residential suburbs. Their image embraces most of the Los Angeles Basin. They share the image of principal edges, pathways, nodes like the downtown civic center, and districts like Hollywood, Watts, Santa Monica, and Pasadena (Fig. 8.8A and B). However, the two maps differ in local detail. Citizens of Northridge are much more familiar with the San Fernando Valley and emphasize the Ventura and Santa Monica freeways, their two pathways to elsewhere. Westwood citizens are more knowledgeable about areas south of the Santa Monica Mountains. By comparison, they know more about the city than do their Northridge status counterparts. Northridge is an outer suburban area with young families occupying single-family, ranch-style homes. Westwood citizens are older; they are primarily students and business and professional people without children and are

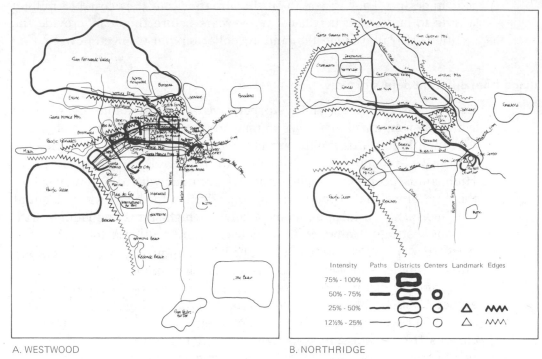

A. WESTWOOD

B. NORTHRIDGE

Fig. 8.8 Composite image for high-status citizens groups: (A) Westwood; (B) Northridge. (Los Angeles Department of City Planning, 1971, Figs. 7B and 8B.)

cosmopolitan in their interest. Consequently, the complexity of their mental maps reflects their varied life styles.

Fairfax, a predominantly Jewish district in midcity, consists of older families residing in a traditional ethnic neighborhood. Both economically and socially, it is a middle-status community. The residents' knowledge is limited primarily to the immediate area, with the beaches, cultural centers, and cemetery recognized as nodes (Fig. 8.9A and B). The prominence of the San Fernando Valley is explained by the relocation of children and grandchildren into this suburban area.

Avalon and Boyle Heights are lower-status, inner city districts. Knowledge of the rest or the city by residents of these areas is limited (Fig. 8.10A and B). The restricted social and physical mobility of the lower-income inhabitants limits their knowledge and understanding of the city. Hospitals and recreational areas like Dodger Stadium and Exposition Park replace cultural and educational centers as nodes and landmarks.

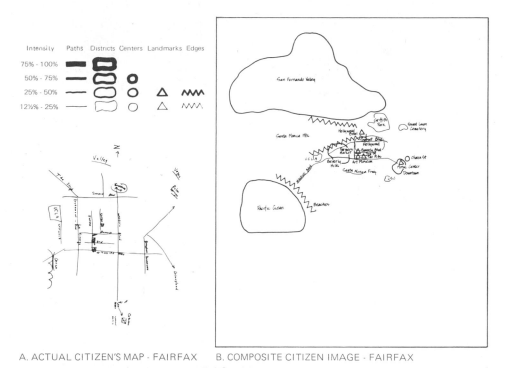

A. ACTUAL CITIZEN'S MAP - FAIRFAX   B. COMPOSITE CITIZEN IMAGE - FAIRFAX

Fig. 0.9 Composite image from Fairfax, a middle-status community. (A) An actual citizen's map. Composite maps (B) were drawn by integrating features which appeared on many maps. (Los Angeles Department of City Planning, 1971, Figs. 9A and D.)

Residents of Boyle Heights, a Chicano community, are further limited by language barriers from interaction with the total city. Inadequate educational and commercial facilities and the paucity of public transportation is their most urgent concern, but they are unable to articulate their need in a manner that would achieve citywide attention.

Policy implications

Different images of the city impede adoption of programs for beneficial change. For most residents, their community is a historical mental map: It is a bag of memories coordinated about familiar paths, edges, nodes, districts, and landmarks. Any change that impinges upon this image is disliked by the community. For this reason, many programs for urban improvement are either stalled until a sufficient level of agreement can be developed to ensure support through the design and implemen-

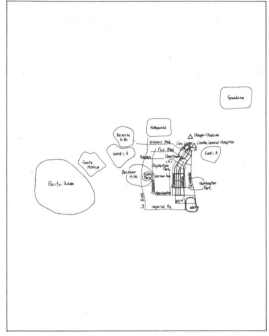

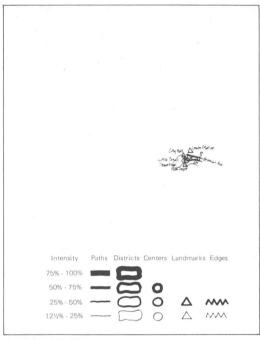

A. AVALON

B. BOYLE HEIGHTS

Fig. 8.10 Composite image for low-status citizen groups: (A) Avalon; (B) Boyle Heights. (Los Angeles Department of City Planning, 1971, Figs. 10B and 11B.)

tation phases, or result from compromise solutions attempting to resolve differences between groups with conflicting objectives.

Most metropolitan areas are involved in airport location disputes. Original airports are too small and too noisy for adjoining residents. The problem is to find a location that will accept the new jetport. Pilots want the safest place; residents support the site farthest from *their* homes; businessmen desire the most convenient site; and ecologists insist that tidal estuaries and marshland cannot be filled in. Development is stalled while a compromise is sought among the various special-interest groups. Travelers are inconvenienced, but tolerate the inconvenience. Perhaps the new airport was not as urgent as the planners had originally indicated. Bigger is not necessarily better. Air travel is not essential. If the inconvenience of traveling increases, people travel less. In many instances a telephone call can be as effective as a business trip.

Airports and freeway planners need to recognize that various groups will perceive their proposals differently. Planning strategies must enable different groups to participate in the planning process early enough so that community interests can determine the alternatives. To resolve differences in opinion between groups, satisfactory rather than optimal plans have to be accepted, because solutions that optimize technical criteria are seldom acceptable to the local community. Attempts to compel acceptance of optimal solutions have been rejected by many communities, and this has brought urban freeway construction to a virtual halt. New federal guidelines for planning insist upon maximum feasible participation by the affected communities. In this way, local groups can influence the location and design, not only of transportation facilities, but also of all construction aided by federal grants.

URBAN DESIGN AND THE DEVELOPMENT OF NEW TOWNS

City design reflects man's desire to reduce his environment to discernible order, to construct environments that represent a culturally defined sense of appropriate and pleasing order. From the earliest human encampments, there appears to have been concern for central locations protected by supporting settlements or walls. The rest of the world was organized about this focus. The Yurok Indian, for example, conceptualized the world centered upon his own village (Fig. 8.11). Young children have a similar view, which is reinforced in social studies by beginning with the home and local community and expanding to encompass the world.

Organization of cities about a central focus has numerous expressions. Peking, from the sixteenth century onward, emphasized the Chinese conception of order (Fig. 8.12). Most sacred activities are centrally located, with the areas of lesser importance located farther away. Spanish colonial cities exhibited similar orientation by emphasizing the central church and plaza.

In British colonial settlements, the post office was the symbol of authority and it, too, was centrally located. To emphasize the importance of the central city, and in keeping with the tradition of military surveyors, greenbelts bordered the central city. Originally, the parkland was intended as a barrier against surprise attack, but today it remains as glorious open space (Fig. 8.13).

The garden city ideal that stimulated the growth of suburbia and new towns results from the same psychological desire to impose cen-

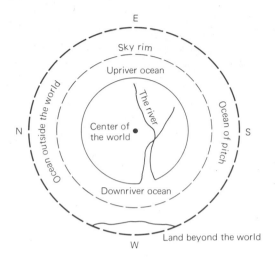

Yurok Indians (Northern California)

Fig. 8.11 Composite image of the world for
Yurok Indians. (Tuan, reproduced by
permission from the Commission on
College Geography of the Association of
American Geographers Resource Paper 10,
Man and Nature, 1972, Fig. 2.)

trifugal order upon urban development. The garden suburbs were to be
residential foci outside the industrial city, connected by mass transit
corridors. Within the new town, order was imposed to reinforce perceptual identity. Emphasis is placed upon creating a visual environment
that will be perceived by the prospective residents as providing a meaningful life style (Fig. 8.14).

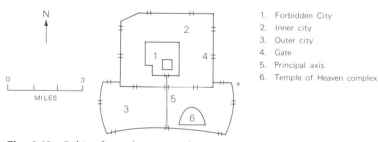

1. Forbidden City
2. Inner city
3. Outer city
4. Gate
5. Principal axis
6. Temple of Heaven complex

Fig. 8.12 Peking from the sixteenth century onward. Rectangular
ideal city, oriented to the cardial directions. (Tuan, reproduced by
permission from the Commission on College Geography of the
Association of American Geographers Resource Paper 10, *Man and
Nature*, 1972, Fig. 5.)

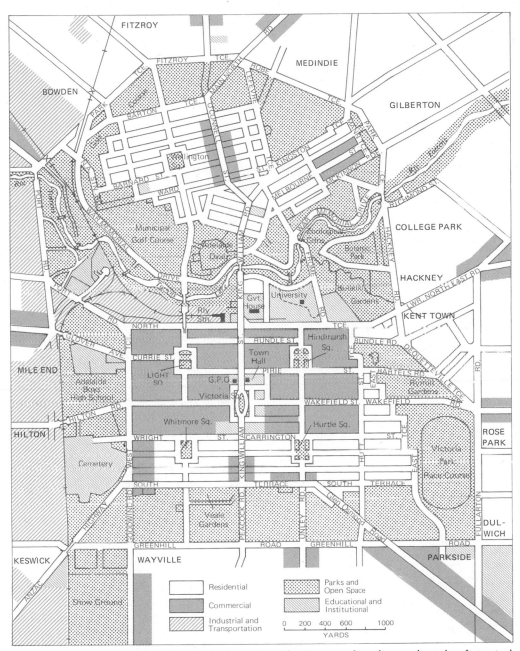

Fig. 8.13 Adelaide, South Australia. The rectangular plan and park of central Adelaide is the result of an early plan reflecting the perception of a modern city.

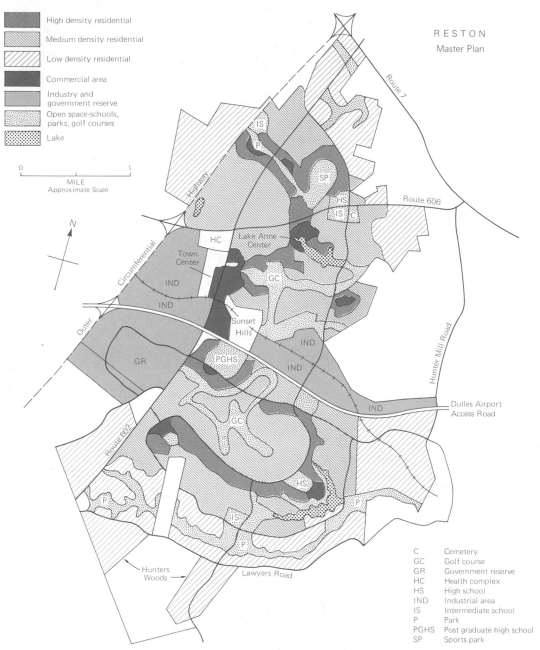

High density residential

Medium density residential

Low density residential

Commercial area

Industry and
government reserve

Open space-schools,
parks, golf courses

Lake

0   1
MILE
Approximate Scale

N

RESTON
Master Plan

Route 7

Route 606

Highway

Circumferential

Outer

Route 602

Hunter Mill Road

Dulles Airport
Access Road

Lawyers Road

Hunters
Woods

IS
P
SP
HS
IS C
Lake Anne
Center
HC
Town
Center
IND
IND
GC
Sunset
Hills
IND
GR
PGHS
IND
GC
IND
HS
P
P
IS
P

C   Cemetery
GC   Golf course
GR   Government reserve
HC   Health complex
HS   High school
IND   Industrial area
IS   Intermediate school
P   Park
PGHS   Post graduate high school
SP   Sports park

Fig. 8.14 General plan for the new town of Reston, Virginia. The golf courses, park
system, lakes, educational facilities, and commercial centers create the visual
images perceived by prospective residents as providing a meaningful life style
and definition of communities. (Burton, 1968.)

Paths and edges

Roads, railroads, and greenbelts are used as edges for planned communities. They not only connect the new town with the metropolitan community, but also separate local neighborhoods. In the successful communities, greenbelts are multipurpose: they relieve the continuity of urbanism and provide parks, walking, and cycling trails. In Reston, Virginia, lakes, golf courses, and pathways provide a continuous link throughout the community: They produce coherence in what might otherwise be a mere supersuburban tract development.

Nodes

Activity centers, like schools and commercial centers, provide the nodes for both community and neighborhood life. The town center is a neighborhood shopping center with forty to sixty functions, serving a hinterland that extends beyond the new town. A high school or college is also a central place for a wider hinterland. Both the town centers and educational facilities provide important nodes for community orientation. Residents know their locations and mention them when describing their community.

Each residential cluster has its convenience shopping center—a cluster of stores representing functions like groceries, hardware, hair-care centers, service station, and bank. Elementary schools are also provided within residential clusters as a convenience service. Playgrounds and local parks are other such activity nodes.

Districts

Residential districts of different density, form, and cost occupy most of the new town area. Developers strive to provide a range of housing in order to appeal to different social status groups. Residential areas are relatively homogeneous and separate. For social reasons, there is a tendency for people to cluster with those whom they perceive to be similar. Separation of these social status residential areas establishes their identity as districts and assists interaction. Although there are some exceptions like Columbia, Maryland, attempts to mix low- and middle-status housing have not been successful.

Manufacturing districts are included in most new town plans as an attempt to develop balanced communities. However, few developers have been successful in attracting manufacturing plants to locate at the extreme fringe of the metropolitan area where new towns are situated. Entrepreneurs prefer established manufacturing plants adjoining the older suburbs. These locations provide a more diversified labor force, better communication facilities, and lower tax rates.

Landmarks

It is one thing to plan a new town and yet another to have the residents perceive this plan and the community identity it is presumed to elicit. Landmarks are important to this achievement. A building, a monument, or even a prominent rock or hillside can provide a landmark that assists individuals to conceptualize their city. Landmarks provide a visible item that can be shared by all.

Greenbelts, lakes, schools, and colleges can help to establish a community identity, but they are perceived from differing points of view. A structure like a monument or prominent rock is devoid of any emotional connotation; therefore, it provides a perceptual image that may be widely and equivalently shared.

How new towns fail

Given their opportunity to provide modern urban growth that is psychologically appealing, new towns ought to be phenomenally successful. They are not. All residents do not derive satisfaction from the perception of paths, edges, nodes, districts, and landmarks. Many people seek the diversity of the older city and reject the aesthetically pleasing new town plans prepared by upper-status planners and architects. As was indicated earlier in this chapter, perception is socially biased. New towns do not appeal to all, and all new towns do not emphasize those elements that might offer psychological satisfaction.

Even those for whom the new towns were built—upper- and middle-status families, and working-status families in the case of some British new towns—find such communities unsatisfying. Economic diversity is lacking. The range of commercial and employment opportunities that exist in an older suburb are not present, and families often move away upon job changes.

Uniformity of social and political life also becomes stultifying. If some residents feel strongly on local issues, there is little community support. Developers control both the pace and nature of development and their time horizon is limited to when the land is sold. Developers resent attempts to control their freedom through local political activity, and the residents who get involved in such activities are soon frustrated. The developer usually commands the skill and the resources to influence public decisions. Local residents, unless they develop the required political skill and knowledge of local affairs, usually lose. Potential local leaders become frustrated by their failures and move away.

It is not uncommon for the developer to build all single-family homes first, sell these and, after selling these, he then constructs high-density residential buildings on the view-commanding sites. The original homeowners resent the loss of their views and the increased activity that the high-density development will create. Attempts to reduce the density are common but, although construction may be stalled for a short time, high-rises are ultimately built. The landowner has a greater interest in pursuing the project than the homeowners who oppose it. Opposition comes primarily from those whose homes adjoin the high-rise structure. People living farther away are uninterested in the controversy.

New towns throughout the world have sparked our imagination as we confront the dilemma of urban policy and metropolitan government. Achievements in the United States, Britain, Western Europe, Israel, and, in fact, in almost every nation, have provided innovations in architecture and urban design. However, from an economic and social point of view, new towns leave much to be desired: They remain attractive to only a minority of the population.

NEW APPROACHES TO THE PSYCHOLOGICAL PROCESS

The analysis of space perception might have continued with themes in personal space. How do individuals respond to different shapes and sizes? Why are hallways confining? Why do businessmen feel more comfortable in spacious surroundings and college professors prefer intimate settings? How should airport terminals be designed to reassure passengers, or how should shop fronts be designed to invite patronage? These are themes that architects, psychologists, and regional scientists strive to understand (Sommer, 1969).

Learning behavior is another theme worthy of geographical attention. How do people learn about other areas? This was mentioned in the section entitled "Migration Behavior," but only superficially. Why is it, for instance, that similar commercial and manufacturing areas tend to cluster? Politically imposed zoning is part of the answer, but it is also possible that imitative behavior is involved. Entrepreneurs observe a successful enterprise and seek to copy the behavior. Like most behavior, location theory is subject to fads.

Attitudes are also influential in spatial behavior. An individual's predisposition to act in a certain way has been learned. It will not only affect the way he behaves, but also the way he perceives information and the way he searches the environment for cues. The value system shown in Fig. 8.3 represents attitudes in their widest connotation. They exercise a pivotal role in structuring spatial behavior.

Psychological processes are inherent in all decision making. During consideration of the economic process, it was convenient to discuss optimum solutions to the location of agriculture, manufacturing, and commerce. However, optimal conditions are seldom achieved: There are limits on available information; entrepreneurs cannot know the consequences of all alternatives. Problems are limited and when solutions are itemized, the least risky, rather than the optimal, solution is normally chosen.

Man avoids risk. Instead of optimal solutions, satisfactory ones are sought. Economic man exists only in textbooks. Farmers, industrialists, and businessmen are psychological men. They make *satisfactory* rather than *optimal* decisions (March and Simon, 1958).

These are but some of the aspects of psychological behavior that challenge geographers. Our focus has been upon the perception of hazards, areas, and man's adaptation to the images perceived. This chapter would have been an appropriate introduction to all human processes, but too little is known about man's appraisal of his environment. As psychologists and geographers unravel the nature of the psychological process, more precise statements will be possible. In this way, our understanding of the spatial patterns resulting from man's organization of society will be improved.

SUGGESTED READINGS

Studies of the psychological process have attracted the attention of many geographers. Reviews of the literature have been provided by:

Abler, Ronald; Adams, John S.; and Gould, Peter. "Individual Spatial Decisions in a Descriptive Framework." *Spatial Organization: The Geographer's View of the World.* Englewood Cliffs, N.J.: Prentice-Hall, 1971, pp. 491–530.

Burton, Ian, and Kates, Robert W. "The Perception of Natural Hazards in Resource Management." *Natural Resources Journal* 3(1964):412–441.

Downs, Roger M. "Geographic Space Perception." *Progress in Geography* 2(1970):67–108.

Three publications have also been published by the Commission on College Geography:

Moore, Eric G. *Residential Mobility in the City.* Resource Paper No. 13. Washington, D.C.: Association of American Geographers, Commission on College Geography, 1972.

Saarinen, Thomas F. *Perception of Environment.* Resource Paper No. 5. Washington, D.C.: Association of American Geographers, Commission on College Geography, 1969.

Tuan, Yi-Fu. *Man and Nature.* Resource Paper No. 10. Washington, D.C.: Association of American Geographers, Commission on College Geography, 1972.

More specialized publications that report the results of research are:

City of Los Angeles. *The Visual Environment of Los Angeles.* Department of City Planning, 1971.

Kates, Robert W. *Hazard and Choice Perception in Flood Plain Management.* Research Paper No. 78. Chicago: Department of Geography, University of Chicago, 1962.

Sommer, Robert. *Personal Space: The Behavioral Basis of Design.* Englewood Cliffs, N.J.: Prentice-Hall, 1969.

White, Gilbert F. *Choice of Adjustments to Floods.* Research Paper No. 93. Chicago: Department of Geography, University of Chicago, 1964.

Wolpert, Julian. "Behavioral Aspects of the Decision to Migrate." *Papers of the Regional Science Association* 15(1966):159–172.

GLOSSARY OF TERMS

accessibility: The relative degree or ease with which a location may be reached from other locations. It involves the variables of time and distance.

adaptation: A change in structure, function, or form that produces better adjustment of man to his physical and cultural environments.

agglomeration: Spatial grouping of activities or people for mutual benefit.

analogue model: A model in which one property is represented by another, for example, as in a map.

arable: Land suitable for plowing and, hence, for producing crops.

arrangement: The relation of occurrences with respect to one another.

assimilation: The cultural absorption of an ethnic group or new individuals into the main cultural body.

barrio: Spanish-American word for slum community.

central business district (CBD): The main business center of a city.

central place: A village, town, or shopping center which offers goods and services to surrounding areas.

centrifugal: Moving or tending to move away from the center, that is, developing from the center outward.

centripetal: Tending to move toward a center.

chaparral: A plant association consisting of moisture-conserving shrubs which grows on the coastal hills of southern California and along the Mediterranean coast line.

choice: How individuals select among several alternatives based on individual perceptions and utility for alternatives.

choice model: A model which assigns an estimate (probability function) to the way individuals will select between alternatives.

choropleth map: A map utilizing statistical areas like counties or states to indicate magnitudes. Figure 2.6 showing the poverty in Illinois is one such example.

coefficient of correlation: A measure of the relationship between the magnitude of two variables. It need not be a causal relationship. People with low incomes may live in areas with high rainfall, but no causal relationship may exist.

cohorts: A group of people of similar age and sex used in forecasting population change.

comparative advantage: An area's suitability for different activities, based on the idea that all locations have certain activities which are more profitable than others.

complementary region: An area in which there exists a mutually beneficial linkage. Commerce is the normal link as is best seen in a town and its hinterland or trade area.

contagion: The process of spreading an idea or disease to others who are receptive.

conurbation: A group of cities which coalesce as they grow although they remain politically independent.

convenience goods: Goods required frequently, such as groceries and gasoline.

coterminous: A continuous area such as the United States without Alaska or Hawaii.

cultural realm: A continental area in which there is some uniformity or cohesion based upon cultural traditions.

culture: A way of life acquired by learning the rules and traditions of society.

deductive research: A method of research where a researcher tests propositions about attributes of a theoretical relationship.

demand: The goods and/or services desired by customers.

demographic cycle: An idealized sequence of changes in the vital statistics of a society.

density: The ratio of frequency of occurrence of an item to the size of the area, usually expressed in terms of average frequency.

dependent variable: The variable under examination which is held constant while the suspected causal (independent) variable or variables are changed.

dichotomous: Divided into two opposite categories like married or single, male or female.

diffusion: The process of gradual spread over space of people or ideas from centers of origin.

direct costs: Costs like labor and raw materials which can be related directly to production costs.

discrete distribution: Separate from other occurrences of the same distribution.

dispersion: A measure of the relative position of occurrences (spread) with respect to the boundaries of the area under study.

distance: The separation between two or more locations.

distribution: The spatial arrangement of occurrences of the same type. The arrangement may be described as discrete, continuous, contingent, random, uniform, or clustered.

dot map: A map on which the arrangement and intensity of a distribution is shown by discrete symbols.

economic rent: The additional return over and above costs of production which an enterprise will return. When it applies solely to the additional return for land with superior accessibility to the market, the term is *locational* or *land rent*.

economies of scale: These are savings in the costs of production achieved by larger enterprises.

environment: The natural and cultural setting within which people live.

equilibrium: A theoretical condition of stability. The value at which producers are willing to supply goods and buyers are willing to purchase them.

exchange: The concept of trading goods and services for labor, money, or affection.

exchange model: Where the allocation of goods is determined by the supply and demand for the commodity or service.

exponential increase: Where the rate of increase of the independent variable is greater than the dependent variable itself. The exponent expresses the rate of increase.

farmstead: The farm home and associated buildings used to house livestock and equipment.

favella: A Portuguese word for slum which usually occupies peripheral or hillside locations rather than the central city.

friction of distance: A measurement used to indicate the effect of distance on economic competition.

functions: A specific type of business or service activity, for example, banks have one function; churches have another.

geographical inertia: The tendency of economic activities to continue in established locations even though new locations might reduce costs of production.

geography: The study of the locations and arrangements of phenomena on the surface of the earth and the processes which generate these distributions.

good: An item or service which is of value to someone else.

gravity model: A representation of the relationship of the interaction between areas and their distance apart. Interaction declines with increasing distance.

hierarchy: The concept that central places are arranged so that some like villages serve a small trade area and others, like the CBD of a metropolitan area, serve a large trade area. Consumers will travel to smaller, nearby places for everyday purchases and to larger, more distant places for specialized goods.

high-order goods and services: Those goods and services needed occasionally like jewelry and medical specialists which are located in the larger centers.

higher-order central places: Places which offer higher-order, specialized, goods and services as well as lower-order goods and services for everyday needs.

hinterland: The area which is dependent upon or dominated by, a central place. The terms nodal region or functional region are synonymous.

hypothesis: A hunch or idea advanced for testing.

independent variable: The variable whose magnitude is changed so that the effect upon the dependent variable may be observed.

indirect costs: Those costs not directly related to production such as advertising.

inductive research: The researcher tests a hypothesis about the relationship between two or more phenomena which have been observed to occur together.

innovator: A person who leads change in individual behavior or production process.

interaction: The interrelations between locations, usually specified in terms of movement of people or communications. The level of interaction varies inversely with distance.

interest group: People who share a common goal or objective. A person usually belongs to several interest groups—work, neighborhood, and social.

intervening opportunity: When the presence of a closer opportunity for shopping or migration diminishes the attractiveness of more distant centers.

isoline map: A map drawn by connecting points of equal value. For example, an elevation map uses contours to join places with equal elevation.

isopleth map: A map drawn so that the lines separate areas with different average values. A map of residential values uses isopleth to separate suburbs in which the average value of homes differ.

isotropic surface: An area that has no difference from place to place or in one direction to another, that is, one in which all places are the same and movement effort is the same in all directions.

land use: The actual use of land whether for a crop, house, or industry.

land utilization: The generalized land use for an area. This refers to a system like industrial zones or commercial areas which may contain several land uses.

law: A generalization which has regularity of occurrence over space and time.

locational rent: A measure of the value to a landowner of superior accessibility to a particular market. Land rent is the same, but economic rent reflects factors in addition to location.

low-order goods: Everyday purchases and services which are conveniently provided at many central places.

magnitude: The measure of size or importance of spatial distributions.

market: A location where goods and services are exchanged. The surrounding area is the market area or hinterland.

megalopolis: Convergence of several metropolitan areas along a communication corridor or national boundary. The northeastern megalopolis extends from Boston to Washington, D.C.

metes and bounds: A system of land survey not related to a systematic grid. An irregular pattern of property lines and roads results, which contrasts with the rectangular land-survey system.

milieu: A French word used to describe the cultural environment of man and his surroundings.

model: An idealized representation of a part of reality, which is constructed so as to demonstrate certain of its properties.

nodal region: An area which is dependent upon a central place. It differs from other areas in respect to its organization.

nodes: Centers of transportation networks.

normative pattern: The theoretical ideal pattern.

norms: Standards against which social behavior is judged as acceptable.

occurrence: An identifiable phenomenon of a specific magnitude.

paradigm: An outline of a theory. A theory which has not been proved, although a process is suspected. Used to explain complex behavioral processes.

parallel analysis: A problem in which multiple causes are hypothesized, each of which is tested in sequence to estimate their contribution to changes in the distribution of the dependent variable.

pastoralism: A system of land utilization which features the grazing of livestock rather than the cultivation of crops.

perception: recognition by the mind of an external object, sound, or smell.

political integration: Where the interactions between people are used to establish and maintain a sense of loyalty to the political unit.

power elite: A small group of people who are able to consistently influence political decisions.

primary activities: Those which specialize in the production and conversion of raw materials from agriculture, forestry, and mining, as distinguished from secondary industry, which utilizes the outputs of primary activities.

probability: The likelihood of an event occurring which is measured by the ratio of occurrences to the whole number of cases in which it was possible.

public interest: A myth that presumes that some actions benefit all people. Most governmental decisions only benefit a small section of the people so that it is more appropriate to speak of public interests.

range: In central place theory, the maximum distance over which a seller will offer a good, or from which a consumer will travel to a center to purchase the good or service.

redistributive programs: Governmental programs which use money derived from affluent people and areas to provide benefits for those not so fortunate.

region: An area which according to specified criteria possesses some degree of homogeneity (*see* "nodal region" and "uniform region").

regression analysis: A statistical technique for explaining as much as possible of the variation in the dependent variable by some measure of the independent variable. Multiple regression occurs when there are several independent variables in the equation. In simple regression there is only one independent variable.

salience: A tendency for people in different areas to be oriented to each other.

sampling: The unbiased selection of a test population or test area. Different types of sample are used to ensure adequate coverage of different distributions.

satisficing: A concept introduced to counter the concept of optimal behavior. Indicates that people seek satisfactory returns rather than optimal returns, when choosing between alternative courses of action.

secondary activities: Those which use the processed raw materials from primary industry to manufacture goods. Processing is primary, manufacturing is secondary, and selling is tertiary activity.

spatial behavior: The decisions individuals make about their use of and actions in specific areas.

surrogate: A measure used to represent a variable when precise information on the desired variable is not available.

target population: The total population in a study from which a sample is chosen.

tertiary activities: The marketing, transporting, and selling of goods produced by primary and secondary activities.

theory: A system of hypothetical statements or laws which explains distributions.

threshold: In central place theory, the minimum level of demand needed to attain profitability.

transactional flow: The exchange of messages and goods between two or more areas.

transferability: The extent to which a good or service can be moved.

transportation network: The system of links and nodes over which movement can occur.

uniform region: An area for which the internal variation of specified criteria is appreciably less than the variation between this area and other areas.

utility: The value or usefulness of goods and services.

variance: The extent of variation from the mean value which is contained in a designated unit.

BIBLIOGRAPHY

Abler, Ronald; Adams, John S.; and Gould, Peter R. 1971. *Spatial Organization: The Geographer's View of the World.* Englewood Cliffs, N.J.: Prentice-Hall.

Adams, John S. 1970. "Residential Structure of Midwestern Cities." *Annals of the Association of American Geographers* 60:37–62.

Alonso, William. 1964. "The Historic and Structural Theories of Urban Form: Their Implications for Urban Renewal." *Land Economics* 40:227–231.

Backstrom, Charles H., and Hursch, Gerald D. 1963. *Survey Research.* Evanston, Ill.: Northwestern University Press.

Banfield, Edward C. 1970. *The Unheavenly City*. Boston: Little, Brown.

Berry, Brian J. L. 1963. *Commercial Structure and Commercial Blight*. Research Paper 85. Department of Geography. Chicago, Ill.: University of Chicago Press.

Berry, Brian J. L. 1964. "Approaches to Regional Analysis: A Synthesis." *Annals of the Association of American Geographers* 54:2–11.

Berry, Brian J. L. 1967. *Geography of Market Centers and Retail Distribution*. Englewood Cliffs, N.J.: Prentice-Hall.

Berry, Brian J. L.; Barnum, H. G.; and Tennant, R. J. 1962. "Retail Location and Consumer Behavior." *Regional Science Association, Papers and Proceedings* 9:65–106.

Berry, Brain J. L., and Horton, Frank E. 1970. *Geographical Perspectives on Urban Systems*. Englewood Cliffs, N.J.: Prentice-Hall.

Berry, Brian J. L., and Marble, Duane F., eds. 1968. *Spatial Analysis: A Reader in Statistical Geography*. Englewood Cliffs, N.J.: Prentice-Hall.

Beyer, Glenn H., ed. 1967. *The Urban Explosion in Latin America*. Ithaca, N.Y.: Cornell University Press.

Boal, Frederick. 1970. "Urban Growth and Land Value Patterns: Government Influence." *Professional Geographer* 22:79–82.

Bowman, Isaiah. 1931. *The Pioneer Fringe*. New York: American Geographical Society.

Broek, Jan O. M., and Webb, John W. 1968. *A Geography of Mankind*. New York: McGraw-Hill.

Burgess, E. W. 1923. "The Growth of the City." *Proceedings of the American Sociological Society* 18:85–89.

Burton, Bess. 1968. "Reston, Virginia." In *Nine Geographical Field Trips in the Washington, D.C. Area*. Washington, D.C.: Association of American Geographers, pp. 29–35.

Burton, Ian, and Kates, Robert W. 1964. "The Perception of Natural Hazards in Resource Management." *Natural Resources Journal* 3:412–441.

Carey, George W.; Macomber, Lenore; and Greenberg, Michael. 1966. "The Regional Interpretation of Manhattan Population and Housing. Patterns Through Factor Analysis." *Geographical Review* 56:551–569.

Carey, George W., et al. 1968. "Educational and Demographic Factors in the Urban Geography of Washington, D.C.: *Geographical Review* 58:515–537.

Chisholm, Michael. 1967. *Rural Settlement and Land Use: An Essay in Location*. London: Hutchinson.

Christaller, Walter. 1966. *Central Places in Southern Germany*. Translated by C. W. Baskin. Englewood Cliffs, N.J.: Prentice–Hall.

City of Los Angeles. 1971. Department of City Planning. *The Visual Environment of Los Angeles*.

Clark, Andrew H. 1959. *Three Centuries and the Island: A Historical Geography of Settlement and Agriculture in Prince Edward Island, Canada*. Toronto: University of Toronto Press.

Coleman, James. 1957. *Community Conflict*. New York: Free Press.

Downs, Roger M. 1970. "Geographic Space Perception." *Progress in Geography* 2:67–108.

Dunn, Edgar S., Jr. 1954. *The Location of Agricultural Production*. Gainesville: University of Florida Press.

Ehrlich, Paul R., and Ehrlich, A. H. 1970. *Population, Resources, and Environment: Issues in Human Ecology*. San Francisco: Freeman.

Fielding, Gordon J. 1964. "The Los Angeles Milkshed: A Study of the Political Factor in Agriculture." *Geographical Review* 44:1–12.

Fried, Marc. 1963. "Greiving for a Lost Home." In *The Urban Condition*, edited by Leonard J. Duhl. New York: Basic Books, pp. 151–171.

Gans, Herbert. 1962. *The Urban Villagers*. New York: Free Press.

Gould, Peter. 1965. "Wheat on Kilimanjaro: The Perception of Choice Within Game and Learning Model Framework." *General Systems* 10: 157–166.

Gould, Peter. 1969. *Spatial Diffusion*. Resource Paper No. 4. Washington, D.C.: Association of American Geographers, Commission on College Geography.

Green, H. L. 1955. "Hinterland Boundaries of New York City and Boston in Southern New England." *Economic Geography* 31:283–300.

Grotewold, Andreas. 1959. "Von Thünen in Retrospect." *Economic Geography* 35:346–355.

Hagerstrand, T. 1969. *Innovation Diffusion as a Spatial Process*. Chicago: University of Chicago Press.

Haggett, Peter. 1965. *Locational Analysis In Human Geography*. London: Arnold.

Haggett, Peter. 1972. *Geography: A Modern Synthesis*. New York: Harper & Row.

Hardwick, W. G.; Rothwell, D. C.; and Claus, R. J. 1971. "Cemeteries and Urban Land Value." *Professional Geographer* 23:19–21.

Harris, Chauncey D., and Ullman, Edward L. 1942. "The Nature of Cities." *Annals of the American Academy of Political Science* 242:7–17.

Hartshorn, Truman A. 1971. "Inner City Residential Structure and Decline." *Annals of the Association of American Geographers* 61:72–96.

Harvey, David W. 1969. *Explanation in Geography*. London: Arnold.

Helvig, M. 1964. *Chicago's External Truck Movements*. Research Paper No. 90. Chicago: Department of Geography, University of Chicago.

Hoover, Edgar M. 1963. *The Location of Economic Activity*. New York: McGraw-Hill.

Isaac, Erich. 1970. *Geography of Domestication*. Englewood Cliffs, N.J.: Prentice-Hall.

Isard, Walter. 1956. *Location and Space Economy*. New York: Wiley.

Isard, Walter. 1960. *Methods of Regional Analysis*. New York: Wiley.

James, Preston E. 1964. *One World Divided: A Geographer Looks at the Modern World*. New York: Blaisdell.

Kasperson, Roger E. 1965. "Towards a Geography of Urban Politics: Chicago, A Case Study." *Economic Geography* 11:95–107.

Kasperson, Roger E., and Minghi, J. V., eds. 1969. *The Structure of Political Geography*. Chicago: Aldine.

Kates, Robert W. 1962. *Hazard and Choice Perception in Flood Plain Management*. Research Paper No. 78. Chicago: Department of Geography, University of Chicago.

King, Leslie J. 1962. "A Quantitative Expression of the Pattern of Urban Settlements in Selected Areas of the United States." *Tijdschrift Voor Econ. en Soc. Geographie* 53:1–7.

Knos, Duane S. 1962. *Distribution of Land Values in Topeka, Kansas*. Lawrence, Kan.: Center for Research in Business, University of Kansas Press.

Lewthwaite, Gordon R. 1966. "Environmentalism and Determinism: A Search for Clarification." *Annals of the Association of American Geographers* 56:1–23.

Lösch, A. 1954. *The Economics of Location*. Translated by W. H. Woglon. New Haven: Yale University Press.

Mackinder, H. J. 1962. *Democratic Ideals and Reality* (paperback). New York: Norton (Holt, 1919).

McCarty, Harold H., and Lindberg, James B. 1966. *A Preface to Economic Geography*. Englewood Cliffs, N.J.: Prentice-Hall.

March, James G., and Simon, H. A. 1958. *Organizations*. New York: Wiley.

March, James G. 1966. "The Power of Power." In *Varieties of Political Power*, edited by David Easton. Englewood Cliffs, N.J.: Prentice-Hall, pp. 39–70.

March, James G., and Lave, Charles. 1974. *The Art of Model Building: An Interdisciplinary Introduction to the Social Sciences*. New York: Harper & Row.

Maryland-National Capital Park and Planning Commission. 1964. *On Wedges and Corridors: A General Plan for the Maryland-Washington Regional District in Montgomery and Prince George Counties*.

Meinig, Donald W. 1965. "The Mormon Culture Region: Strategies and Patterns in the Geography of the American West, 1847–1964." *Annals of the Association of American Geographers* 55:191–220.

Meinig, Donald W. 1972. "American Wests: Preface to a Geographical Introduction." *Annals of the Association of American Geographers* 62:159–184.

Moore, Eric G. 1972. *Residential Mobility in the City*. Resource Paper No. 13. Washington, D.C.: Association of American Geographers, Commission on College Geography.

Morrill, Richard L. 1965. "The Negro Ghetto: Problems and Alternatives." *Geographical Review* 55:339–361.

Morrill, Richard L. 1970. *The Spatial Organization of Society*. Belmont, Calif.: Wadsworth.

Morrill, Richard L., and Wohlenberg, Ernest H. 1971. *The Geography of Poverty in the United States*. New York: McGraw-Hill.

Murdie, Robert A. 1965. "Cultural Differences in Consumer Travel." *Economic Geography* 41:211–233.

Murdie, Robert A. 1969. *Factorial Ecology of Metropolitan Toronto, 1951–*

1961. Research Paper No. 116. Chicago: Department of Geography, University of Chicago.

Newman, James L. 1973. "The Use of the Term 'Hypothesis' in Geography." *Annals of the Association of American Geographers* 63:22–27.

Novak, R. T. 1956. "Distribution of Puerto Ricans on Manhattan Island." *Geographical Review* 46:182–186.

Oates, Joyce Carol. 1969. *Them*. New York: Vanguard.

Paulson, William; Butler, E. W.; and Pope, H. 1967. "Community Power and Public Welfare." *American Journal of Economics and Sociology* 28: 17–27.

Prescott, J. R. V. 1965. *The Geography of Frontiers and Boundaries*. London: Hutchinson.

Rees, P. H. 1968. "The Factorial Ecology of Metropolitan Chicago, 1960." Master's thesis, Department of Geography. Chicago: University of Chicago.

Reitsma, Hendrik J. 1971. "Crop and Livestock Production in the Vicinity of the U.S.–Canada Border." *Professional Geographer* 23:216–223.

Richards, J. Howard. 1968. "The Prairie Region." In *Canada: A Geographical Interpretation*, edited by John Warkentin. Toronto: Methuen, pp. 396–437.

Rose, Harold M. 1969. *Social Process in the City: Race and Urban Residential Choice*. Resource Paper No. 6. Washington, D.C.: Association of American Geographers, Commission on College Geography.

Rose, Harold M. 1971. *The Black Ghetto: A Spatial Behavioral Perspective*. New York: McGraw-Hill.

Rushton, Gerard. 1969. "A Computer Model for the Study of Agricultural Land Use Patterns." *Computer Assisted Instruction in Geography*. Technical Paper No. 2. Washington, D.C.: Association of American Geographers, Commission on College Geography, pp. 141–150.

Russell, Peter, ed. 1966. *Nationalism in Canada*. Toronto: McGraw-Hill.

Saarienen, Thomas F. 1966. *Perception of Drought Hazard on The Great Plains*. Research Paper No. 106. Chicago: Department of Geography, University of Chicago, Department of Geography.

Saarienen, Thomas F. 1969. *Perception of Environment*. Resource Paper No. 5. Washington, D.C.: Association of American Geographers, Commission on College Geography.

Sabbagh, Michael E. 1968. "Some Geographical Aspects of a Plural Society: Apartheid in South Africa." *Geographical Review* 58:1–28.

Sharp, Lauriston. 1952. "Steel Axes for Stone Age Australians." In *Human Problems in Technological Change*, edited by Edward H. Spicer. New York: Wiley, pp. 69–90.

Shibutani, Tamotsu. 1961. *Society and Personality*. Englewood Cliffs, N.J.: Prentice-Hall.

Simmons, J. 1964. *The Changing Pattern of Retail Locations*. Research Paper No. 92. Chicago: Department of Geography, University of Chicago Press.

Skinner, B. F. 1971a. *Beyond Freedom and Dignity*. New York: Knopf.

Skinner, B. F. 1971b. "Beyond Freedom and Dignity: Pre-publication Summa." *Psychology Today* 5:37–80.

Smith, David M. 1971. *Industrial Location: An Economic Geographical Analysis*. New York: Wiley.

Soja, Edward W. 1968a. *The Geography of Modernization in Kenya*. Syracuse, N.Y.: Syracuse University Press.

Soja, Edward W. 1968b. "Communications and Territorial Integration in East Africa." *The East Lakes Geographer* 4:39–57.

Soja, Edward W. 1971. *The Political Organization of Space*. Resource Paper No. 8. Washington, D.C.: Association of American Geographers, Commission on College Geography.

Sommer, Robert. 1969. *Personal Space: The Behavioral Basis of Design*. Englewood Cliffs, N.J.: Prentice-Hall.

Sopher, David E. 1967. *Geography of Religions*. Englewood Cliffs, N.J.: Prentice-Hall.

Spencer, J. E., and Horvath, Ronald J. 1963. "How Does an Agricultural Region Originate?" *Annals of the Association of American Geographers* 53:74–92.

Spencer, J. E., and Thomas, William L. 1969. *Cultural Geography: An Evolutionary Introduction to Our Humanized Earth*. New York: Wiley.

Spykman, Nicholas. 1944. *The Geography of Peace*. New York: Harcourt Brace Jovanovich.

Taaffe, Edward J., ed. 1970. *Geography*. Englewood Cliffs, N.J.: Prentice-Hall.

Tabb, William K. 1970. *The Political Economy of the Black Ghetto*. New York: Norton.

Thomas, Edwin N. 1960. *Maps of Residuals from Regression*. Report No. 2. Iowa City: State University of Iowa, Department of Geography.

Thrower, Norman J. W. 1966a. *Original Survey and Land Subdivision*. Monograph 4. Association of American Geographers. Chicago: Rand McNally.

Thrower, Norman J. W. 1966b. "Relationship and Discordancy in Cartography." *International Yearbook of Cartography* 6:21.

Tocqueville, Alexis. 1955. *Democracy in America*. New York: Vintage Books.

Tuan, Yi-Fu. 1972. *Man and Nature*. Washington, D.C.: Association of American Geographers, Commission on College Geography, Resource Paper No. 10.

U.S. Council on Environmental Quality. 1971. *Environmental Quality, Second Annual Report*. Washington, D.C.: Government Printing Office.

Wagner, Philip. 1960. *The Human Use of the Earth*. New York: Free Press.

Warkentin, John, ed. 1968. *Canada: A Geographical Interpretation*. Toronto: Methuen.

Webber, Melvin M. 1964. "The Urban Place and the Nonplace Urban Realm." In *Explorations into Urban Structure*, edited by Melvin M. Webber. Philadelphia: University of Pennsylvania Press.

White, Gilbert F. 1964. *Choice of Adjustments to Floods*. Research Paper No. 93. Chicago: Department of Geography, University of Chicago.

Whittlesey, Derwent. 1936. "Major Agricultural Regions of the Earth." *Annals of the Association of American Geographers* 26:199–240.

Wolfe, Roy I. 1963. *Transportation and Politics*. Princeton, N.J.: Van Nostrand Searchlight Book No. 18.

Wolpert, Julian. 1964. "The Decision Process in Spatial Context." *Annals of the Association of American Geographers* 54:537–538.

Wolpert, Julian. 1966. "Behavioral Aspects of the Decision to Migrate." *Papers, Regional Science Association* 15:159–172.

Wolpert, Julian; Mumphrey, Anthony; and Seley, John. 1972. *Metropolitan Neighborhoods: Participation and Conflict over Change*. Resource Paper No. 16. Washington, D.C.: Association of American Geographus, Commission on College Geography.

Yeates, Maurice H., and Garner, Barry J. 1971. *The North American City*. New York: Harper & Row.

Zelinsky, Wilbur. 1966. *A Prologue to Population Geography*. Englewood Cliffs, N.J.: Prentice-Hall.

INDEX

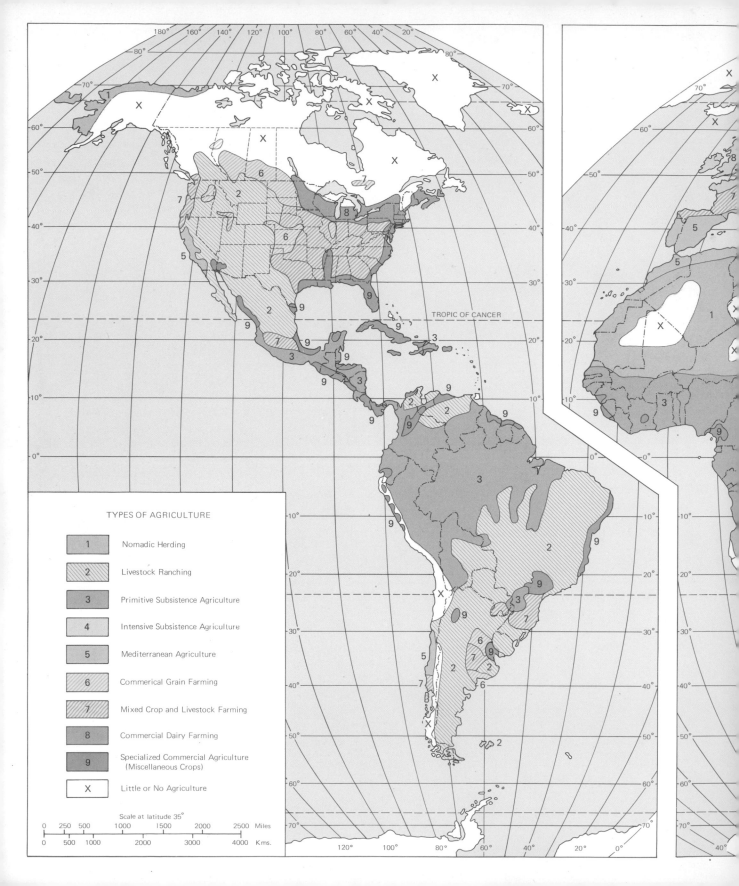

TYPES OF AGRICULTURE

1	Nomadic Herding
2	Livestock Ranching
3	Primitive Subsistence Agriculture
4	Intensive Subsistence Agriculture
5	Mediterranean Agriculture
6	Commerical Grain Farming
7	Mixed Crop and Livestock Farming
8	Commercial Dairy Farming
9	Specialized Commercial Agriculture (Miscellaneous Crops)
X	Little or No Agriculture

Scale at latitude 35°

0   250 500   1000   1500   2000   2500 Miles

0   500   1000   2000   3000   4000 Kms.

TROPIC OF CANCER